Chicken Soup for the Soul.

The Magic of Moms

Chicken Soup for the Soul: The Magic of Moms
101 Stories of Gratitude, Wisdom and Miracles
Amy Newmark

Published by Chicken Soup for the Soul, LLC www.chickensoup.com

The publisher gratefully acknowledges the many publishers and individuals who granted Chicken Soup for the Soul permission to reprint the cited material.

Front cover photo courtesy of iStockphoto.com/dszc (©dszc)
Back cover and Interior photo artwork courtesy of iStockphoto.com/SelectStock (©SelectStock)
Photo of Amy Newmark courtesy of Susan Morrow at SwickPix

Cover and Interior by Daniel Zaccari

Distributed to the booktrade by Simon & Schuster. SAN: 200-2442

Publisher's Cataloging-In-Publication Data
(Prepared by The Donohue Group, Inc.)

Names: Newmark, Amy, compiler.
Title: Chicken Soup for the Soul : the magic of moms : 101 stories of
    gratitude, wisdom and miracles / [compiled by] Amy Newmark.
Other Titles: Magic of moms : 101 stories of gratitude, wisdom and
    miracles
Description: [Cos Cob, Connecticut] : Chicken Soup for the Soul, LLC,
    [2020]
Identifiers: ISBN 9781611599985 | ISBN 9781611592986 (ebook)
Subjects: LCSH: Mothers--Literary collections. | Mothers--Anecdotes. |
    Mother and child--Literary collections. | Mother and child--Anecdotes. |
    Grandmothers--Literary collections. | Grandmothers--Anecdotes. |
    LCGFT: Anecdotes.
Classification: LCC HQ759 .C456 2020 (print) | LCC HQ759 (ebook) | DDC
    306.874/3--dc23

Library of Congress Control Number: 2019953003

PRINTED IN THE UNITED STATES OF AMERICA
on acid∞free paper

25 24 23 22 21 20   01 02 03 04 05 06 07 08 09 10 11

Chicken Soup
for the Soul.

The Magic of Moms

101 Stories of Gratitude, Wisdom and Miracles

Amy Newmark

Chicken Soup for the Soul, LLC
Cos Cob, CT

Changing the world one story at a time®
www.chickensoup.com

Table of Contents

❶
~There's No One Stronger~

❷
~Mom Knows Best~

❸

~Only She Would Think of This~

❹

~Always There for Us~

❺

~Grand Moms~

❻

~Honorary Moms~

❼

~Mom Can Make Anything~

❽

~Wise Words~

Introduction

Barbara Kingsolver wrote something that I loved in her book *Homeland and Other Stories*. She said, "Sometimes the strength of motherhood is greater than natural laws." Any human being knows that's true, and that mothers are not only incredibly strong but at the same time gentle, forgiving, creative, clever, and wise.

That's the magic of moms, and that's what we're sharing with you in this new collection of stories. My fellow editors and I are all mothers and daughters, so we get it. It was with that understanding that we lovingly compiled this collection of stories from our library. With twenty-seven years of publishing history, we had some amazing stories to choose from.

We don't just honor mothers in this book. We include stories about grandmothers, stepmothers, mothers-in-law, and the other "moms" in our lives. These touching stories will sometimes make you laugh, occasionally make you tear up a little, and most importantly, they'll make every mother feel great about the impact she has on her children. Take it from me, any mother who reads these stories will feel appreciated!

There's a special twist to this book, too. The contributors who wrote these stories have selected a number of charities they want to support with the royalties from this book. We'll be providing royalties on their behalf to four nonprofits that help moms keep the magic going.

We decided to start this volume with stories about strength and Chapter 1 is called "There's No One Stronger." Cynthia M. Gary leads off with "The Other Bus Story," in which she relates her mom's experience as a young black girl on a segregated bus in South Carolina in the 1950s, and how a white woman invited her to sit beside her in the front seat. Cynthia's mother shared that story with her children and Cynthia says, "My mother's decision to share this story helped me focus on the common thread of humanity that is sewn into all Americans."

The title of Chapter 2 is a phrase that all of us mothers love to hear: "Mom Knows Best." We start off with the ultimate "I told you so" story, "The Matchmaker," in which Lisa Leshaw's mother sets her up with a guy she declares is "delicious." It turns out that Lisa's mother had forced him to go along and he was just as reluctant as Lisa was to go on a blind date. Of course, Mom was right. That first date lasted four hours, and Lisa and Stu have been married more than three decades now.

In Chapter 3, "Only She Would Think of This," we read tales of creativity, quirkiness, and kindness. We start with "Mom's Secret Mission" by John Dorroh. John's mom would disappear every Christmas Eve for a few hours and he never knew why. It was only after her death that he learned where she had gone. A man wrote to him and explained that John's mother had gone to their house every Christmas Eve for the past seven years, dressed as Mrs. Claus and bringing gifts for the whole family.

It's amazing that mothers have enough time and energy to do for others, when they do so much for their own families. But, as we show in Chapter 4, they are "Always There for Us." Tiffany Mannino starts off that chapter with "Never Too Old to Want My Mommy," in which she recalls the day that she had to tell her mother that she had been diagnosed with breast cancer. Tiffany's mother helped her through every step of her treatment and Tiffany says, "She was attending to my every need, both physically and emotionally, but who was attending to her needs?" She adds, "I know what my mother would say if I asked her that question. She would say, 'That's just what you do when you are a mother.'"

That goes for grandmothers, too. Having just spent the Thanksgiving holiday helping as much as possible with my newborn grandson, I know that we are "always there" for our children, and then for our grandchildren, too. Sometimes that special relationship between a grandmother and grandchild makes all the difference. Who doesn't feel better knowing that grandmothers love unconditionally and with the wisdom of having lived a lot longer than parents?

Matt Caprioli's story "Lord Knows" is how we begin Chapter 5, which is all about the ladies we call "Grand Moms." Matt's grandmother was quite decisive when it came to showing her displeasure when someone disappointed her. She would just say she didn't know anything about that person if asked, making it clear the relationship was over. Matt was afraid to tell his very religious grandmother that he was gay, but he finally decided that he had to when he started college. He sent her a letter, and when he got back a thick envelope filled with his childhood photos he thought she was saying goodbye. But in fact there was a note in that envelope as well, and it said that she loved him.

Most of us have honorary moms too, whether they are a dear aunt, or a mother-in-law, or even the kind neighbor down the street. In Chapter 6, "Honorary Moms," we share stories about those special relationships, starting with Nikki Loftin's story, "Excellent Stock." Nikki always resented her mother-in-law Liz's interference, which took the form of doing everything perfectly and helping Nikki — with everything — even though it made her feel inadequate. That very special lady even managed to help out while she was dying from cancer, and Nikki could only cry when she found a delicious meal waiting for her in the freezer after Liz was gone.

Speaking of cooking, we honor the creativity and ingenuity of mothers in Chapter 7, which is called "Mom Can Make Anything." There are a lot of great meals described in this chapter, but also many other forms of creativity. Alicia Rosen leads off with her story "Note to Self," in which she recounts how her enterprising mother stayed up all night making hand-drawn stationery for Alicia's class pen-pal project. Alicia stopped complaining about the fact that they couldn't afford to buy fancy stationery at the store, and proudly used her mother's creations instead, sending them to pen pals around the world.

We moms impart lots of great advice to our children and grandchildren — whether they want to hear it or not. So, Chapter 8 is titled

"Wise Words." The first story in that chapter is "Thank You for the Reminder," a phrase that Andrea Fortenberry learned from a very wise mother she met while on vacation. This is her recommended response when someone reminds you of something that you already know. Instead of getting mad, or saying "I know" in an exasperated tone, just say "Thank you for the reminder." Andrea's whole family uses this strategy now, and it has headed off a lot of arguments.

The magic of moms indeed. They never cease to amaze us. But telling them is something we don't do often enough. So we hope this new *Chicken Soup for the Soul* collection will help you say "I love you and appreciate you" to all the mothers in your own life.

—Amy Newmark—
Author, Editor-in-Chief, and Publisher
Chicken Soup for the Soul
December 1, 2019

Chapter
1

There's No One Stronger

Chicken Soup for the Soul

The Other Bus Story

*It ought to be possible, in short, for every American
to enjoy the privileges of being American without
regard to his race or his color.*
~President John F. Kennedy

In the early 1950s, in a small South Carolina town, a little girl refused to sit at the back of the bus. Her mother gave her the evil eye and insisted she move. But the little girl continued her protest as she sat in a front seat beside a white woman, leaving barely enough room for air between them. The white woman looked back at the little girl's mother and said, "Oh, it's okay. She can sit here beside me so she can have a better view." The bus doors closed, and they all proceeded to their destinations without incident.

This story has not been recorded in any history books or newspapers because I am finally writing it down for the first time. My mother was that little girl, and the white lady is an unnamed character in a story that has helped to shape my image of life in this country. I remember my mother telling this account to my sister and me on more than one occasion, and it has stuck with me all these years. That incident on a bus in segregated South Carolina is the picture of America that I am determined to keep in my heart. While numerous outrageous lines were drawn throughout the southern United States at that time, every person on the bus that day, black and white, made a conscious choice to maintain peace.

Hearing this story as a child was significant to me in a few ways.

First, it demonstrated that, regardless of how dire the circumstances, there is hope. At the very core of American life, there has always been hope. Despite the obvious turmoil that plagued the country during that time, there was hope that great things were still possible. On that day, my mother hoped that her determination would result in a better seat, and she prevailed. It was a small victory for a little girl, but an enormous victory for humanity that would reach the next generation.

Second, I learned that "we the people" are just trying to make it — just trying to live a good life and make it home without incident. I do not know if that white lady was just tired, a secret freedom fighter, or a mother who had a little girl waiting at home for her. But I feel certain that she, like most Americans, believed in "life, liberty and the pursuit of happiness" for all people. It can be hard to cancel out the chaos that surrounds us, but that lady was able to focus on doing the right thing.

And, third, this story taught me the importance of storytelling. How many other little girls and boys of color were brave like my mother? How many small victories have been won in some quiet corner of this nation? The only way to begin to answer these questions is through storytelling, so that we can help paint a more complete picture of this place we call home. I have shared this story with a few people over the years, and they always seem happier after having heard it. I have often wondered if that lady shared this story with her children. I like to believe she did, and that they, too, were inspired and encouraged to share the story as I am doing now.

No, my mother's name is not famous, nor is the name of the white lady. And, no, my mother's actions did not lead to the desegregation of South Carolina buses. But that one incident has survived history because it helped shape the heart of a post-segregation African American woman: me. My mother's decision to share this story helped me focus on the common thread of humanity that is sewn into all Americans. I am constantly grateful that my parents chose to tell positive stories like this one. Their memory sharing helped me form a more complete vision of the world around me — one that acknowledges the trials, but is not embittered by them. I definitely have my tough moments when I am sure that hell in a hand basket is just around the corner. But remembering the incident that took place on a bus in the 1950s helps me know that moments like that have happened all throughout our history and continue to happen today.

— Cynthia M. Gary —

A Gift of Time

If you don't ask, you don't get!
~Stevie Wonder

January 20, 1965

Dr. Michael DeBakey
Methodist Hospital
Houston, Texas

Dear Dr. DeBakey,

I am a widow of 52. My husband died three years ago after an illness of almost ten years, which kept him at home and under the care of many doctors. I have supported my family for the last 12 years and with additional odd jobs on the weekends. With the aid of scholarships given to my two fine sons, 18 and 21, who have always worked during high school and college and summers, they have been attending the University of Connecticut, one in pre-med and one in pre-law — high aspirations out of very difficult youth.

Life is very dear to me, at least until my sons have completed their education and can stand on their own feet in this world, particularly since they have lived the greater part of their lives in the dark shadow of their father's illness.

There may be other surgeons who can perform the operation I have been told I must have to survive (removal of a blockage in my main aorta) but to my mind there would be no other who could give me the gift of life. I *ask you to do this operation although logic tells me that there may be others who may be almost as competent as you, and I have no right to expect that you will grant my request.*

The trip to Houston can be managed, and hopefully, if your fee can be within the realm of possibility for me, my prayers would be answered. You are, I am certain, besieged with the same request from people all over the world but I shall continue to hope that you will find it possible to help me.

Sincerely,

Mrs. Edith Sherman

I knew Mom was sick but only my nine-year-older sister knew how serious it was. My brother and I were away at college and they thought it wise not to share it with us until there was a plan. Mom had been diagnosed with a very dangerous aorta-blocking aneurism. Her internist explained there was only one doctor who had successfully performed the needed procedure and his most recent patient had been the Duke of Windsor. Not a lot of hope for Edith Sherman. But this was my mother, after all. She demanded more time to be there for us and for herself after decades of a really difficult marriage.

She went to the library and researched her heart out. There was no Google back then. Research of this nature was tedious, but she read about Houston's suddenly famous Dr. Michael DeBakey and his groundbreaking "bypass" surgery. The Duke had called Dr. DeBakey who was, at the time, in the White House conferring with President Lyndon Johnson about the findings of the President's Committee on Heart Disease, which Dr. Debakey chaired.

So my mother wrote that letter.

Six days later, she received a reply.

Dear Mrs. Sherman,

Thank you for your letter of January 20, 1965.
I shall be very happy to take care of you, particularly in light of what

There's No One Stronger | ⹀

you have accomplished under obviously adverse conditions to make it possible for your children to obtain a good education.

The least I can do will be to offer my professional services at no charge to you. I am sure my colleagues here would also be pleased to offer their professional services to one who is of such admirable character.

With all good wishes, I am
Sincerely yours,
M. E. DeBakey, M.D.

My mother and sister went to Houston. The life-saving Dr. DeBakey could not have been kinder. There were lots of painful, "iffy" days in ICU but she fought hard and recovered. Aortic plaque buildup would lead to four more bypass operations by the good Dr. DeBakey over thirty years. Dr. DeBakey always greeted her like family and bragged that she was his oldest living patient.

My mother lived for thirty more years and during that time she gave back with gusto. She became very active in the community and she soon was elected to the legislative body of Stamford, the Board of Representatives. The city of Stamford was undergoing great change in the downtown area. My mother was appointed to the Urban Renewal Commission and soon she became Chairman of that Commission. In ten years as Chair, she moved mountains, mayors, governors, congressmen and senators in her tireless efforts to rebuild this city of 110,000. My words cannot do justice to the praise that covered the front page and editorial pages of the local papers when she died at eighty-two.

Front-page headline: *Edith Sherman, driving force behind downtown revitalization, dead at 82.*

Another front-page headline: *Edith Sherman really had the drive to make the city better.*

Editorial: *Stamford yesterday bid a final farewell to a woman whose leadership and vision have left an indelible imprint on this city.*

My mother sat on every charity board within ten miles. Her walls were covered with "Citizen of the Year" awards and other such honors.

She spoke her mind. She was famous for her candor and her

chutzpah. The local media editor said it best:

Edith Sherman and the Politics of the Possible

Here is the thing to remember about Edith Sherman. She liked politics not in spite of the fact that it was complicated and contentious, but because of that fact.

Mom didn't waste a single day of the thirty years Dr. DeBakey gave her. She traveled the world in her own style. While most women her age would be content to cruise to the Caribbean, my mother was ballooning over the Serengeti. All she wanted for her seventieth birthday was to have the entire family share a craps table at Bally's in Atlantic City. We did it and, as if scripted by Frank Capra, the whole family won a boatload of money on my mom's roll of the dice.

Mom and a close friend of hers, Lillian, decided to go to India. My mother wound up sitting next to a very pleasant woman who happened to be India's Minister of something. More amazing, the woman was the college roommate of Prime Minister Indira Gandhi. By the time the plane touched down in India, my mother and the Minister — now an expert in all things urban renewal — were best friends. Her new friend arranged lunch with the Prime Minister. The photo of Mom, her friend and Indira Gandhi was hung prominently on her "good job" certificates wall. She went back to India a couple of years later and hooked up again with Prime Minister Gandhi. Not long after that, the legendary leader was assassinated.

My mother made the best possible use of her thirty extra years until she passed away at eighty-two. Dr. DeBakey, who died at ninety-nine, had an impact on my family that cannot be measured. And without knowing it, he had a huge impact on our small city as well.

A couple of years after my mother died, they named the street that leads into the mall "Edith Sherman Drive." She had basically built that mall and the mayor wanted to acknowledge her great contributions to the revitalization of the downtown area. The local cable news crew was there. "So Mickey," the mayor proudly said, "Do you think your mom would have liked this?"

I paused, wanting to say something appropriate. "Y'know Mayor, it's really nice. But you knew my mom pretty well. I think she would have preferred I-95 or a major bridge."

— Mickey Sherman —

One Last Dance

Someday I may find my Prince Charming,
but my daddy will always be my King.
~Author Unknown

For most fourteen-year-old girls living in a border town, the world revolves around *quinceañeras*. Yet there was no mention of such an event in my household. There was no talk about *damas* and *chambelanes* or about the color schemes or the dresses. There was no planning about where to hold the coming-of-age celebration or what music to select. There was no discussion about the guest list or the main course.

I helped my friends plan their parties and went to what seemed like dozens of *quinceañeras*. I must've had five to six fittings for all the ruffled dresses I wore as a *dama* that year. Whenever anyone asked if I was having a "quince" or "¿*Que van a ser tus colores?*" my go-to response was always, "I'm saving up for a car." I even had myself convinced until that night when I cried while the band played "*Tiempo de Waltz*" at my friend's *quinceañera*.

I went home early from the party, and although I tried to conceal my runny nose and red eyes, my mother could tell something was wrong. I did not want to lie, but what I feared most about telling her the truth was that I didn't want her to think I was selfish. You see, it's pretty petty and self-serving to be pining over a silly party when your dad is dying.

I finally confessed. I shared with my mom that I wanted nothing more than to have my own father-daughter dance. My dad had been diagnosed with Stage 5 cancer and given five months to live. By this time, he was in a wheelchair and had trouble remembering his children's names.

My mother pawned the little bit of jewelry she owned, and borrowed money from friends and family in order to raise enough money for my *quinceañeras*. In two weeks time we had printed homemade invitations and cleaned up and decorated my back yard by wrapping peach ribbons around the mesquite trees. We covered the borrowed tables with white plastic tablecloths, and set up a makeshift dance floor by draping Christmas lights around the basketball hoop. My *madrina* baked a three-layer cake covered in white frosting with peach flowers. My friends gathered with me in our satin, peach dresses and high heels on December 7th, six months before my actual fifteenth birthday, so I could have my very own father-daughter dance with my dad.

As the music started my mom pushed my dad's wheelchair up the ramp toward the center of the basketball court where I stood waiting. My dad motioned for her to stop and slowly raised himself from the chair and took my hand for the first and last waltz we would share.

— Erika Chody —

Free a Marine to Fight

*Marines everywhere can take pride in their
contributions to our great nation.*
~General James L. Jones, USMC

Mom could hardly contain her excitement as we packed the car. We were headed to Washington, D.C. to visit my sister Marie. This family get-together had been planned for months. Mom had baked for the past two days. I'm pretty sure we loaded more food storage containers than luggage into the car that day.

Mom's dedication to being prepared was no surprise. She had been a United States Marine during World War II.

At the tender age of twenty, as President Roosevelt implored all Americans to do their part, Mom heard the call and took it more seriously than most young women. A poster she saw on the subway wall convinced her to join the U.S. Marine Corps. The sign read, "Be a Marine. Free a Marine to Fight." In the picture a young woman smartly dressed in uniform stood holding a clipboard in front of a military plane. By the end of the day, Mom had signed on the dotted line.

Her decision met with enthusiastic negativity on the home front. Mom's younger brother had already quit high school and joined the Navy. He was headed for the South Pacific. My grandmother was, to say the least, perturbed to learn that her only other child was leaving home for the military. Hiding her feelings was never my grandmother's strong suit. She pitched a fit. My grandfather, on the other hand, cried. Mom stood her ground though, and in March of 1943 she headed off to Hunter College in New York where the first platoon of United States Marine women recruits gathered to train.

By the end of the war she had been promoted to Sergeant and served in Washington, D.C. and Philadelphia. She put her secretarial skills in high gear so that she could "Free a Marine to Fight." That's exactly what she would tell you if you asked why she enlisted.

Fast-forward about fifty years and her own platoon of children was plotting to surprise her with a tour of the National Museum of the Marine Corps.

"Where are we going?" she said, as we all piled in the car.

"Thought we'd take in some sights, Mom. You must know your way around Washington."

"I haven't been here in fifty years!"

"That's okay, Mom. I heard they haven't moved any of the important stuff," I said.

She rolled her eyes at me. "Oh you! Behave yourself."

The National Museum of the Marine Corps is located in Triangle, Virginia, so Mom began to get suspicious as we left D.C. and were passing through Arlington.

"Okay, give it up," she said. "Where are you taking me?"

"Um… We found a neat restaurant we thought you'd like. It's in Triangle, Virginia."

"Oh," she said. She didn't believe a word of it.

When we pulled into the museum parking lot she was dumbstruck.

"Whose idea was this?"

"Ours," we said in unison.

"Can we go inside?"

"Sorry Mom, it's only for active military. We just thought you'd like to see the parking lot."

"You're not too big to smack, Annie! Now get out of my way. I can't wait to get in there."

My mom's new hip replacement slowed her down a bit, so while my sisters helped her out of the car and up the steps I scooted inside to purchase tickets.

Down the hall a bit and off to the right sat the reception desk with a fine looking Marine behind it.

"Good afternoon, how can I help you?" he said.

"I'd like to purchase tickets to tour the museum please. That's my mom and sisters coming through the front entrance. My mom was with the first class of United States Marine Corps Women's Reserves in 1943."

"She was?"

"Yes, indeed!" I said. "She read 'Free a Marine to Fight' on a poster and she decided to do it."

"What is her name?"

"Back then her name was Marie Sherin. She was a sergeant."

He grinned at me and said, "There's no charge for the tour Ma'am. I look forward to meeting your mother."

Then he watched Mom, with her slight limp, slowly make her way to the reception desk. When she stepped up to the counter the young Marine stood at attention, snapped my mother a crisp salute, and barked in drill sergeant style, "The National Museum of the Marine Corps is ready for your inspection Sergeant Sherin!"

Slightly stunned, Mom saluted back and told him to stand at ease. Then we watched as a shy smile crept across her face. I think she had trouble coming to grips with being recognized.

The young Marine emerged from behind the desk to shake her hand, but Mom would have none of it. Instead she hugged him good and strong with a force that transcended time. Marine to Marine, they embraced. She held him fast in thanks for his genuine kindness and respect for her.

"Semper Fi, young man."

"Semper Fi, Sergeant Sherin. You get the royal treatment when you've freed a Marine to fight."

For a second I really think she had the notion he was psychic until she caught a glimpse of me winking at my sisters.

My mom smiled. "Oh, that was a long time ago," she said.

"A Marine is a Marine, Ma'am—forever. We never forget our own."

I still tear up when I remember the look on my mother's face and how touched she was by that young man's sincerity. Without his recognition of her service, she'd have walked through that museum and never mentioned that she was with the first class of the United States Marine Corps Women's Reserve in 1943. Mom would've spent the entire time pointing out everything that related to my Dad's United States Marine Corps enlistment. She'd have talked about nothing but how proud she was of him. That was always her way.

Her new young comrade in arms ignited a flame, a sense of pride, and a willingness to share her experiences with us as we made our way through the exhibits. I'll always be grateful to him for making her feel so special and appreciated.

I have often heard my mom's age group referred to as the "greatest generation." I don't believe she ever felt that way until the kindness of a single Marine from the current generation honored and recognized that she did her part when she answered the call and "Freed a Marine to Fight."

—Annmarie B. Tait—

The 115-Pound Miracle

Nothing has more strength than dire necessity.
~Euripides

"Hand me that wrench, Tammy." I did what my Pappaw Luther said. I was about ten years old, and hunkered down near a car he had jacked up and was working on. A light gray one with a black top.

I didn't give his mechanic work a second thought. He'd lain under cars before, fixing them, and I'd seen him do it a dozen times. He lay on his back underneath in the gravel, only his head and shoulders visible. The rest of him, from chest down, was under the car.

It was a pretty summer day. Life on my grandparents' farm was quiet that day, with almost everyone having attended the funeral of a relative. My mother didn't want to attend, so she volunteered to babysit all the kids — my siblings and cousins. Usually the yard would be full of running, playing, laughing kids.

It was a one-hundred-acre farm, and my pappaw worked on the car in front of his house. I liked hanging out with my pappaw once in a while. He was a man of few words, but when he talked, he liked to explain how things worked and what he was doing. He was a diesel mechanic and farmer, and could build or fix anything with his hands. I looked up to him and thought he could do anything — invincible.

That's why my brain was so frozen and stunned when the jack slipped and the car fell straight down onto his chest with a sickening thump. He couldn't move, and the only sound was a slight gasp of "Get Dana," so I ran as fast as I could toward the trailer my mother, sister, and brother lived in.

My mouth opened to scream to my mother as I ran, but no sound would come out. My voice had frozen in my throat.

Finally I reached the door, and I screamed, "The car fell on Pappaw! The car fell on Pappaw!"

My mother and I ran back to the car, and he still lay as he had when I left — trapped under the car on his back. My mother gripped the bumper of the car and lifted it, urging, "Scoot out! Scoot out!"

Pappaw scooted in the gravel, and my mother scooted the car over and set it back down.

My mother couldn't have weighed more than 115 pounds.

I couldn't believe my eyes. At ten, I knew something extraordinary had happened, but, on the other hand, it seemed like a perfectly normal thing for a person to do when a car crushes someone's chest.

My mother ran to the farmhouse to call an ambulance.

"I don't want to go to the hospital," my pappaw said. "With this hole in my sock."

Well, he did go to the hospital, and the doctors were amazed that he only had some bruises.

"It should have killed him," the doctor said.

At the time I thought of the incident as amazing, but now as an adult, I believe it was a miracle. Two miracles really. One, that my mom lifted the car and scooted it over. And, two, that Pappaw had only some bruises.

People claim adrenaline, and I don't doubt that. But the truth of the matter is, not everyone in a state of panic can lift a car, and not every person who has a car fall on his chest survives with just a few bruises.

All I know is that I witnessed firsthand the power of miracles that summer day so long ago.

— Tammy Ruggles —

Beacon

We are each gifted in a unique and important way.
It is our privilege and our adventure to discover
our own special light.
~Mary Dunbar

There is something graceful about a well-made hurricane lamp. Especially the antique ones. The kind that were made with all the love and pride a true artisan has for his work. Heavy, hand blown bowls to cradle the oil. Tightly woven braid wicks bridging the distance between fuel and flame. Tall tunnels of thin glass entrusted to guard the dancing light inside them. Such fragile glass to be so strong, to stand up against the elements, against the inevitable night. Mom had a great affection for the lamps. They were designed to keep their light lit through the harshest of moments, no matter how dark the night or windy the storm. She needed something like that in her life.

I can remember searching through countless flea markets, antique stores, and garage sales for them. She had a huge collection of hurricane lamps in every shape, size, and color. Heavy, cut crystal bowls with short hurricanes, squat and sturdy. Delicate cylindrical bowls with paper thin hurricanes, too fragile to be used but beautiful. Plain, round functional ones filled with red tinted oil. Mom tried very hard to buy the lamps in pairs but her favorite of all the lamps had no mate.

This one unmatched lamp was rather large, standing about two feet tall with the hurricane glass. Its bowl was octagonal and clear. A simple, elegant lamp, one that could stand on its own. It didn't need a partner to be spectacular. She found it just after we moved 3,000 miles away from everything we knew, after she left my stepfather. It was the first beautiful thing she bought for our new home without the fear that it would be smashed to pieces. On rough nights, when she was down or lonely or frightened, she would light her lamp and sit for hours until she could sleep.

Through the long, fearful nights at the height of a miserable divorce, she'd sit there until the sun came up, fear beating out her exhaustion. When she first found the two marble-sized lumps on her back, Mom found her comfort in the lights that danced untouchable behind glass, lights that would shine forever if she fed them. The night she got the official diagnosis of cancer, she let me help light them.

The spring after Mom's first battle with malignant melanoma, we went to a local craft fair to pass the time, to keep busy. We were still waiting to hear from the doctors on the results of her follow-up tests. She was feeling less than herself, and she wanted desperately to do something, anything, that would make her feel normal again. If not normal, then at least better.

Everything about the fair is a blur to me; I was so intent on seeing her smile, on not letting my brother see us panic, that I don't think I noticed anything. All I wanted was to make her smile. I hadn't seen her smile, heard her laugh, in months and I missed both.

Intent on my search, I bounded ahead of my mom and baby brother as they meandered along the tables and displays. I didn't make it far before something caught my eye. The recognition was immediate, a sizzle-snap-synapse moment, the kind that makes the hair on your arms rise up to face the synchronicity. Standing proud on the display table sat a lamp. Not just a lamp — this was a tall hurricane lamp with an octagonal bowl.

I was excited, frantic, as I raced back through the crowd to my mom. She was inspecting a pair of small lamps at another vendor's table. Normally, I was not one to interrupt, but this was important. Even at twelve, I understood how much it would mean to her. "Mom! You have to see something!" I said.

"Hang on. I think I'm going to get these lamps. What do you think?" She held them up so I could see them but I didn't even look at them.

"You've got to see what I found first." I tugged on her jacket, unrelenting. She sighed, said something to the person behind the table and set the lamps down.

I dragged her through the fair, not letting her stop to look at anything else, not letting her waste time. She had to see that lamp. When she did, I knew I'd done well. She squeezed my hand and her eyes teared up. As she picked up the lamp, she ran her fingers over the bowl, over the hurricane glass, inspecting it closely. "See this?" She pointed at a very small mark in the glass on the bottom of the bowl. I nodded. "The one at home has the same mark." She smiled. It was the first time I had seen her truly smile since the doctors first found the melanoma.

When the lamp took its place on the mantle, next to its mate, she cried. After my brother and I were both in bed, she went back downstairs. I knew she went to light the lamps and sit in their glow until she could sleep. She'd done it before. I fell asleep knowing that I'd made her feel better — even if only for one night.

Years later, I understood her need for those lamps, those inextinguishable beacons through the darkest moments of her life. They didn't help her survive her last bout of cancer, nothing could have done that, but maybe they made those days less frightening. I love those lamps but I don't need them the way that she did. My memory of her is all I need. She was my hurricane lamp. She was inextinguishable — through the darkest moments, she lit my way without fail. She still does. In those hours when my life is storm-tossed and wind-battered, the light around me shines bright with hope shielded by her hurricane spirit.

— Sarah Wagner —

Heroine

Let your love be like the misty rains,
coming softly, but flooding the river.
~Malagasy Proverb

S he is so short, less than five feet now as more than eight decades of life have shrunken her. She moves slowly, the arthritis of course, but mostly her breathing, her lungs damaged and diseased. The various medications, the pills and inhalers help somewhat when she takes them.

Her appearance belies the truth. She is a heroine, strong, determined, relentless.

She is my mom.

"He's never coming home, is he?" she asks me, her son the doctor, a few weeks after my dad has been admitted to the nursing home.

"No, Mom, he isn't." I answer as gently as I can.

And of course he is not. Parkinson's disease has made getting about difficult, and he is so very frail. But it is the theft of his mind by the continued progression of dementia that has made continued living at home impossible and, after a brief hospitalization, led to his admission to the nursing home's dementia unit.

Nobody ever comes home from the dementia unit.

It is a wonderful nursing home. The rooms and corridors are sparkling clean; it is brightly lit and cheery, and the care is provided by a staff that is skilled, caring, kind and patient. It is literally just down the hill and across the street less than half a mile from their home.

A few months later she tells me, "I'm bringing him home."

And she does. She has live-in assistance for a few months, but thereafter cares for him herself. He lives in his own home, with his wife, for another three years. He is the only person ever discharged from the dementia unit.

Six decades of marriage, of love, of loyalty and commitment.

She is a heroine.

She is my mom.

—Harvey Silverman—

Granny's on the News

*Have the fearless attitude of a hero
and the loving heart of a child.*
~Soyen Shaku

I received an urgent call from my aunt. "Turn on the TV. Granny's on the Channel 10 news."

I clicked on the TV just in time for the teaser: "And stay tuned for a daring story that happened just this afternoon, and a criminal who didn't realize what he was getting into."

What on earth?

I stayed on the phone with my aunt through the commercials. Finally, the newscasters were back, ready to tell this heroic story.

It turned out that Granny had made a sandwich run for her office and was stopped at a red light downtown. She had the window rolled down to enjoy the breeze when a man rushed up to the driver's side window, intending to carjack her.

Now, what the would-be carjacker couldn't have known was that this woman simply wasn't "a granny." This was Nancy Johnson — the same woman who owned and lived on a Texas cattle ranch, drove her own tractors, and dug her own post holes to lay fence. The week before, she had shot a rattlesnake and chopped off its head with a shovel. She was the proud owner of the new minivan she was driving, as one of her Brahma bulls had head-butted her former car into oblivion after seeing its own reflection gleaming in the door.

In other words, she was not your normal kind of granny.

The carjacker leaned into the open window, one hand stuffed in his pocket, and said, "Get out of this car. I have a gun, and I will shoot you."

A statement like that would have terrified anyone else. Instead, Granny saw it as a challenge.

"If you really had a gun in your pocket, you would've pulled it out and led with that first," she snapped at him, completely unfazed.

She was right. The criminal didn't have a gun. She had called his bluff, so he instead lurched into the window, grabbed her, and tried to pull her out of the van. He yanked open the door, wildly clutching at Granny's arms.

Granny leaned her shoulder into the steering wheel to blast the horn and started yelling to make a scene. With the door now open, she looped one arm through the steering wheel and started kicking the man anywhere her foot could make contact. At 5'9", the woman has quite a reach.

After a well-placed kick to the crotch, the man was done, and attempted to release her and run. But Granny wouldn't stand for that.

It was now her turn to grab onto him, her hands made strong from hours and hours of ranch work. That poor fool didn't have a chance.

She yelled for help to bystanders, and they rushed to her aid. With Granny leading the charge, a group of strangers came together and pinned the man to the sidewalk, holding him there until the police came.

A silver-haired woman — who loved being out on her tractor as much as she loved making brownies and crocheting — had just made a citizen's arrest.

When asked by the starry-eyed young reporter covering the story why she fought back and wasn't scared, Granny's answer was surprisingly simple: "No, I wasn't scared of that little twit. I'd had my brand-new van for less than two days and a pack of good sandwiches for my office. And there was no way he was going to get either of those!"

And this was quintessential Granny. The local newspaper ran it as their lead story the next day. She proudly clipped it to her kitchen fridge, wedged between pictures of her grandkids.

At first, we were furious with her. "Granny, don't you realize you could've gotten yourself killed?" we said.

But we all learned an important lesson from her that day — the same lesson that had been building through the years, all centered around one theme.

It was there when she would kick us grandkids out of the house at 8:00 a.m., telling us to be back at sunset. It was there when she taught us how to climb into the tractor, which at the time seemed scary yet simultaneously thrilling, surrounded by unknown machinery and perched well above the fields. It was there when she very carefully showed us how to load and shoot a shotgun.

She encouraged us to push boundaries and expectations. But even more so, she taught us fearlessness.

— Kristi Adams —

9

Losing Gracefully

Loss is nothing else but change,
and change is Nature's delight.
~Marcus Aurelius, Meditations

How do you spell old age? L-O-S-S. I know. I was there to bear witness.

After my father-in-law's unexpected death that Independence Day, Velma decided to move to Colorado to join her three sons, to immerse herself in their families. But the cost of love and companionship was high: My mother-in-law traded her rural hometown, her beloved house, and most of her worldly possessions to be with us.

In the process, she chose to leave behind other members of her family — her brother, sister, nieces, and nephews. She waved goodbye to her pastor, her girlfriends, her old classmates, her long-time hairdresser, her Sunday school class. She uttered her final farewells at the headstones of her parents, grandparents, and younger sister.

And her husband.

It was my privilege to spend time in Kansas that winter, helping her dismantle the household she'd established decades earlier when her boys were young, her days full, and her dreams rosy. The idea of old age and ill health in those years was still so distant it hadn't even seemed possible.

"What do you want to do with these?" I nodded toward the kitchen counter where rows of vases stood at attention, soldiers waiting for orders.

She blew a tired breath. "Box 'em. The hospital auxiliary will fill them with flower arrangements."

"And those?" I pointed at mountains of craft supplies, rainbows of embroidery floss, and packages of straight pins glinting like mica.

"Well, I was thinking some of the ladies at church might use those up. I've already set aside my scraps and quilting books. They go with me." When she reached for a stack of crocheted doilies on her desk, her hand trembled — a symptom of the disease we suspected but was as yet undiagnosed.

Each closet held surprises. The white Tonka truck my husband treasured in his childhood. A vintage game of *Chutes and Ladders*, still in its original box. Brittle photographs of ancient relatives. We unearthed a lifetime of memories and a flea market's worth of goods amassed throughout six decades of marriage.

"Look here." Velma leafed through her wedding scrapbook. "These gift cards came from Germany, relatives we hadn't heard from during The War." Two heads, one copper and one silver, angled over the pages as we identified signatures and sighed over photographs.

She pawed through boxes and sorted file cabinets, handling each old receipt and rereading every yellowed letter. After a thorough romp through recollections, she left them behind — along with almost everything else she owned.

"No room for any of this in my new apartment at Good Samaritan."

She was right, of course. Space in her new quarters was limited. Even so, I was stunned at how easily she deserted the possessions she'd spent her entire life accumulating and treasuring and storing.

Velma loved her new digs and segued smoothly into assisted living. She contacted old friends from the twenty-five summers spent at our local campground. She made new friends at the facility, engaged a hairdresser, and purchased yards of fabric to quilt. She attended church services, sang, and sewed baby quilts for her professional caregivers.

But more loss was on the horizon. In a few short months, the doctor diagnosed progressive Parkinson's disease. It wasn't long before

Velma's physical needs outgrew the parameters set by the assisted-living facility. As a family, we stepped in to take up the slack. As she steadily declined, we drove her to appointments, escorted her on shopping expeditions, mediated with doctors, oversaw dentures, nursed her through a broken hip, purchased an electric cart, gave her "driving lessons," sat with her at the hospital, and hosted her graduation to a wheelchair.

One by one, she lost her motor skills. Toward the end, we did for her the things her muscles were no longer capable of. We spoon-fed her; we painted her fingernails with her favorite polish — Creamy Carnation — and clipped on her favorite jewelry; we dialed the phone and held it to her ear; and we wiped spittle from the corners of her mouth, straining to catch the words she struggled mightily to speak.

Through it all, she kept up with family near and far. She knew which of the nursing home staff were on vacation, who was expecting a baby, whose teenager was having trouble in school. She read her hometown newspaper and celebrated each victory of the Denver Broncos.

By the time she died, Velma had lost so much — her spouse, her home, and her health. But, ever gracious and accepting of life's circumstances, she set an example for us all. Without complaint or grieving, she willingly gave UP a lot. Yet she never gave IN.

The real loss, I came to realize, wasn't hers… it was ours.

— Carol McAdoo Rehme —

10

My Mother's Daughter

*That which seems the height of absurdity
in one generation often becomes
the height of wisdom in another.*
~Adlai Stevenson

Mom used to be carefree, a happy-go-lucky woman. She dealt with the endless mishaps of raising five kids with take-it-in-stride abandon. No sooner was one hurdle cleared than a new one surfaced. She was the ball in a game of pinball—constantly bounced to and fro with bells ringing.

Decades ago, one by one, we left her nest to begin nests of our own. I don't recall Mom worrying much as we packed up and moved out. Instead, we heard an audible sigh of relief, quickly followed by a frenzy of re-decorating the rooms we had just vacated.

Now in her late sixties, she's still a lot of fun to be with, she's still hard-working, and she's still a beautiful woman inside and out. But she's acquired a new habit that's beginning to make me uncomfortable. She worries. And since she retired, her life has slowed down and she has even more time to worry.

Throughout the years of raising my own kids, I sometimes called Mom when a mishap occurred. But lately I'd been fighting the urge, hesitating to burden her even more.

"Mom, how did you do it?" I finally asked one day while we lunched.

My husband Chuck and I had deposited our son Chase for his freshman year at college. The pain of cutting the cord from our firstborn was so raw I couldn't even say his name without a lump clogging my throat. I thought I had been prepared, and I was; he had everything he needed for his dorm room, and then some. But what I never expected were the grief-like symptoms of not having one of my children at home anymore.

I was just getting a handle on raising him, and then he's gone?

Daughter Chelsea was next in line. It wouldn't be long before I'd have to do this once again. My mother, however, let go five times.

"How did you ever get through this?" I asked, dabbing at my eyes.

"Ahhh, yes," Mom nodded her head slightly and smiled reflectively.

She's smiling? I couldn't believe it.

"There was such constant commotion for so many years that I guess I reached a point where I became anxious to get my own life back."

"But you made it look so easy."

"Oh no, it was never easy. It's just that there was always so much to do. I worried while I worked. As a mother yourself, you know you start worrying from the moment you find out you are pregnant. And it never stops."

It never stops? I shook my head in dismay. Why did I think this job had an end to it?

For years, I had daydreamed about what I would do after the kids moved out. I assumed I would go back to being my carefree self again. And that's when it dawned on me.

It wasn't my mother who had been the lighthearted one — it was me. Mom had always worried about us; I just hadn't noticed. I had been so busy spreading my wings and then making my own nest that I never stopped to think about the adjustments Mom made at each leave-taking.

That is, not until now.

As I glance into my son's empty room, I once again resist the urge to call him, just to "check in."

"He'll let us know if he needs something," my husband constantly reassures me.

Still, he could be sick, or out of money, or...

I flip the page in my daily calendar and realize it's been three days since I've heard from Mom. I pick up the phone to call her, suddenly needing the comfort of her reassuring voice.

"Mom, it's me. I'm just checking in," I hear myself say.

And suddenly it becomes clear. As I watch my children spread their wings in anticipation of leaving our nest, I, like my mom, want them to know my wings are bigger and will always be able to wrap around theirs.

From the generations of women preceding me, the worry torch has been passed. I am my mother's daughter, after all.

— Connie Sturm Cameron —

Chapter 2

Mom Knows Best

11

The Matchmaker

He that would the daughter win,
must with the mother first begin.
~English Proverb

With the hairdryer going during our phone call it was possible that I hadn't heard her correctly so I turned it off in time to hear her say, "So I gave him your number and he'll probably call you on Sunday evening."

"Mom," I said with quiet anger, "who exactly will be calling me?"

"You'll love him. He's delicious," she cheered.

I turned the hairdryer back on, first to muffle the rest of the conversation and second to dry my hair so that I could leave my apartment and go over to my mother's to kill her.

At twenty-one, I had been on my own for two uneventful and relatively successful years, although according to my mother I was living like a rat in a dark hole.

Yes, my studio apartment had a shower stall in the kitchen and yes, my laundry basket doubled for my bookshelf and coat closet, but I was living without any parental assistance (financially at least) and working my buns off to stay proud and independent. I often times reminded my mother that it was her splendid job of raising me right that had given birth to this competent and newly minted young adult.

For some reason though my mother lacked confidence in two of my abilities — choosing the right foods and choosing the right men.

I'll give her the one in the nutrition department as I lived entirely on pasta and peanut butter. After all, they provided the necessary protein without the unnecessary expense.

When it came to the romance department however, I was never quite sure what she was quibbling about.

After all I had had just two boyfriends in my life thus far. Kevin, my first true love, forgot to mention to me that he was gay. When I chased him half way across the country to find out what was bothering him he introduced me to Paul and told me I was the problem. You can't fault me for this outcome though somehow my mom managed to question my judgment as if I should have figured this all out at the tender age of sixteen.

The second love of my life, my boyfriend Wally, loved me through senior prom weekend and then decided (with urging from his mother) that he was too young to go steady and needed to play the field.

It was then and there that I developed this strong belief: true love existed only in the minds and imaginations of talented authors.

When I arrived at her apartment, my mom was humming softly while braiding my younger sister's hair.

"Hi honey, I didn't know you were stopping by."

"Could you please leave the room?" I asked my younger sister. "I need to talk to Mom alone." I realized I couldn't kill her... yet. After a heaping serving of meatloaf and mashed potatoes I calmed down long enough to listen to her story.

"I was attending a meeting at the local library and the moderator asked for comments and questions after his speech. This very handsome young man raised his hand and said some things that sounded as if they had come directly from your mouth. I couldn't believe my ears! The two of you have so much in common and I thought that you absolutely have to meet." I left without saying goodbye but I think (although I'm not 100% certain about this) I called her to complain again as soon as I got home.

When I regained my composure the following week I found out more details. My mom had become enthralled with this mystery man and approached him near Biographies as he was preparing to leave.

I'm aghast at what supposedly took place next. She signaled for him to come over with the "bended and slightly moving pointer finger gesture" accompanied by the "psssst" sound.

Apparently, (whether through kindness or embarrassment) he walked towards her and the following exchange took place.

"I have a daughter you would love."

"Thank you but I'm really not in the market for dating right now."

"You're not married, are you?"

"No, actually I'm recently divorced from my childhood sweetheart and I have two very young children as well."

I guess he thought the above information would be substantial enough to send my mother home.

Oh no, not my mother. She proceeded with gusto!

"You seem very bright and I love what you said in there."

A nod from the kind stranger.

"May I ask how old you are?"

"I'll be thirty-two."

"My daughter is only twenty-one but she's incredibly mature for her age and I would love for you to meet her. The two of you seem to have so much in common. Here's her phone number. Why don't you give her a call next Sunday evening? She's usually home by seven or eight."

"By the way my name is Beth and my daughter's name is Lisa."

"I'm Stu. It was nice to meet you."

He didn't call the following Sunday (much to my mother's chagrin) because I imagine he wanted to avoid any daughter whose mother had to go out canvassing for her love life.

Unfortunately for all concerned though, they met up again two weeks later and this time there was no avoiding the inevitable. Stu approached my mother first and assured her he would be calling soon.

He called three days later. I thought he sounded very nasal (which I dislike immensely) and his name reminded me of beef. Nothing he said sounded remotely like anything I would ever think or say, so the "you have so much in common" comment lost its credibility. We agreed to meet the following evening at a local café.

I decided that I would have to prevent any future matchmaking attempts on the part of my mother. My plan was to embarrass and humiliate myself so that my mother would be embarrassed and humiliated too, and would never try to be a matchmaker for me again.

The evening of the dreaded date I borrowed a top from my landlady who just happened to be sixth months pregnant at the time. It looked like an elderly woman's housedress and managed to cover up any shape I might have had. Next I proceeded to plaster tons of hair gel on top of my head, creating a Mohawk effect, and then I tied my long hair into a tight ponytail to accentuate the look. I used enough black eyeliner to be competing with Morticia of *The Addams Family* fame. For the finishing touch I wore striking red lipstick that would have made Bozo proud.

Stu did not describe himself and my mother's description of him could not be trusted, so I sat in the predetermined location to be sure we spotted one another.

An unappealing man walked in, so I figured it was Stu. But he passed me by. One bullet dodged; one to go.

Moments later in walked the man I wished my mother would have realized was my type — rugged and muscular, with blue eyes and a boyish grin.

"Lisa?"

I looked directly at him.

No way, I thought. This can't be happening.

"Stu?" (I think I whispered but I can't be sure.)

He smiled and shook my hand.

I excused myself and bolted to the ladies room. Down came the hair. Off came the eyeliner. On came a delicate shade of pink lip-gloss. The muumuu had to stay. That or risk indecent exposure.

I think I tried to breathe deeply. I don't think I was successful.

It was too crowded in the café and Stu suggested the diner across the street.

We sat for four hours and shared our life stories and even some of our secrets.

He told me he gets cold sores every few months. I told him I would never marry a man who gets cold sores and drinks chocolate milk.

He told me he hadn't asked me to. I told him he would.

There were no future matchmaking attempts on the part of my mother. She got it right on the very first try. This year Stu and I will celebrate our thirty-third wedding anniversary. The children Stu had mentioned to my mother so very long ago are now forty and forty-three with five magnificent children between them. Stu's childhood sweetheart (and ex-wife) is one of our dearest friends.

And the woman who made all this joy possible for me will turn eighty-eight this month.

And don't think she doesn't remind me on a regular basis what a marvelous job she did indeed.

— Lisa Leshaw —

12

Unbreakable Faith

Every tomorrow has two handles. We can take hold of
it by the handle of anxiety, or by the handle of faith.
~Author Unknown

Like most moms of her generation, our Italian mother has mantras for every life event. For medical ailments — whether a broken bone or toothache, her advice is to "take two aspirin and grease it with Vicks." When something she predicted didn't exactly happen the way she believed it would, Mom's reply is, "I may not always be right, but I'm never wrong."

One of the most inspiring attributes of our mom is her ability to face adversity and not come out defeated. She always emerges with a renewed spirit and infectious sense of hope. Her outlook on tragic events is typically met with: "Hey, nobody died, nobody has cancer; we'll get through this, too!" But by far, our mother's most widely used mantra is, "For the love of God, count your blessings! It could be worse!" And she should know. Four of my parents' five children, myself included, are afflicted with a rare genetic bone disease called Osteogenesis Imperfecta, known as "brittle bones," as are three of their grandchildren. Having children who have collectively broken more than 300 bones would lead some parents to question their faith, but our mom refused to let others pity her or let us feel sorry for ourselves. "Hey, it's just a broken bone... it'll heal. There are worse things children could have. If this is the worst thing I ever have to deal with in my lifetime, I'll take it."

I, on the other hand, needed a little more convincing. Let me illustrate a typical day in my O.I. history. I woke up one morning, slipped on something innocuous, fell and broke my wrist. After Dad splinted my arm, we went to the ER, and I was sporting a heavy white plaster cast before 10:00 AM. Most parents would allow their injured child to stay home from school for the rest of the day, but not my mother. She scrubbed floors to pay for all five of us to get a Catholic education and by God's grace, she was going to see to it that we didn't miss a day. Whining was out — and so was reason when it came to dealing with my mom.

"But Mom, I have a broken arm. Can't I stay home?"

"It's just an arm, Jodi. You still have two good legs — now get out of the car and use those good legs to walk into that school."

"But Mom, it's my right arm... I'm right-handed. How am I supposed to write?" Protesting was fruitless because Mom had an answer for everything.

"Hey, that's why God blessed you with two hands — use your other one."

Did I mention I'm now ambidextrous? Not by birth, but by counting the blessing of my two hands. Years later, when I learned that I was carrying twin girls, my joy became short-lived when they were born sixteen weeks early. Weighing in at one pound, three ounces each and just under twelve inches in length, my daughters had a large medical mountain to climb. My mother, by my bedside, holding her rosary in one hand and my own hand in her other, told me with great conviction, "They may be tiny, but they're mighty. Count your blessings." Even after Hayley succumbed to pneumonia and died three weeks after she burst into our lives, my Rock-of-a-Mother was there helping me find a way to go on in spite of my incredible grief.

"I know you want your baby here with you," she said in a gentle, loving voice, "but God must have another plan. Maybe he needs Hayley in heaven to be her sister's guardian angel here on earth. Hayley will watch out for Hanna so Hanna can survive." Mom was right; Hanna did survive. Each day for the past seventeen years, I've looked into my daughter's blue eyes and I've known firsthand that I am indeed blessed.

When Hanna was diagnosed with O.I. and people around me

started to feel sorry for us, I replied, "Hey, she's not dying and she doesn't have cancer — she'll survive this. Broken bones heal." Then I started to laugh… I had finally turned into my mother.

In 2003, our mother took ill and had to have surgery. When the doctor relayed the unthinkable diagnosis to my siblings while Mom was in recovery — post-menopausal ovarian cancer — my sister called me and said, "Now what do we tell her? We can't say, 'No one's dead, no one's got cancer!'"

As it turned out, we didn't have to say a word. Mom knew even before she was told, and she soothed us when we should have been comforting her. "Hey, let's count our blessings; the doctor got it all and I'm not dead yet. Let's have some faith." As usual, our wise mother was right. She survived not only this bout with cancer, but five years later, she rebounded from another round of cancer — colorectal. She never needed chemo or radiation because miraculously both cancers were contained and surgically removed; and she has been cancer-free for nearly two years and counting.

"Faith; that's all you need," my mom says firmly as she taps the table. "Feeling sorry for yourself doesn't help anything or solve the problem… pity just adds to your problems. Spend your time counting your blessings instead. You'll see just how well off you really are. That's my motto."

And now we have the good sense to reply, "Yes, Mom… we know, we know!"

Counting blessings is not just a mantra drilled into our heads by our mom. It's become a way of life for all of us. So much so that when I count my blessings, my wise mother is always near the top of the list.

—Jodi L. Severson—

The Bully and the Braid

Kindness is in our power, even when fondness is not.
~Samuel Johnson

"Somebody's gonna get beat up," announced May Jordan while casually leaning against the monkey bars. Frozen by fear, the group of students surrounding May silently hoped that her latest victim wasn't among them, but they knew full well that there was always a chance. "We'll see after school," she said before flexing her large muscles for effect. Meanwhile, I hugged my Cabbage Patch Kid on a nearby bench, trying desperately to ignore the lump in my throat; it now felt the size of a small tangerine. I couldn't wait for recess to end.

I loved school, I really did. But since May had transferred in, Elliott Elementary had become an uncomfortable place. At approximately five feet eight inches, May was the tallest kid in our fifth grade class, and, in fact had already sprung well above every student in the school. Although her height was intimidating, it wasn't a problem—her attitude was. No part of the student population was beyond the reach of May's menacing taunts: She routinely hurled insults at innocent third graders who were too afraid to defend themselves; she blatantly bullied boys during gym class; she even threatened to snatch the patches off the sashes of Girl Scouts.

After carefully looking over their shoulders so as to ensure that

May wasn't within earshot, many students contended that she was all bark and no bite. But I wasn't so sure. I had managed to fly under May's radar — and I wanted to keep it that way. But all that changed when I showed up for school one morning with a new (albeit unoriginal) hairstyle. Apparently, by wearing my hair in a French braid, I had managed to change my fate.

It all started when my best friend, Jaime, said my hair looked nice. I noticed May's piercing glare — and it made me uncomfortable — but I remained focused on my math worksheet. Then came May's daunting proclamation as she passed me in the cafeteria: "Nice braid. Somebody might cut it off."

I was scared. But what really sent me into a tailspin was when May, who was now clear across the room, moved her fingers to imitate a pair of scissors in motion. My stomach dropped to my knees, and I immediately came up with a plan, which involved hiding out in the bathroom at the end of the school day so as to avoid running into May on the walk home.

I awoke the next morning with a start and scurried to the bathroom to watch my mother get ready for work. Although my watching her had become routine, she knew something was up.

"What's wrong, Courtney?" my mother said, while sweeping the apples of her cheeks with blush.

"Nothing," I replied.

"You're lying. Tell me the truth," she persisted.

"May Jordan wants to cut off my braid," I sputtered with a mouth thick with saliva; tears began to fall.

"She's a bully," my mother said earnestly while taking my chin in her hand. "She thrives on making others scared, that's all. Don't be afraid of her, Courtney. If she can see that you're not afraid, she will stop. I'll bet she's like everybody else — she just wants to fit in and make friends. Perhaps she just doesn't know how."

I rolled my mother's words around in my head. She did have a valid point. May wasn't so great at making friends. Maybe — just maybe — underneath all that toughness was a regular fifth grader who simply wanted to be liked. Did I have what it would take to befriend

May? I wasn't sure, but I wanted to find out.

Later that morning, I told Jaime that I had made the tentative decision to talk to May.

"You're crazy," she said. "Do you know what she could do?"

"Maybe not," I replied. I didn't quite believe my own words, but I realized that, for the first time, my curiosity outweighed my fear.

After lunch, I approached May at the pencil sharpener and went for broke: I invited her to come to my house after school. "We could walk home together, if you'd like. Maybe watch the Nickelodeon Channel?" I offered. (I'd be lying if I didn't admit that I was somewhat pacified by the idea that I'd be on home turf, under the watchful eye of my parents, where little could go wrong.) Still, I was proud that I had extended the invitation.

Then, something unprecedented happened. Something that I would not have believed had I not seen it with my own eyes. May smiled. And then she said yes.

I don't remember what we watched on television, or what my mother prepared for our after-school snack. But I do know that I went from ruing the day I wore a French braid to school to realizing that it had become the catalyst for a new friendship.

May Jordan never bullied me again, and, in fact, we became pretty good friends. After spending countless afternoons at my house, I quickly realized that, yes, underneath the tall girl's armor was an insecure fifth grader who wanted nothing more than to be accepted.

I've since learned that the old adage, you can't judge a book by its cover, certainly rings true, and that someone who looks different on the outside can really be just like you.

— Courtney Conover —

Sure-Footed Faith

I remember my mother's prayers and they have always
followed me. They have clung to me all my life.
~Abraham Lincoln

y mother gripped my feet and ankles firmly but with tenderness. "This will work," she said to herself as she looked at me. I was lying on a thick blanket folded into a makeshift bed that was sitting on the dining room table. I cooed and stared at my mother, unaware of the prayer she said while she moved my feet around. "Please, God, make this work."

My feet were pointed inward when I was born. My condition was a mixture of being severely pigeon-toed and a minor case of being club-footed. My legs were twisted a bit like corkscrews, in that the tips of the big toe of each foot touched naturally and the knees bumped together when bent, making it impossible for me to walk if left uncorrected. I wasn't in pain. I was unaware of the crippling effect that my legs could have on me in my future. Instead, I lay on the bed my mother created on the dining room table and watched my mother turn my little legs from the inward position in which my toes touched to the outward position in which they pointed forward. I smiled each time.

"This isn't going to work," my father had bellowed at the doctor who began fitting my little legs with braces a week before in his office. I was squealing uncontrollably, as if the metal of the braces burned me with every touch. "No, this is not going to work. Get them off him."

"He needs them to realign his legs," the doctor said, holding the tiny braces up for my father to see. They looked like torture devices from the Inquisition. "We talked about this."

"Jimmy," my mother said. She had scooped me up in her arms. She held me close to her bosom, and her raven hair fell across me like a veil, protecting me from the suffering of the world. "He won't be able to walk."

"There's got to be another way. If you think I'm going to let him put that on my son," he pointed at the braces the doctor was holding, "well, it's not going to happen. I'm not letting that happen to my son."

"We'll have to operate then," the doctor said. He dropped the braces onto the table in the room; they clanked heavily, silencing my father. "We'll need to operate on him when he's older if we don't use the braces."

"He's not going to wear those," my father roared before he stormed out of the room.

"Is there anything else we can do?" my mother asked. Tears ran down her cheeks. She was not going to challenge my father. "Please."

The doctor said nothing for a minute before he looked up at my mother. "There's an exercise," he said. He opened a drawer and pulled out a prescription pad. He began to write on it. "There's an exercise you can do with his legs that has been known to work."

He eased me from my mother's arms and touched my chin briefly. There was a bluish line on it intersecting another like-colored one, although shorter. Like an X, he thought to himself, even as he checked the mark to ensure that it was made up of veins still visible through my slightly transparent skin.

"Like this," he said as he knelt on the carpeted floor and placed me on the ground gently. My mother knelt next to him. She looked as if she were in prayer. The doctor held my feet loosely, deciding what to do, and then slowly turned my feet so that the toes that faced inwards faced forward. My knees rolled with my toes and my feet, which were turned on their side, adjusted accordingly. I cooed again. "You try."

My mother slid over, exchanging places with the doctor. She took my feet in her hands and did what the doctor did.

"If you do this every day for half an hour," he said, trying to calm my mother, "there's a small chance that the surgery will be easier."

"Easier?"

"Just do it," he said. "It'll help you."

"It'll help him," she said. "This will work."

"Come back in three months."

After the appointment, my mother took me home and placed me on a blanket in the living room. She bent her head slightly and folded her hands and prayed for her son's legs. "This will work," she whispered to Him. "I know You will make it work."

She took my feet into her hands and began to exercise them while reciting nursery rhymes and singing children's songs and religious hymns. She talked about my brother and my father. She talked about her faith in God.

Ten minutes turned into twenty, and twenty turned into an hour. Soon, she and I sat together for the better part of every day. And as the minutes turned into hours, the days turned into weeks and those weeks turned into months.

"This will help you," she said to me again and again. "I have faith in Him."

"Where's your son?" the doctor said to my mother three months later as he examined my legs.

"This *is* my son."

He smiled awkwardly. He looked at my legs and didn't recognize them.

"This is not your son. Your son's legs were twisted like the roots of a tree," he said and checked his chart again. He calmed himself. "This child's legs do not look like your son's legs."

"He's my son," my mother said quietly. She picked me up. "He's my son."

The doctor examined my legs as I cooed at him. They were straight, with the toes pointed toward the heavens and the knees only turned in slightly. Then he looked at my face before touching my chin softly.

"It looks like a cross now," he said out loud, but to himself. He allowed his finger to trace the intersecting lines on my chin. He had remembered the mark from before. "He is your son."

"He is," my mother said, smiling through her tears. "And he is healed."

"What did you do?"

"I did what you told me to and more."

"It shouldn't have worked," he said. He looked at my mother apologetically. "There's no such exercise. I made it up. It shouldn't have worked."

"It wasn't the exercise that cured him, doctor."

And in my file in a doctor's office in Pennsylvania is a note pinned to the documents pertaining to my crippled legs. It reads simply Cured by Divine Intervention.

—James Foltz—

15

Grateful for Stew

It's bizarre that the produce manager is more
important to my children's health
than the pediatrician.
~Meryl Streep

When I was a young girl my mother made the same dish for supper five nights a week. She boiled potatoes, carrots, and occasionally, other vegetables, in a big, shiny pot on the kitchen stove. The vegetables were cooked fresh every day and small amounts of the roast beef that she cooked once a week were added to the bowls. She called it stew.

I would often hear the other children at school talk about the delicious meals they had for supper. Many of the children ate from fast food restaurants, which were expensive at the time. They got hamburgers, fries, and milkshakes. I wished we could eat like that once in a while, but my parents couldn't afford it. We only had take-out food once or twice a year — for special occasions.

Now I look back and I think how blessed I was. My mom took the time to cut up and prepare those vegetables and potatoes every single night. Her portions were right — focusing on the vegetables and not on the meat — and we weren't eating the grease and fat and salt we would have had in take-out food.

I'm pretty sure I had a lot fewer head colds and flus than my classmates. If I did get sick, I'd be home for a day or two, not a whole week like many of them.

Mom Knows Best | 53

When I was in my thirties I became ill and was diagnosed with hereditary high blood pressure. I have to admit I had been eating a lot of fast food, making up for not getting it as a child. But when I went back to preparing homemade meals without all the extra grease and salt I started to feel healthier.

Today I often find myself craving a bowl of my mother's stew. I realize how blessed I was to have a mother who took the time to prepare a healthy meal for her family five evenings a week. That stew was made with love and it has left me with a memory that will warm and nourish me forever.

— Shawna Troke-Leukert —

16

Three-Dollar Miracle

We all have a guardian angel,
sent down from above. To keep us safe
from harm and surround us with their love.
~Author Unknown

I braced myself against the biting spring wind as I walked through the pharmacy's sliding doors into the parking lot. I stuffed my empty hands into my coat pockets. They were empty, too. Disgusted, I shook my head. What had my life come to? I didn't even have enough money to refill my prescription. The time had come to admit it. I was broke.

How quickly I had stepped over that line. One day I was holding a paycheck and the next day I was holding a pink slip. Twenty-two years of employment hadn't meant much when my company decided to cut costs. With a mortgage and plenty of other bills to pay, I blew through my savings in no time. Now, here I stood, unable to purchase a simple necessity for the lack of three dollars.

My feet felt leaden and I stood outside that pharmacy for a long time, despite the gusting wind, pondering my dilemma. I felt so desperate, I even entertained the idea of asking the next customer who walked toward the pharmacy for the three dollars I needed.

My late mother would have taken a different tack, I thought, as I stood there contemplating my next move. Mom had long subscribed to the notion that we are each assigned a guardian angel — ready to help out in tough situations, waiting to be asked for assistance. Mom made no apologies to anyone about her firm belief and much to the amusement of many naysayers had actually given her guardian angel a name.

I had been one of those naysayers. Yet at that moment I felt so hopeless, a cry came from deep inside me: "I've tried to do everything right. I worked hard and now I have nothing to show for it. I'm scared. If my guardian angel is really out there," I pled, "please help me." Then I tipped my head down to keep the dust in the air from blowing into my eyes. And right in front of me, three dollar bills floated directly toward my feet.

While my practical side prefers to maintain a healthy skepticism about such things, I no longer count myself among the doubters. That experience in a windy parking lot seems like proof positive that I do have a guardian angel. I've been pondering names for her for quite a while now. I'm not sure, but think I'll call her "Mom."

— Monica A. Andermann —

What This Virginian Learned about OHIO

One good mother is worth a hundred schoolmasters.
~George Herbert

My mom is the most positive person I know. She has an encouraging spirit, sees the good in all people, and always sees the silver lining in any situation. The world needs more people like my mom to view a glass as "half full" rather than "half empty." I grew up in a loving, positive home environment, where there were always family activities and lots of laughter.

I have fond memories of my mom taking us to volunteer at a food pantry every other Saturday morning. While my brother and I would have rather stayed in bed or watched cartoons on our day off from school, she had us tag along with her for her volunteer shift of interviewing and counseling people in Roanoke, Virginia who needed groceries to feed their families. While she did her service role, we helped in the food pantry, sorting, stocking and preparing bags of food. Surprisingly, this got to be something we looked forward to! My brother and I made a game out of filling each food bag for the families, and we always left feeling good about what we did.

My sweet mom even made household chores enjoyable. The best advice I learned from her that sticks with me today is "O-H-I-O." Growing up, my mom would hand me a stack of clean clothes, and I would immediately set them on the floor, promising to put them away later. My mom would say, "Kids, you've got to remember: OHIO! That means Only Handle It Once. When I give you clothes, put them away in your drawers as soon as I give them to you so they are only in your hands once." It got to be annoying during my high-school years when having a messy room was the norm. She'd gently remind my brother and me, "Kids, OHIO!" and we knew exactly what that meant. She said it in such a sing-songy tone, too, that it was hard *not* to follow her instructions since OHIO is so sensible!

Sadly, I never got the neat gene, if there is one. My college dorm room, my first apartment, and my current house are never that tidy. It is easy to forget this simple piece of advice my mom gave to me and leave stacks of mail or clothes lying around. Today, as a forty-two-year-old wife and stepmom, when I pick up my mail or bring clean, folded laundry to my room, I hear my sweet mom's voice in my head: "Remember, OHIO!" Most of the time, I take those extra two minutes to handle things only once and put them in their proper place. Who knew that this girl from Virginia would learn such a valuable lesson about OHIO that stays with me still today? Thanks, Mom!

— Kate Tanis McKinnie —

18

The Third-Room Rule

Never settle for anything less than you want.
~PJ Harvey

I learned many valuable things from my mother, a woman who developed a number of methods for coping with life's little challenges. Our family called the strategy she developed for checking into hotels "Mom's Third-Room Rule."

"Always hold out for the third room," she told us. "It's only after you reject the first two rooms that they realize you mean business and will give you a Good Room."

When you check into a hotel, she explained, the folks at the front desk size you up. Are you a business traveler in an expensive suit? You'll get the best the hotel has to offer. But our Midwestern family of four — Dad and Mom and two little girls — in two adjoining rooms? They probably figured that we'd settle for less.

Mom was never the kind of woman who'd settle for less. And she taught me well.

For instance? My recent stay at a resort hotel in California. When I checked in, the desk clerk gave me a room that had a pair of double beds, not the king-sized bed I'd requested. I was traveling alone; the last thing I needed was two beds. Plus, the beds were rather small — as, for that matter, was the room itself.

I returned to the front desk and politely asked for another room.

Room Number Two did have a king-sized bed, but the room faced a wall! The view from the window was of a vast expanse of cement.

I'd looked forward to a nice view of a lovely California town. But this room gave me a view of nothing but an alley. Plus, because of that vast wall, the room was rather dark. And it had a noisy air conditioner.

"The second room they give you will usually be worse than the one you've rejected," Mom always told us. Why? Perhaps to punish you for not just accepting that first room? Or maybe they assume that you'll give up and take what they've given you.

Not my mother!

I grew up watching Mom do the Three-Room Shuffle whenever the Warren family checked into a new hotel. (My dad, who wasn't persnickety about this kind of thing, wisely left these negotiations up to his wife.) As my sister and I got older and became more aware of the situation, it became a game to critique what was wrong with Rooms Number One and Two.

Our favorite place to play this out was at the Waldorf Astoria in New York City, where we stayed for a week each December while my dad attended a conference. In a classic hotel like this, the rooms within a price range can vary wildly. Our goal? To get good ones.

The first set of rooms they gave us was always mediocre. We promptly rejected them. "This won't do either," Mom would say after a brief look at their next offer. Once again, we'd troop back down to the front desk with all our luggage, where Mom's perseverance would finally be rewarded.

I have fond memories of our family—after turning down the first two sets of small, dark, noisy rooms we were offered—walking into an adjoining set of splendid, large, high-ceilinged hotel rooms with wonderful views.

"This is more like it," Mom would say happily. That was our signal to unpack and settle in.

With this in mind, I took one look at The Room That Faced a Wall and returned to the front desk. "Call me a *kvetch*," I told the desk clerk, "but a room that faces a cement wall doesn't say 'spa vacation' to me. It says 'incarceration.' Can we try again?"

As she handed me yet another room key, I thought of Goldilocks and the Three Bears. First room? Beds too small. Second room? Faces a wall. But the third room?

It turned out to be a large, quiet corner room on the fourth floor. There was a comfy-looking, king-sized bed, a lovely reading chair, and a view of Walnut Creek with the California hills in the distance.

Perfection!

Thanks, Mom, I thought, as I opened my suitcase and settled in.

— Roz Warren —

19

Chicken Soup for the Soul

From Attitude to Gratitude

*Sometimes the strength of motherhood
is greater than natural laws.*
~Barbara Kingsolver

The day my mother saved me from being killed, or at the very least, from severe injury, I was awakened from a peaceful sleep by the incessant ringing of the phone. I glanced at the clock. It was not yet eight. Who had the audacity to call so early? The phone display said "Unknown Name, Unknown Number."

To be roused abruptly and by a call I did not invite or want always makes me cranky. Then on my nightstand I noticed Larry's note. "Forgot. Have early tee time. Later. Love you, L."

Oh, great! It was Saturday morning and I had planned on a leisurely breakfast with my husband. "But I guess his precious golf was more important," I mused grumpily.

Breakfast? In the kitchen I found his other note: "We need milk. Ours is sour." I don't ask for much in the morning except for my cup of coffee with two sugars and milk — fresh milk.

Grabbing five dollars, I grudgingly threw on my yoga pants and top. There was no need for underwear, I decided. After all, I was only going two blocks away. I drove to the 7-Eleven. I had almost reached the store when a policeman stopped me.

I wasn't wearing a seatbelt and had left my driver's license on the dresser. His professional disinterest added to my foul mood and it was evident he didn't like my attitude either. He gave me a ticket.

At home, I took my coffee, a blanket for my legs and my latest novel out to the back patio.

It had rained overnight. But now it was a perfect spring day. The flowers on the Bradford pear tree created a stunning canopy of snowy white.

The yard was alive with energetic squirrels and the birds provided a sweet symphony of background music. The pleasing sight caused me to question why I was in such bad humor when I was, in fact, so fortunate.

I had good health, a loving husband, a family and friends. Oh, sure, it would have been nice to be ten years younger and have a million dollars, but all things considered, I led a charmed life.

I thought of the officer who had ticketed me. "At least he didn't do a strip search," I spoke out loud, laughing as usual, at my own joke.

I stretched out leisurely on the wooden bench, surrounded by the beauty of nature. My thoughts turned to the bench on which I reclined — my bench. Larry had sanded and stained it a red brick color to match our concrete patio floor.

I smiled as I recalled when we had first discussed marriage. He had good-naturedly warned me that he was not a "honey-do" kind of guy, but his cooperation and eagerness to help over time belied those words.

I must have dozed off. The shrill ringing woke me. Jumping up with a start, I heard my mother shout, "Answer the phone."

I ignored her, until her voice penetrated my ears again, this time with more urgency.

"Eva! Answer it!"

"Can't you pick it up, Mother?" I called out, but she didn't reply.

The phone was on the window counter across the yard. Untangling myself from the blanket, I rushed towards it. A startled little squirrel had been caught up in the blanket and had scampered away in fright.

The phone's display showed those annoying words, "Unknown

Name, Unknown Number." My pet peeve struck again.

I'll never know what prompted me to pick up the receiver instead of pressing the "off" key.

The caller seemed hesitant, wanting to talk despite having dialed the wrong number. For some reason it didn't frustrate me like it normally would have. Very politely, I took the time to explain that there was no one in our home by that name. As I was about to hang up there was a deafening thud behind me.

The beautiful Bradford pear tree had uprooted and its enormous trunk had crashed onto the bench where my head had been resting only a minute before. I gazed with horror at the demolished bench, gasping as I realized what had almost happened.

When I had recovered from the shock, I reflected on the miracle that my mother's voice could rouse me from such a deep sleep, sparing me from being injured — or worse — from possible death. What was even more astounding is that it happened on the one-year anniversary of her death!

We later learned that Bradford pears, although exquisite in appearance, are trees that are notorious for uprooting and breaking.

My early morning funk was replaced that day with profound gratitude — gratitude for something even as simple as a wrong number.

— Eva Carter —

20

R You Listening?

For years, I'd go to the movies and see guys doing
Boston accents and think, "Oh please, God, I hope I
never have to do that."
~Michael Keaton

I am the product of a mixed marriage — my mother was a Red Sox fan from Boston and my father was born and bred in New York City. I live in Greenwich, Connecticut, in staunch Yankees territory, but only twenty miles south of the Red Sox Nation border. The American League East is at war in my blood. My cousin on my mother's side has worked at Fenway Park his whole life and he gave me a Red Sox hoodie that I love wearing when I am safely outside my local area.

But where I live? Forget it. I dared to wear my Red Sox hat *once* while walking in our neighborhood. And sure enough, I took it off for one second when I got hot, and a bird pooped right on my head — a big pile right where the emblem with the two red socks had been. Even the local birds had noted my treachery.

Boston is on my mind a lot because my son and daughter-in-law live there now, surrounded by people who sound just like my mother. Why do I bring this up? Because I remember fondly the day more than twenty years ago when I was talking to the kids about "foreign countries" and they insisted they had already been to one. They explained that every time we visited my parents we went to a foreign country.

In reality, my parents lived twenty minutes away. Where had they gotten the idea that Grandma and Grandpa lived in a foreign country? Well, they explained, Grandma had a foreign accent and she lived in a place with a foreign name — Chappaqua — in New York State. So "New York" must be a foreign country. I had no idea that for years I was getting credit for taking my children on exciting weekend trips out of the country!

My mother's "foreign" accent was always a source of amusement in our family. When she drove me to my freshman year of college, she actually said the very clichéd "oh look, they opened the gates so we can pahk the cah in Hahvahd Yahd" as we pulled up to the front of my dorm. I always teased my mother and dared her to pronounce words with an "r." She would struggle and slowly enunciate the words, with only the faintest trace of an "r" no matter how hard she tried. But give her a word like "idea" and up popped an "r" right where it didn't belong. What's an "idear" anyway?

One of my favorite stories about my mother's accent was when she tried to buy some dark chocolate bark a few years ago in a candy store in touristy Annapolis, Maryland. Mom told the salesclerk that she wanted some of the "dahk bahk" in the glass case. Considering all the foreign tourists who visit Annapolis, the home of the Naval Academy, the clerk assumed that English was not my mother's first language. She explained that she couldn't understand my mother's accent, so would she please spell what she wanted? My mother proceeded: "D-A-AH-K B-A-AH-K." No luck. She left the store empty-handed, foiled by her Boston accent.

After my mother had a stroke, which resulted in her losing some language skills, I had to pull the speech therapists aside and explain to them that her Boston accent was not the result of aphasia. I didn't want them to try to reinstate an "r" sound that had never been there anyway. They had actually been trying to teach her how to say words with R's in them, so they appreciated the heads-up.

At my mother's memorial service I told some stories about her various unique characteristics, including her Boston accent and how she was often misunderstood. My cousin who works at Fenway "Pahk" came up to me after and said it was the best funeral speech he ever heard but he didn't really understand my comments about my mother's accent because he "had never noticed that she had one."

And that's why I love going to Boston, where the pahking is difficult and the snowy, cold winters are hahd. In the meantime, I still get to talk to the other side of the family, the New York side, which can't pronounce R's either. It wasn't until my Park Avenue aunt died that I learned that her best friend's last name wasn't "Shera," but was "Sherer." And we love to tease my Brooklyn-born husband about his R's. And his L's too. He can't for the life of him pronounce one of his favorite beverages, the "Arnold Palmer," so he always has to order a half-iced-tea-half-lemonade.

— Amy Newmark —

21

Chicken Soup
for the Soul

Seventeen

When you re-read a classic you do not see in the book
more than you did before. You see more in you
than there was before.
~Clifton Fadiman

"I can't wait to get out of here!"

My mother didn't answer; she just turned and left the room. Left me standing in the middle of the floor with the echoes of my angry words to keep me company.

Looking back on it now, I suppose she was either too hurt to respond to my teenage tantrum, or couldn't understand it. The oldest of eleven, my mother had never harbored such a fervent wish as mine. She had never wanted to leave home, and only did so because "it was time." I knew she didn't remember being a teenager. She was too old.

Our differences were irreconcilable. She was trying to hold me back, to keep me the baby. I would be graduating in a few weeks, and in two months more, I would be eighteen. No one would be able to tell me what to do then.

Was it so hard for her to understand my desire to be on my own?

Due to my father's job transfer, I was uprooted my senior year in high school. We moved from Oklahoma to West Virginia, and I was anxious to get back to my old friends, to the life we'd planned for our post-high school years.

Those plans included moving from the small rural Oklahoma community we had grown up in to the hustle of the metropolis: Oklahoma

City. The five of us planned to rent a large house, find jobs, and make it "out there" on our own.

Our plans didn't include going to college. After all, we reasoned, plenty of people made it in the world without a college degree. My own parents were examples of that. So what was the big deal? And how could I bear living at home one minute longer than absolutely necessary?

Mom and I never really talked about that day again. It had been a particularly heated argument. She said things she shouldn't have. She was unreasonable. Set in her ways. And spoiled. She wanted everything her way. Why couldn't she see my side of things?

I flopped down on the bed, and let the tears come. I would remember this, I vowed. And I'd never treat my own children like that.

For all my wisdom and forethought, life didn't work out as we had planned. Two of our five-some got pregnant the last two months of high school; another decided to move in with her older sibling. That left just two, and it would prove to be nearly impossible to find a place we could afford. The reality of rent payments, utility fees, and spartan meals held little appeal. Our dream of being independent lost its luster.

I decided maybe I could live at home a while longer and go to college. But I didn't have to like it. After all, I had a mother who couldn't possibly understand me. She had called our plan foolhardy! Five girls, banded together, were indestructible. We could have taken Oklahoma City by storm. If what she had predicted hadn't happened quite so… predictably.

Besides, she was one of the oldest moms I knew. My friends all had younger moms; moms who weren't so set in their ways, moms who would at least try to understand.

Today, as a mother myself, I breathe a sigh of relief for the headstrong, willful teenage girl that I was. I live in Oklahoma City and there are places I will not venture, even now. As a young girl, I wouldn't have had the good sense to stay home. My mother knew that.

When my daughter, Jessica, turned seventeen, her birthday came with an attitude. Suddenly, her mom just didn't "get it" anymore.

Amidst her tears, eye-rolling, and fits of temper, I tried to remind myself what it was like to be seventeen. I remembered that long-ago time when I felt so misunderstood and insignificant, when I thought I knew it all, when I felt invincible.

And seeing it all replayed over thirty years later, I silently asked for forgiveness. Forgiveness for my own youthful inability to understand how great a parent's love, how boundless a mother's wisdom and understanding.

"I can't wait to get out of here!" Jessica yells, tears threatening.

I pull her to me and hug her. She tries to remain stiffly defiant, but finally, I feel her relax, her arms coming around my waist.

"I can't wait to get out of here!" I'm sure there were times when my aged, out-of-touch, controlling mother couldn't wait either.

I once promised myself to remember that argument. And I do. Only now I truly understand what those words meant to my mother: A loss and a longing, a promise and a prayer, an escape and an exile.

In another thirty years, perhaps Jessica will be standing on the other side of the fence and hearing those same words. I can only hope she, too, will always remember seventeen.

— Cheryl Pierson —

22

Lessons from a Six-Carat Diamond

Through darkness diamonds spread their richest light.
~John Webster

My mom was not a vain person, but a natural beauty who spent very little time on her physical appearance — especially in terms of fancy clothes, manicures or hairstyles. She declared herself a tomboy and didn't care about stuff like that. She kept beautiful her way: rest, water, exercise, vegetables, and laughter.

Some say it was a generational thing, being raised in and around the Great Depression. From a young age, my mom had her mind conditioned about money. She would tell me that her father was tight-fisted and miserly with a touch of lazy, and he had her run his little corner store from the age of ten. She saw the poor people of her neighborhood come in, heads hung low, scrounging for food and making hard choices, like meat or cheese, powdered milk or juice. She took their coins with an eye on the bottom line. It was up to her, though just in elementary school, to make sure the register balanced at the end of the day. That experience taught her early that life is all about making choices — the seemingly small salami or bologna choices that direct a person's long-term security.

For all of her thriftiness, my mom had one weakness: diamonds. In 1958, my teenage dad gave her a diamond chip as an engagement ring, which she proudly wore until she had squirreled away enough for an "upgrade." By then, she was in her late thirties, and had worked hard and done without in order to acquire a beautiful Tiffany two-carat solitaire ring. I witnessed the small sacrifices and hard choices she made to get that diamond. Over the years, with patience and perseverance, my mom also acquired other gorgeous diamond pieces like earrings, pendants, and bracelets. Mom wore those diamonds proudly, whether she was pulling weeds, going to Walmart, or at the bridge table. She simply loved the way her diamonds sparkled. Sure, her clothes may have looked like floral draperies, and her hair may have been a mess, but she didn't care — as long as she was garnished with her precious diamonds.

Years passed, and it came time for my parents' 50th wedding anniversary. My only brother and I did it up big for our parents, whisking them away to Atlanta to treat them to dinner at our mother's favorite restaurant. It made her happy, but Mom had her eye on a very big diamond to mark the occasion. "The bigger the better," she said. And she had earned it, after all. Her wholesale (naturally) diamond guy found her a six-carat, round-cut one. Mom cooed over that rock, exclaiming that each carat represented a decade that she loved my dad, plus one to grow on. Mom had that gorgeous stone mounted with baguettes showcasing it on both sides. For the next six years, she never took it off her finger. She loved it and what it represented.

One summer day, out of the blue, things changed on a dime. There we were six years later, hearing the word "incurable." What a powerful word when it is directed at someone you love.

My mom proudly wore her diamonds to all of her chemotherapy appointments. Occasionally, as I sat with her, I would catch her glancing sadly at the six-carat ring on her IV-bruised hand. Many nurses would remark on its beauty, as my mom would proudly announce that she had earned every last carat. Indeed, she had.

Knowing how my mom loved that diamond made it all the more special when she left it to me. After wearing it on my hand for a year or so, I decided to set it into a necklace where it would be closer to my heart. It reminds me of my mom every day, no matter what I am doing, and it speaks to me in weird ways.

There was the time when I was tempted to buy asparagus at $5.99 per pound. Just as I was putting a bundle into my cart, I inadvertently touched the necklace. A wave of practicality washed over me as I headed over to the green beans instead. It wasn't about what I could afford, by any means. It was as if I was genetically programmed to suddenly be practical. Another time, I thought I should buy a new car because my old one needed a tune-up and a good mechanic. "Hold on a sec. Think about what you really want and then go get it," I could almost hear her whisper in my ear. It made me pause and think about how happiness isn't derived that way. What did I want? What would make me happy?

My mom's example of practical frugality taught me a lot about how making little sacrifices along the way can bring far more satisfaction in the end. That six-carat diamond, especially, brought my mom joy without fail. For Mom, diamonds made her feel empowered even though she may have eaten canned beans for years to afford the luxury. Diamonds were her kryptonite. One thing is for certain, though: Not even my mom could have known that her beloved six-carat diamond represented both a carat for each decade that she loved my dad and a carat for each year she had left to enjoy the pleasure that diamond gave her.

In some ways, it makes me *carpe diem* the hell out of life. What does "stuff" matter, anyhow? Other days, it makes me say and do whatever I want. Again, what does it matter anyway? Life is tricky that way.

My mom was far from perfect, and we fought sometimes. I was so obtuse, though. I never realized how much I dug her until it was time to dig her grave. All the diamonds in the world don't sparkle as much as she did.

— Kim Kelly Johnson —

23

A Lesson in Failure

*Most of the important things in the world have been
accomplished by people who have kept on trying when
there seemed to be no hope at all.*
~Dale Carnegie

The text said *I think I made a mistake in coming here.* My twenty-year-old son Aaron is a biology/pre-med major at Morehouse College in Atlanta and at the time of the text was a rising junior. But the "here" referenced in his text wasn't Morehouse; it was Case Western Reserve University in Cleveland, Ohio. He was there for a ten-week summer internship.

Why? What's wrong? I texted back.

I'm frustrated… I'm wasting my time here.

I wrote back. *Let's talk about it.*

But he responded, *It's gonna have to wait till later.*

I remember how helpless I felt as I ended the exchange. *Okay. Keep the faith, son. Things happen for a reason.*

From previous conversations, I fully understood his angst. Aaron's experiments exploring the connection between fructose and hypertension weren't going well. He couldn't figure out what he was doing wrong. His repeated requests for in-house assistance left him feeling incompetent and further confused. His feelings of isolation and his inability to bond with the other research students compounded the already precarious state of his emotions.

Plus, I suspected a recent encounter at a science conference had chipped away at my son's self-esteem. A couple of attendees implied that students from historically black colleges and universities (HBCSs), like my son, were not as intellectually gifted as those who attended other institutions of higher learning. The emotion I heard in Aaron's voice every time he mentioned the incident suggested the instigators had succeeded in making him doubt his ability and his academic choices.

When my son finally called, I did my best to encourage and reassure him. I reminded him of his proven capabilities and past achievements. He'd scored in the 95th percentile on the ACT. He'd been named a National Achievement Finalist. He'd been offered scholarships at a variety of colleges and universities. He was at Morehouse College on a full academic scholarship. The Case research coordinators wouldn't have selected him if they thought he was incapable of doing the work.

I even offered suggestions for coping with the situation — meet privately with the professor in charge, do the same with the administrator who recommended you to the program, solicit advice from friends with research experience at other programs, stay hydrated, get plenty of sleep, and try to exercise.

But what I didn't do was suggest he leave the program. Instead, I said, "You know you can't quit, don't you?" His silence indicated that wasn't what he wanted to hear. Nonetheless, I continued, "Because if you do, you'll always wonder what might have happened had you stayed. Besides, sometimes it's better to be dismissed than to give up on yourself."

Later, while second-guessing my response, I gave in and said he could leave the program if the situation didn't improve. But when I spoke with my seventy-five-year-old mother about her grandson's struggles, she instructed sternly, "Do not let him come home!" Furthermore, she said as soon as our phone call ended, she was contacting her morning walking partner so they could go into full prayer-warrior mode. She vowed to do the same with the ladies in her Christian fellowship group.

As amused as I was by my mother's impassioned church-lady response, I, too, am a firm believer in the power of prayer. My husband and I both sent up daily prayers on our only child's behalf, but with the understanding that the outcome — good or bad — was one we would have to accept.

In Aaron's case, not only did his experiments continue to fail, but a series of additional bad breaks and setbacks transpired. One morning, while making breakfast, he inadvertently set off the fire alarm, which drew the fire department and led to his dorm's evacuation. His plans to shadow a local emergency room doctor vanished in a never-ending shuffle of administrative paperwork. A black male medical student from whom he'd hoped to seek advice all but ignored him. And just when we all thought it couldn't get any worse, Aaron's efforts to relax and stay fit led to him hyper-extending his knee during a pickup game of basketball.

It pained me, not only to watch my child fail, but to witness him do so in such a devastating and spectacular fashion. Deep down, though, I knew learning how to gracefully accept a catastrophic outcome was an experience he needed. Any attempt by me to assist in his rescue would only impede his growth and maturity. His life wasn't in any real danger, I reminded myself repeatedly. He wasn't being harassed or discriminated against. And the internship, not to mention his suffering, would be over by summer's end.

Aaron informed us that his lack of lab results meant he would have no research findings to exhibit on presentation day. He would also likely have to forfeit the program's final paycheck. Resigned to such an outcome, I began focusing on how to help my son manage his disappointment and care for his bruised ego upon his return home. So imagine my shock and disbelief when I received a text message on July 13th — accompanied by several crying emojis — that read: *THE EXPERIMENT WORKED!!!*

It turned out that my son's failures in the lab were due, in large part, to a bad chemical reagent. Once the error was discovered and corrected, everything took a turn for the better. Not only did he present his findings at Case upon his return to Morehouse in the fall, but my son and another Morehouse student were selected to present their research projects at Icahn School of Medicine at Mount Sinai in New York City. More recently, the same summer research landed him an invite to the Annual Biomedical Research Conference for Minority

Students (ABRCMS 2017) that was held in Phoenix, Arizona. Last but not least, there's been talk that the work might be published in a science-related academic journal.

In the end, my son experienced a victory that no one privy to his situation could have ever predicted. It was a victory that, in my opinion, can best be described as miraculous. What I most hope he takes away from the experience is a greater appreciation for the power of patience, persistence and prayer. I think what my son and I both learned is that sometimes, just on the other side of what you're convinced is a total and complete failure, is actually a win so stunning and bright that you have no choice but to bow your head in acknowledgement and appreciation.

—Lori D. Johnson—

Chapter 3

Only She Would Think of This

24

Mom's Secret Mission

When I was young, I admired clever people.
Now that I am old, I admire kind people.
~Abraham Joshua Heschel

My mother grabbed her car keys and said, "Be back in a few hours."

"Where are you going?" I asked, puzzled that she'd be leaving on the busiest day of the year — Christmas Eve.

"There's an errand or two that I forgot to do. Be back soon," she said as she scurried out the back door.

Since we had company coming for Christmas dinner the next day, there were still things to do. I asked my dad if Mom had left us a to-do list, and he said no. We both knew that something was up.

"Maybe she forgot to get someone a gift," he said.

"You know how she despises going out on Christmas Eve," I reminded him. Mom never failed to start her shopping in August and was finished with her list by Thanksgiving.

Her temporary absence was indeed a mystery.

She was back at the house a few hours later, just as she had promised, and I asked if she got her errands done.

"Yes," was all that she would say, and I didn't feel like pressing. Maybe she had gone out to get that telescope that I wanted.

The next year, my mother disappeared again during the day on Christmas Eve. She continued to do so every year for the rest of her life. We didn't question it anymore.

The year she passed away I got a sweet letter from a man named Robert, who wanted me to know what my mother had done for him and his family for the last seven years.

Dear Johnny,

I just wanted you to know how much my family and I appreciate what your mother has done for us for all these years. Every year on Christmas Eve day your mom comes to my house dressed like Mrs. Claus and gives my kids a Christmas that we can't afford to give them. She has given them shoes, shirts, jeans, toys, and candy. I know your heart is heavy and that you are missing Miss Sue. We do, too. We loved her and just wanted you to know what she has done for us.

Love,
Robert and Nellie and the kids

That short note was the best gift that I ever received from anyone, better even than that silly old telescope.

—John Dorroh—

25

Holiday Harpooning

*Decorate your home. It gives the illusion that your life
is more interesting than it really is.*
~Charles M. Schulz

arly morning phone calls on a holiday weekend are always
cause for alarm. When I saw that it was my neighbor on
the caller ID I feared the worst.

"Cathi," she said, "I hate to bother you this early, but I
wanted to apologize for trashing the side of your house."

"Wait. Trashing our house?"

"You mean you don't know?"

"Know what?"

"Go outside and take a look."

I hopped out of bed and walked out the front door. My neighbor
called me to the side yard, where she held up the twisted and tattered
canvas of her patio umbrella.

"Wow. Where's the rest of it?" I asked.

She pointed above my head. I turned to find the umbrella pole
lodged in the side of the house with the accuracy of an Olympic javelin.
"What on earth?" I asked.

"Remember the big wind gusts last night?"

I recalled the fierce howling of the wind before bed. "Yeah."

"Well, we ran out to grab the patio furniture before it blew off
the deck, but we were too late. The wind picked up the pole, and it
shot through the air like a missile."

"Obviously." I looked at the pole's location in relation to the inside of my bedroom. "Uh, that's awfully close to our bed." I cringed. "And it's my side, too."

"We thought your bed might be along that wall, but we figured you were okay because we didn't hear a scream."

"I hate to point this out, but if it had impaled me in my sleep, I wouldn't have had time to scream."

"Good point." She winced.

We stood there a moment, taking in the sight of the pole suspended from the siding. "I suppose I'll call my insurance company to file a claim."

"Do you want us to help you remove the pole today?" she asked.

"I think we'll leave it there because they'll have to assess the damage. But thanks."

"We're so sorry," she offered.

I wagged my finger at her. "It's because our dogs bark early in the morning that you're trying to kill us, isn't it?"

"No, actually, it's because you accidentally set off your house alarm one too many times."

I looked toward the death spear. "Well, the alarm certainly didn't go off when this thing came barging into the house unannounced."

My neighbor and I parted on amicable terms, and I went back inside to find my husband standing in the kitchen. "What's all the commotion?" he asked.

I motioned for him to follow me. We walked into the bedroom, and I pointed to the visible drywall chips on the floor by the bedside. On further inspection, we saw that my nightstand had cracked in half. The pole had sliced through the siding, the wall, and the piece of furniture.

"What the heck is that?" Michael asked, pointing to the pole's end, which protruded a good ten inches through the bedroom wall.

I nodded toward the neighbor's house. "Their patio umbrella."

He stood for a moment trying to comprehend what happened. I explained the wind gust and my near harpooning while we slept. "I don't know what disturbs me more," he said, "the fact that a pole came slicing through the side of our house, or that we failed to notice."

"If it had sounded like one of the kids sneaking in after curfew, or one of the dogs barfing on the bedroom carpet, I would've shot right up in bed," I offered.

Later that day Michael called the insurance agent to report the incident, but due to the holiday weekend it would be a few days before an adjuster could come out.

"A few days?' I said. "What do we do in the meantime?"

"Just ignore it."

It seemed like we could ignore it, but others had a more difficult time. When I went back outside, a woman walking her dog stopped on the sidewalk and called out, "What happened there?" Then a few phone calls from neighbors came in, followed by cars stopping curbside. It appeared the pole had become a public spectacle of sorts, so I decided to make the most of our newfound celebrity status.

I hung an American flag on the pole. It was, after all, Memorial Day weekend. After a day of stares, snickers, and headshakes from passersby, I decided to try a new décor — hanging planters — petunias, impatiens, ferns, and moss roses, which caused more cars to slow and take a gander. People hung out of their car windows, pointing and laughing.

Two days later, our son Holden came home from his friend's house and asked, "Mom, why are there bras and underwear hanging from the pole on the side of the house?"

"Because they can," I replied, smiling at my creativity.

Piper, our daughter, laughed and said, "What the heck, Mom? Cars are stopping in front of the house. Can't we have a little privacy around here?"

"Privacy?" Michael chuckled. "We no longer have privacy since your mother decided to air our dirty laundry in front of the neighbors."

"Can't we just go back to normal?" Holden asked, tired of the parade of people.

"Normal? Oh, you mean just the pole jutting from the side of the house?"

"Exactly," he said.

Fearing the display of intimate apparel might eventually cause a traffic accident, I removed the garments from the makeshift clothesline.

By the end of the week, the adjuster arrived at the house. He stood, shielding his eyes from the sun while peering at the now barren pole. "Isn't this the strangest thing you've ever seen?"

Michael glanced at me and smiled. "Close."

— Cathi LaMarche —

Only She Would Think of This

26

Dinner for My Boyfriend

As a child my family's menu consisted
of two choices: take it or leave it.
~Buddy Hackett

Bringing a boyfriend home to meet my mom could be cause for concern. Even after I was grown and living on my own, I still worried how someone I brought home would react to Mom's eccentric ideas. She was unlike other mothers, and not everyone understood or appreciated her unconventional ways.

Reared by parents who emigrated from Transylvania, she was greatly influenced by the customs they brought from their homeland. Growing up dirt poor during the Depression, in the Yuma desert, Mom learned the value of hard work and frugal living. Her old fashioned ways were many and she was determined to hang onto them whether we liked it or not.

A fan of organic gardening, long before it was popular, Mom grew fruits and vegetables in a large plot behind our house on our five-acre farm. No insecticide or pesticide ever touched her plants. She didn't believe in being wasteful, either. Wormy and bird-pecked fruits and vegetables, that others might not find so appetizing, made it into the kitchen. She insisted that they could be salvaged, no matter how much had to be cut off to make them fit to consume.

Mom also raised animals for us to eat. While the men in the family butchered the larger animals, Mom had no trouble dealing with the chickens. All she needed was a stump and a hatchet. One chop and it was all over. Then the real work began.

The chickens were dunked in a pot of scalding water. Then we'd pluck the steaming hot feathers. The worst part for me was singeing the pinfeathers over crumpled newspaper. The smell was horrible and it seemed to take forever to get rid of the odor on my clothes.

Every part of the chicken that could be eaten was used. Gizzards, liver, and heart were either fried or cooked in soups. Chicken feet were considered a delicacy to our mom, no doubt a tradition brought over by her parents from the old country. She was the only one in our family who ate them, and after many years of adamantly refusing to take even a taste, she knew better than to try to give me one. Looking back, I'm sure she enjoyed my explosive reaction to her teasing, since it was obvious that she wanted to keep them all for herself. I can still envision her holding a chicken foot over her plate and gnawing on it.

A great cook, Mom made everything from scratch. She baked cakes and pies that always drew raves. Mom was also known for serving a variety of meats that some friends and family had never eaten before — and never planned to. Besides traditional meats most people were accustomed to eating, guinea, peacock, rabbit and goat meat were regularly on the menu at our house while squab, burro, and beef tongue and brains were served on occasion. No animal was completely safe on our farm.

Mom didn't feel it necessary to tell her guests what she was serving unless they asked. She couldn't wait to see the horrified expression on someone's face when she offered them food they had never imagined eating. Returning guests with a squeamish stomach or sensitive conscience would not eat any meat Mom prepared, until it had been positively identified. When some unsuspecting newcomer came for dinner, they were sometimes unhappily surprised when they were told what they had already eaten.

So, when I took my new boyfriend to dinner at Mom's house for the first time, I worried about what she would be serving. I could only hope that she had prepared something he would recognize and was willing to eat. When we got to the house, I was relieved to find out we were having chicken soup. Who doesn't like chicken soup?

With the pot of hot soup already on the dining room table, we sat down to eat and Mom began serving the soup. True to her upbringing, Mom made certain her guest was served first and she poured a large ladle of soup into his bowl. Then... oh, no! Before I knew what was happening or could stop her, she added a special treat to his bowl. A chicken foot! Though my boyfriend was completely shocked and disgusted by the chicken foot in his soup, he did not say a word about it. But he didn't eat much soup, either!

I sometimes wonder if the chicken foot in my boyfriend's bowl was really just a test to find out what my boyfriend was made of, to determine if he would be able to adjust to our unique family traditions.

That boyfriend eventually became my husband, with no help from my mom. Over the years I've made countless pots of homemade chicken soup, just like my mom did, except I used chickens purchased from the grocery store, chickens with the feet already removed. But my husband was so traumatized by the chicken foot that, for twenty-eight years he refused to eat chicken soup, unless he knew for certain it came out of a can.

— RoseAnn Faulkner —

27

A Call a Day Keeps the Loneliness at Bay

We cannot direct the wind but we can adjust the sails.
~Author Unknown

For much of my childhood, my mother filled the evening hours doing something for someone else. Sometimes she knitted hats for preemies, and at other times she cooked chicken soup for sick neighbors. Therefore, I wasn't surprised when one evening my mother announced she'd undertaken a new project.

"I'm going to telephone seniors," said my mother.

"Every night? But you don't even know these people."

"Doesn't matter," she said. "What's important is that I listen."

I was sixteen years old and couldn't fathom why my mother was willing to spend her evenings talking to strangers. She had friends and my two older sisters to call if she felt lonely. "They'll talk your ear off," I said.

My skepticism didn't diminish my mother's enthusiasm for the project. That evening, after washing up the dishes from supper, she settled on the sofa with the heavy rotary phone in her lap and dialed.

For a while, I listened as she asked the woman on the other line about her day, inquired what she had eaten for dinner, and asked if she had noticed that the daffodils in a neighboring park had begun to bloom. When she finished the call I said, "What do you care whether she had Jell-O or rice pudding for dessert?"

My mother grasped one of my hands and gave it a slight squeeze. "I'm the only person she talked to today."

It took me close to thirty years to fully understand the significance of that statement. Now, as my mother is nearing eighty, I find myself thinking about those nightly calls she used to make.

I am often the only person who telephones my mother, and sometimes I'm the only person she speaks to all day. I ask her what she cooked for dinner, but mostly I just listen as she recounts a walk she took, or how her dog Lucky stole a bunch of Brussels sprouts from the refrigerator.

I realize now that my mother's calls were lifelines that ensured housebound seniors remained connected to the world. Without her, their world would have been eerily empty. Somehow, she managed to juggle working full-time and raising a family while improving the lives of others. That kind of service requires commitment and superior organizational skills — traits and skills I do not possess. While she lifted the shroud of loneliness from the lives of five seniors, I struggle to call just one — my mother.

— Alicia Rosen —

Dog Gone Clean

Visits always give pleasure — if not the arrival,
the departure.
~Portuguese Proverb

Money was tight in our household, but my mother always shared what we could, as long as there was a genuine need. But that generosity had limits, limits which Mom handled in her own inimitable fashion.

We had some neighbors who finally pushed Mom over the edge. One day, they stopped by just as Mom was finishing dinner preparations, so she invited them to stay. But then it happened again a few days later — and then again after that! It actually became a regular thing. They would come knocking just before dinner and stay for a free meal. One thing I should mention is that they were in the same financial situation as we were. They could afford the same food we could. So, it was often frustrating to us kids. We knew these neighbors were taking advantage of us.

But Mom took care of the situation one night.

Right on schedule, the neighbors showed up for dinner again. Mom served it the same as always. When the meal was finished, the neighbors offered to wash dishes (a first for them). My mom said, "No, I can take care of it." Without missing a beat, she took all the dirty dishes and put them on the floor. Our dogs came rushing into the kitchen and happily lapped the plates clean, after which my mom put them back in the cupboard. Then she smiled at the neighbors and told them they were "ready for tomorrow."

Of course, tomorrow never came as far as our neighbors' dinner raid was concerned. For some strange reason, they stayed away after that!

— Betty Maloney —

Pajama Party

*You know children are growing up when they start
asking questions that have answers.*
~John J. Plomp

Every Christmas Eve, Mom let us open one present. I always hoped that the one I got to open would be a book, or maybe a toy, to keep me occupied the next morning until everyone else was awake.

But no, every single Christmas Eve it was the very same thing: pajamas!

When Mother handed each of us the selected gift to unwrap, she knew exactly which present held each kid's nightwear. But how did she know? It just couldn't be a coincidence!

At first I thought maybe she was stacking the gifts in a certain area under the tree to make sure all four of us got new PJs when it was time to get ready for bed. So one year I mixed up the placement of all the presents. No change. The girls still got nightgowns, the boys still got action figure designs, and it was all still flannel.

The next year I ruled out the color of the wrapping paper, since everything was wrapped in different designs. So I examined the tags of every package. Written on each tag was one of our names and a funny-looking squiggly design. Some squiggles looked like an exclamation mark with a twist. Some looked all loopy and flowery.

Two days before Christmas, I saw that there was one package for each of us with the same specific matching design on it. And that year, those were the very packages we got to open! It must have been some kind of secret code!

Try as I might, year after year, I couldn't make any kind of sense of the squiggles. By my junior year in high school, my problem-solving skills had sharpened somewhat. Christmas Eve I asked Mom if I could be the one to select our "night before Christmas" gifts to open.

"Okay," she said slowly, "but I have to approve your choices first."

I quickly picked out all four presents. She smiled. "You know which ones, but you're not sure why, are you?"

I agreed that that was the case.

My senior year in high school I took several secretarial preparation classes. I didn't want to be a secretary, but I wanted to be sure my typing and other skills would serve me well in college.

Mid-December rolled around, and suddenly the Christmas code made sense. I picked up package after package from under the tree and knew exactly what was inside.

Smugly, I went into the kitchen and confronted my mother. "The jig's up, Mom," I told her. "You're going to have to stop writing what's inside the presents on everyone's gift tags."

She looked up from her cookie icing, tilted her head and said, "And why's that?"

"Because..." I smiled and stole a frosted cookie from the racks, "...I'm taking shorthand this year, and I'm at the top of my class."

Her eyebrows nearly hit her hairline and she jumped to her feet. "Janet Marie!"

There were no more squiggly marks on package tags after that day, but I still got a new nightgown to wear on my last Christmas Eve at home. Marked in bold blue felt pen all across the red and green wrapping paper, it clearly said, "PJs for Jan."

—Jan Bono—

Thanksgiving Dressing

Most turkeys taste better the day after;
my mother's tasted better the day before.
~Rita Rudner

I gave my mother her wake-up call, as requested, and she assured me that she had been up since six and everything was fine. The giblets were boiling on the stove and the turkey was in the pan, ready to go.

Despite her confidence, I had an uneasy feeling something was amiss, although I wasn't sure what. I was only certain of one thing: My quirky, independent mother had insisted on making the Thanksgiving turkey this particular year.

Mom said, "I have to find something to cover the turkey breast, or it'll be dry. I need cheesecloth. But the oven's already hot, and I hate to go running out last-minute to the market. Besides, it's probably a madhouse. Well, I'll figure out something. Lemme get off the phone."

I heard a click as she hung up. Actually, I shouldn't have been concerned. Improvisation was second nature to Mother. After all, she was a former nightclub singer, and a rather creative thinker, too.

The nutty thing about my mother was that she heard music where the rest of us didn't. Music for Mom could be anyplace. Even a watercolor painting in the living room might serenade her. To me, you, or anyone else, it was merely a picture of a branch. To Mother, it was a line of musical staff. The drawing on the wall showed three small birds sitting in a tree. A larger bird (their parent) perched slightly below to the right. I knew from its colorful beak that the fourth bird was a toucan. For the longest time, Mother walked by the picture without giving it so much as a blink. Then one day she suddenly stopped and froze, staring at it intently.

"Reminds me of Beethoven," she muttered.

"Who?"

"You know. Beethoven. The composer."

A week later, she walked past it again. Only this time…

"Now I get it!" she exclaimed. "Beethoven!"

"Ma-RONE, Mom. What's with you and Beethoven?"

Rolling her eyes, she pointed to the birds. As she did so, with infinite patience she sang each note slowly. One after the other.

"Da-Da-Da-DUM! See?"

I did. Sort of. Those four birds represented to her the opening notes of Beethoven's Fifth Symphony.

My mother definitely thought outside the box, and she was continually surprising me. My uneasy feeling about our Thanksgiving dinner continued to bother me. Later that day, I called her again. "Hey, Mom, it's me again. Everything all right?"

"Terrific." She sounded happy, almost elated.

"Did you get the cheesecloth?"

"Ah, no. But I found something else. Don't know why I didn't think of it before."

"What'd you use?"

"You'll see when you get here. Oh, be sure and bring some more butter."

Relieved to learn things were on track, I began wrapping the foods I had prepared to accompany the turkey: cranberries with grated orange zest, bourbon yams, and green beans sautéed in broth. My sister was bringing a pie. It was going to be a great Thanksgiving! I grabbed the canvas tote bags, tossed in my keys and wallet, and walked out the door.

Hurrying down the hall in Mom's building, I could hear sounds of dishes clanking and happy voices in conversation coming from behind apartment doors. I was anticipating a warm, delightful family celebration with no surprises. Mom greeted me with a hug. I caught the aroma of cinnamon as our cheeks touched. I put the butter in the fridge and unpacked the food. Then I turned my attention to the turkey.

"Can I baste it?" I asked.

"Sure," Mom smiled, handing me a large spoon. "You know," she added, "I was right. The covering I used for the turkey worked great!"

Slowly, I opened the oven. A blast of hot air hit me, mingled with the heady scent of roast poultry. The oven had no light so I peered in, took a mitt, and slid the enamel pan toward me. There it lay. Brown and fragrant, the ten-pound bird reclined, flanked by glazed onion slices. Its ankles were tied with string. But my brain needed a few seconds to fully comprehend what I was seeing. The turkey was wearing a pair of white cotton underpants.

I started to giggle and couldn't stop.

"Mom, this is too weird!" I gasped between chuckles. "You've outdone yourself this time!"

"What's the matter?" she snapped. "I used a new pair that was in the back of the drawer. Jeez, it's not like I wore them or anything!"

With the help of trusty kitchen scissors, we snipped away the undies and eased them down, effectively disrobing the turkey. It was done to perfection. Moist, not dry as Mother feared it might be.

I had just dropped the fabric shreds into the wastebasket when the intercom shrilled. Our guests had arrived.

Soon, we were carving off the slabs of meat, and all of us tucked into a splendid holiday meal. Our neighbor, his mouth full of food, noted a stripe across the turkey's breastbone. The panty's elastic waistband had left a mark.

"Oh, that," Mom said casually. "I tied an extra string nice and tight. Can't let the stuffing spill out."

"Good thinking," he nodded. With that, he tossed another dollop of yams onto his plate. Mom shot me a quick sidelong glance. I decided to keep quiet and eat.

— Cindy Legorreta —

31

The Package

Christmas is not as much about opening our presents
as opening our hearts.
~Janice Maeditere

As surely as turkey and dressing followed jack-o'-lanterns, every December since I left home a package from my mother arrived signaling the official beginning of the holidays in my household. Upon its arrival, I would place the package in a prominent place and ponder the ethics of opening a parcel clearly labeled with the admonition, "DO NOT OPEN 'TIL CHRISTMAS!" In the battle of ethics versus curiosity, ethics never prevailed.

I rationalized, "What if Mom sent perishables?" I do confess that in all those years, I never opened a parcel containing tuna sandwiches and potato salad.

The packages did contain a mixture of items that were so varied and unrelated, they were worthy of inclusion in a time capsule prepared in a moment of pure whimsy. Over the years, there were jewelry caddies, address books covered in simulated zebra skin, swizzle sticks with cute sayings like "Alexander Graham Bell had hang-ups," and a gold electroplated Rudolph the Red Nosed Reindeer necklace, complete with "genuine ruby Nose."

The one constant was my mom's date and nut loaf, not to be confused with fruitcake. The date and nut loaves became legendary among my friends and work associates. The day after Thanksgiving, my friends became unusually solicitous. "How's your mom?" Or "Have you heard from your mom lately?" Finally, when subtlety failed, "Has the package arrived yet and when will we get some of that wonderful cake?"

As my children became worldly enough to understand the package also contained things for them, they joined the post-Thanksgiving vigil. They viewed the package as a mystical link to a grandmother they rarely saw, but were utterly convinced loved them without reservation. My children were quick to differentiate between the somewhat conditional nature of Santa's gifts and their grandmother's, which were given with no expectation of scholastic achievement or moral fortitude. This phenomenon puzzled me until I had grandchildren.

The package never contained big-ticket items and we never expected any. The pleasure came from not knowing what to expect. My mom had a talent for finding mutant variations of rather ordinary things. I remember the wooden salad spoons with hula dancer handles, the Indian Head pennies, and the children's sunglasses with pink plastic ballet dancers on the frames. My daughter wore them to dance class and was a sugarplum sensation.

An item that perplexed and then delighted me with its diabolical logic, when explained, was a book bag emblazoned with the name KIM. I did not have a child named Kim. Mom explained that she had heard on *Oprah* that it was not a good idea to allow young children to carry articles with their names in plain view. Some "bad person" could trick children into believing he knew them because he called them by name. Since my daughter's name was not Kim, she could not be tricked. Flawless in its simplicity.

Mom was one of those rare people who understood completely there was more to gift giving than going to Macy's. She knew anticipation far outweighed dollar value.

Even though we knew the package never arrived earlier than December 7th, we started actively discussing it at Halloween and then seriously looking for it after Thanksgiving. By the time it arrived, we had worked ourselves into a giddy frenzy. We adopted an almost Victorian formality when accepting the package from the postman:

It's here! Let the season begin.

My mom died in mid-October, too early for the package to have been mailed.

While cleaning Mom's house in preparation for sale, I found a package, wrapped in brown paper, tied with string, addressed to me. I have never opened that last package, but every Christmas, sometime around December 7th, I take the package, now somewhat tattered, and gently place it under our Christmas tree.

Let the festivities begin!

—Barbara D'Amario—

32

Busted

Nature abhors a vacuum. And so do I.
~Anne Gibbons

"Okay, now I am nervous," my boyfriend Jesse said, steering his Corolla onto the street where I lived as a child. It was the first time I was taking him home to meet my parents.

"Don't be nervous. I am not worried about them meeting you," I assured him. "I am worried about what you will think when you meet them."

My innermost thoughts were a little different. "Please, God, don't let him think we are a bunch of Froot Loops."

I loved my family, but their nutty characteristics, especially those of my mother, challenged my own sanity. Even I, who had been subjected to their eccentricities for thirty years, considered taking up drinking for family get-togethers.

In the past, I had a strict rule for myself — keep any potential mate away from the family as long as possible. But this guy was special, and against my better judgment, I broke my rule and took him to my mom's autumn dinner — the one she had every year to "welcome fall." I know. How could I not see it coming?

As we pulled into my parents' driveway I breathed a sigh of relief because we had dodged the first landmine. When one of my college roommates came home with me for a visit once, my jaw dropped when we drove up to a yard full of lumpy sheets. When I explained that my mom hated losing her flowers to fall's homicidal freezes, my friend said, "Does she tuck them in and tell them a goodnight story, too?" Taking guests home during the summer wouldn't alleviate the problem. The fruit trees would be covered with aluminum pie pans to scare away the birds.

That day, I looked at the bright red front door and took a deep breath. Beyond the threshold lay a minefield of idiosyncrasies waiting to be triggered.

I cringed to think of the sticky notes lying around willy-nilly. Mom is a little forgetful, so she leaves herself notes. One time, one of my friends pointed out a sticky note on the refrigerator that simply said, "Satan 7 p.m." PBS was airing an educational documentary on dangers of the occult, and Mom didn't want to miss it, so she left herself a reminder note. You can't fault her for a lack of brevity.

Then there were Mom's decorations. She has a special place in her heart for silk flowers, artificial plants, and a host of fake woodland creatures. She could run a Hallmark store out of her house. The fireplace mantel in the living room is her special showcase, elaborately decorated each holiday. Thank goodness it wasn't February. With all the heart-shaped lights, the living room looks more like a Vegas wedding chapel. Rightfully, that would have made my boyfriend of a month run pell-mell from the house, never to be seen again.

The dinner itself would involve everyone sitting down and starting to eat, only for my mother to suddenly yell out, "Oh, I forgot the salt!" Or, "Oh, I forgot the butter!" Years ago, I began putting the salt and butter right in front of her plate before dinner, but Mom is a creature of habit and yells anyway. Then there was the worst-case scenario. She could burst out with "Oh, I forgot my Beano!"

Then my younger sister, who might drop in for dinner, could display her conversational finesse. At one Christmas gathering, she described target practice with her new gun in one breath, and then in the next declared herself legally blind.

She and my mom would probably get into a colorful "discussion." My dad, who has complained for years about his hearing loss, would sit and watch, eyes volleying between wife and daughter like he was at a tennis match. Then he would leave the room and "not hear" anyone for an hour or longer, depending on the escalation of the debate. I'm tempted to tell him that no one would blame him if he were faking. Really, it's a coping mechanism. My brother realizes we are a normal-challenged family. He wouldn't be able to make it that day.

I took another deep breath, took Jesse's hand, and we walked to the door. My dad let us in and explained that my mom was downstairs finishing a few tasks.

At first, she had her back to us, rag in hand when we stepped off the basement stairs' landing. Then she turned around. I stared in horror. She was wearing a filtration mask on the lower quadrant of her face.

"Oh, hello," Mom said, cheerful voice muffled by the mask. She said it unabashedly as if she welcomed first-time guests into her home every day wearing a face mask. Who knows, I hadn't lived there in a while, so maybe this was her new thing. She finally put the dust rag down and slid off the mask.

"I have to wear this mask while I clean," she explained. "You know how my allergies act up if I get dust up my nose." No, I didn't know. And no, I didn't want to know. But when you live in a family like mine, you find out regardless.

We made it through the introductions and the dinner, and other than the business with the mask, we made it through the night without incident. Almost... until I picked up the family calico and rubbed her head while she purred. When I put her down, there was cat hair all over my red sweater. I asked Mom if she had a lint roller I could use.

"No, but wait just a minute," she said. She disappeared for a few seconds and returned with her hand vacuum. I froze. No, she wouldn't. But, yes, she would. She flicked the on switch and came toward me. Panicked, I sprinted down the hall like she was Leatherface with a chain saw. She caught me and started running the Dustbuster over my sweater. All the while, I was flailing and wailing, "No, no! It's okay!" But the damage was done. I had been Dustbusted by my mother in front of my boyfriend. When most people I know tell stories of being "busted" by their parents, it has a whole other connotation.

It was clear that I had found the right man when, despite the fact that my mother hand-vacuumed me the first time he met her at that fall dinner, Jesse continued to date me. One day a few years later, we even said "I do" while my whole family watched, admittedly looking and faking normal effectively. And amid the shiny white wrappings on the church gift table was a present from my mother that still graces our home today: a Dustbuster.

Don't worry. I don't have any plans of "busting" my own kids. At least not the way my mother "busted" me!

—Janeen Lewis—

33

A Mother's Help

God could not be everywhere, so he created mothers.
~Jewish Proverb

M y dad continued living in his home of forty years after we moved Mom to a secured dementia assisted living center. One Saturday, I decided to take my mom with me on the seventy-five-mile trip to check on my dad and their house. At this stage, Mom enjoyed riding and being outside. Plus, I knew how much the visit would mean to my dad.

We had a great day together: We enjoyed a meal at the kitchen table, got all the bills paid and mailed, laundry done and put away, the house was fresh and clean, and we made plenty of meals for Dad to enjoy throughout the week.

It was time for Mom and me to head back. Leaving Dad like this was always difficult for me. I knew he wanted us to stay longer, or even to have Mom return home permanently. We both knew that wasn't possible. I always fought back tears as I said goodbye.

We got Mom in the car and safely buckled in. Dad thanked me over and over again for the help. I knew he was grateful for the visit, and I promised him that we would come back again soon. Then we drove off.

Mom entertained me with stories and anything that she could see from her window. I listened quietly as I was pretty exhausted. Then, less than half a mile from Mom's facility, I drove through a green light at the intersection — or at least that would be my story when the red and blue lights flashed behind me.

I pulled over and explained to Mom that this would only take a second. By now, she was seeing a marvelous light show reflecting off the front windshield. Red. Blue. Red. Blue. Totally fascinated, she never noticed the officer approaching my car or the conversation between us. The officer asked where I was headed and I told him my mother lived at the facility nearby and I was taking her back there.

Fortunately, he was all too familiar with the facility because the police station was just two driveways east. Occasionally, some of the residents would get access to a phone and place emergency calls. These calls would soon to be followed by a visit from an officer responding to a call from someone claiming to be "kidnapped."

When he asked for my driver's license and registration I explained that my billfold was in the trunk because Mom had a tendency to take things out of it and hide them, but if he didn't mind I would get it for him. He agreed. I jumped out of my seat and headed to the rear of the car. But when I got there and tried to raise the hatch, the door was locked. I returned to the driver's door, where luckily I had left the window open, to unlock it. Again, I got to the hatch door and again it was locked. Starting to panic, I said to the officer, "Let me try again. I know I unlocked it."

After the third try, the officer suggested that maybe Mom was locking the door as I walked to the hatch. I couldn't hear it because our cars were still running. He said he would hit the unlock button once I got to the back of the car. He was right. As soon as she heard the unlocking sound, my mom would hit the button on the driver's side door, which locked all doors.

Both the officer and I could not contain ourselves. We laughed so hard and shook our heads. What else could we do? He saw the embarrassment and stress on my face. He was so patient and understanding. He simply asked me to be careful because drivers often have bad accidents at that intersection. He told me to take care and offered a blessing for the huge responsibility I had. I expressed my heartfelt appreciation for his understanding and promised to heed his advice.

Within the next sixty seconds, I had Mom back at her place, safe and sound. I headed home to enjoy the alcoholic beverage of my choice and to reflect on yet another moment that would make me laugh and smile for many days to come.

— Cheryl Edwards-Cannon —

A Second Chance at Love

*A bargain is something you can't use
at a price you can't resist.*
~Franklin P. Jones

My mother's home has a revolving door. Not really, but she loves to shop and then she needs to give things away since her house gets too full. It's a constant battle for her. She needs to get rid of stuff but she's not able to resist buying things. Fortunately, she likes to shop at tag sales, thrift stores, and Goodwill, since she doesn't like to spend a lot of money—and every day there are new things to buy!

Although her house is jammed with stuff, she is diligent about getting rid of it—since she has also acquired all the books about organizing, throwing out, and the joy of living with less! We've tried to help her rein in her shopping habits over the years, but the bottom line is that she can afford it, it gives her enormous pleasure, and it keeps her busy. The rest of us just shake our heads when she comes in excited about her new purchase.

One day when I was at her house she showed me a small, beautiful bone china pitcher that she had just bought at one of her favorite haunts. Although it was mostly white, the bone china had a delicate pattern, and it was hand painted with a green decorative line, small tulips and other flowers.

Only She Would Think of This | 107

I looked more closely at the pitcher. It actually looked very similar to one that I had seen before at her house.

"Mom, don't you already have one just like it?" I asked.

She stopped and looked at it. She thought for a moment. "Huh, yes, I guess you're right," she replied. "But I gave it away."

I looked at her wondering if what I thought had happened, had in fact happened.

She burst out laughing. "You know, I think I might have bought back the pitcher I gave away!"

"Yes, Mom, I think you did," I said, incredulous.

I waited a beat before I continued, "So much for that bargain. You bought it twice!"

"Don't look at it that way," she replied, happily. "I just fell in love with it all over again!"

— Gwen Daye —

| Only She Would Think of This

35

A Giant Box of Love

If the whole world were put into one scale,
and my mother in the other, the whole world
would kick the beam.
~Lord Langdale

I t couldn't have been easy for my mom — a single mother with three energetic kids ages ten to sixteen, who worked long hours to provide us with clothing and food. Somehow she did it, keeping us busy and out of trouble. Sometimes she had to be really creative.

One Christmas, Mom came home from work with three boxes... three refrigerator boxes. Seriously. Refrigerator boxes. That weekend, she sent us out to the garage with those boxes and several cans of paint. Our only instructions were to paint them however we wanted. We had no idea what those boxes would be used for and I painted mine my favorite color: bright purple. To add a touch of whimsy, I added huge yellow and orange flowers. It was the 1970's, after all. I can still picture that box; it was awful, really quite hideous, but my ten-year-old self was so proud!

After our day of painting, my siblings and I put those boxes out of our minds and began to look forward to Christmas Day. We knew Mom didn't have a lot of extra money; we shopped at the thrift store for school clothes, gathered supplies at Pic-N-Save, and bought day-old bread at a local bakery. But that certainly didn't keep me from wanting something very special that year. A just-for-me gift that wasn't a hand-me-down from my older brother or sister.

I knew, though, it was unlikely. We didn't have the money for the one gift I wanted and I was okay with that.

Christmas Eve came, and we followed our tradition of going to Christmas Eve service at church. We sang all the standard Christmas songs. Our pastor spoke of the birth of Jesus, the choir sang, the nativity scene was played out. Afterward, we sipped apple cider and munched on sugar cookies. My friends and I talked about what we hoped would be under the tree. I didn't even mention the special gift I wanted.

I kept telling myself that it wasn't going to happen. I would be happy with whatever my mom gave me.

We headed for home and followed another tradition of opening our stockings and one gift. Just one. As always, our stockings were full of candy, small toys, and a pair of socks. Finally, we opened that one gift — matching pajamas. We drank hot cocoa and sang a few more carols. Then it was off to bed.

On Christmas morning, we were not allowed to even peek in the living room before breakfast. This Christmas was no exception. After inhaling eggs, bacon, and toast, we ran to the living room... and stopped dead in our tracks.

Those refrigerator boxes were in front of the tree. But we still weren't allowed to open them. We had to sit quietly in our matching pajamas and read the story of Christ's birth from the book of Luke.

After prayer, we were finally allowed to open the giant boxes.

My sixteen-year-old sister's box was hiding a bright red beanbag chair, a very cool thing for a teenaged girl. She immediately settled in to what would be her favorite seat. My fourteen-year-old brother found a refurbished drum set in his box.

And in mine?

My very first, all-for-me bicycle! Exactly what I wanted! It too was refurbished, but that didn't matter. It was sparkly and purple with pink and white tassels! The basket was white with purple flowers! It was perfect. Just perfect. I could ride all I wanted without having to wait for my brother or sister to let me use theirs, which was never as often as I would have liked. I don't know how she did it, but my mom had once again made a Christmas wish come true.

Yes, it couldn't have been easy, but somehow, my mom made that Christmas one of the best I'd ever had… and few since have topped it. No other refrigerator boxes have appeared before my tree. And no other gift has illustrated a mother's love in quite the same way.

— Sauni Rinehart —

36

One Nice Thing

*When you look at your life, the greatest happinesses
are family happinesses.*
~Dr. Joyce Brothers

There comes a time when every mother reaches the end of her rope. That's what happened the Christmas of 1983 when we experienced Mom's version of *Shock and Awe*.

I am the oldest of six kids — five girls and one boy. Growing up, our different personalities often clashed, and Mom found herself repeatedly refereeing petty arguments. Each of us fiercely defended our viewpoint because if Mom couldn't determine who was at fault, we all got in trouble.

That Christmas, Mom was determined to put an end to the arguing, even if it was only for a little while. She had had enough. She loudly declared we weren't going to get any presents until we said one nice thing to each other.

Cue the groans and eye rolling. It made no difference. When Mom makes up her mind, that's it.

The compliments came slowly at first, but she didn't care. She was perfectly content to sit and stare at us all day if that's how long it took.

As Mom tells the story, the compliments were random and rudimentary. We barely looked at each other, focusing instead on the presents waiting in our laps.

Begrudgingly, Mom and Dad finally gave us our presents since technically we had fulfilled her request, and Christmas went on as usual.

But that wasn't the last of Mom's big idea.

The next year, she made the same proclamation. This time, she wasn't settling for anything less than sincere. We wondered what everyone was going to say.

By the third year, we were getting the hang of it. One nice thing became many. In the months leading up to Christmas, we would take note of a kind deed or special achievement so we could use it come present time.

After a while, being nice came easier. Mom would smile proudly, taking in every word we said as we sat around the living room... hoping the good feelings would last a little longer before the next petty argument erupted.

I was thirteen when she first had that ridiculous idea. I am forty-seven now, and we still can't open presents until we say something nice to each other.

What began as a punishment all those years ago has become a beloved family tradition. Even spouses, who aren't quite sure what to make of it at first, learn to enjoy it.

Over the years, our compliments became more and more meaningful. It is the moment in our family Christmas celebration that we all look forward to most. It gives us permission to say what we don't take time to say throughout the year. It is a moment often filled with belly laughter as inside jokes and funny stories from the year are woven into a meaningful pat on the back.

We can most certainly count on a few tears as well. The tears come not just from the person to whom the kind words are spoken, but also from the giver of the kind words, overwhelmed and reminded that our family is strong and we have each other's backs — always.

The six of us, now grown with our own families, are spread out all over the country. We don't have nearly as many opportunities to argue, and we've come to terms with our differences. In fact, we love hanging out together.

Maybe it's because Mom taught us to overlook the irritating parts and notice the good in each other. Maybe it's because Mom taught us to look each other in the eye and really talk. Maybe it's because we learned we could disagree sometimes and still find reason to offer sincere praise. Thanks, Mom.

—Allison Andrews—

Christmas Lilly

Compassion brings us to a stop, and for a moment
we rise above ourselves.
~Mason Cooley

Everyone has heard the saying that life is what happens while we're making other plans. In our case, it proved to be true. My daughter crawled out of bed one cold December morning, kissed her husband, confirmed their future reservations for New Year's Eve with friends, and went to work like any other day. By sundown, she'd made a decision that would change all of our lives... forever.

I remember the phone call well. With Christmas only a week away, she'd been busier than usual at work, a treatment center for troubled teens. So I was surprised when she called me in the middle of the afternoon from Walmart.

"Mom, I have to make the decision tonight," she said.

"Tonight?" I tried to hide my concern. She'd often hinted that I worried too much, but then my dear daughter had never been a mother.

Recently, however, she'd been mentoring a young, single mother who was now asking my daughter to keep her baby over Christmas. Until now, I'd been completely supportive, but this latest development baffled me. "Isn't this a bit... risky?" I asked.

"Risky? Seriously, Mom, you should come to work with me one day. On second thought, bad idea."

She'd never been afraid of a challenge, that's for sure. But this?

This felt different.

"I think I can handle a baby for a couple of weeks."

"Of course. You're great with kids." That wasn't what concerned me. "But what if someone all pumped up on drugs or something comes banging on your door?"

"Well, fortunately, I have a relationship with both DHS and the police if trouble comes knocking. Don't worry. It's only until a spot opens up for her and the baby at the unwed mothers' home."

"I still don't understand why her older brother is willing to let her stay with him, but not her baby. Do you think she's giving you the whole story, honey? And are you sure she's been accepted into…"

"Slow down," my daughter interjected. "I spoke with both her brother and the program director. The brother is sharp. His place is tiny. Honestly, they probably have a better shot at reconciliation without a baby around."

"And the program?"

"Both baby and mother are guaranteed residency at the end of the month. It's an excellent facility. If anyone can help her succeed, they can. Everything will be fine."

Fine, she'd said. An optimist by nature, my daughter had also become a realist as a result of her profession. She knew the risks. I had to trust her. And God knows I wanted that baby to be safe and warm while the young mother tried to work things out with the only family member willing to help.

Still, I couldn't help but be concerned for my own daughter. The mother had run with a pretty rough crowd. And what if she didn't follow through? Suppose she took off — then what?

"What does your gut tell you, honey?" I asked finally.

"I believe she loves her baby the best way she knows how. I also believe she can learn the skills to become a responsible parent if she wants to."

I admired my daughter's courage and compassion and was proud of her, in spite of my concerns.

"Sounds like your decision has already been made. What does your husband think about having a little one around for Christmas?"

"I'm not sure." She hesitated. "We haven't had time to talk yet."

Had I just heard my daughter correctly? For the second time in fifteen minutes, I was speechless.

"Mom? You there?" she asked. I could almost feel her eyes rolling. "It's not like I'm keeping anything from him. Someone has to do something, and apparently that someone is me."

My daughter and her husband had always talked about having children, but so far their only family walked on four furry feet — two dogs and a cat. I thought my beloved son-in-law would be okay with his wife bringing home a child for a day or two, but two weeks?

"Mom, this is happening so fast. I texted him earlier with as much info as I knew at the time. I told him we needed to discuss something really important, and I asked that he please not say 'no.'" Her voice choked. "At least, not tonight."

I wanted to reach through the phone and hold her — my brave, sweet, and fiercely independent girl. She'd always been respectful of her husband's opinions, even when they differed. I heard the dilemma in her voice.

"I understand, honey. Dad and I are behind you both."

"Thanks, Mom."

I thought our conversation had come to a close, but there was more.

"Mom? I have to tell you something else. I guess I have made a decision, as much as is up to me anyway, but not just for the reasons we've discussed. Something happened today. Here, of all places." I could hear the emotion in her voice. "For the first time in my life, I stood in a shoe department completely bewildered."

That was something. My daughter loved shoes, and shopping for them had always been cathartic for her. I almost chuckled.

"I held these two little boxes of shoes but had no idea what to buy. Mary Janes? Sneakers? High-tops? So many selections. Even more confusing was the range of sizes. All I know is that her little toes nearly ruptured the pair she has now," she continued. "And the price tag, wow! With Christmas coming, our budget has already been stretched. I seriously began to question if I was doing the right thing. I started thinking, *What if?* And then I heard a voice say, *What if you are buying shoes for your daughter?* Mom, the voice wasn't audible, but the words were clear as day. And, suddenly, so was my decision." She sobbed. "I knew exactly what I was supposed to do."

Tears spilled from my eyes. I took a deep breath and straightened my shoulders. How could I have ever let fear and doubt question my daughter's willingness to be the hands and feet of Jesus? Especially at Christmas. "Lord, please forgive my unbelief," I prayed.

I, too, knew what my daughter and son-in-law would be doing that cold December night. They'd be making room at the inn… for Lilly. And now, my precious granddaughter Lilly is five, and Christmas is her favorite time of year. In fact, she starts planning for it in October, asking me when I'm coming to visit. Somehow, I think she remembers….

—Julia M. Toto—

38

Play Ball

A hot dog at the ballgame beats roast beef at the Ritz.
~Humphrey Bogart

"**M**om..." I tried not to sound too condescending, but my displeasure was evident. "You can't wear that to the ball game."

Mom stood up straight, looked me square in the eye, and said, "Give me one good reason why I can't wear this shirt to Safeco Field." She puffed out her chest. "It's my eightieth birthday, and I can wear anything I want!"

I sighed. "The Mariners are playing Boston, Mom. Boston Red Sox fans will be wearing red."

"Your point?"

"I'm not sitting next to a woman who dresses like a Red Sox fan."

"But I look good in red."

I sighed a second time, picked up a wrapped present I'd earlier set on her kitchen counter, and handed it to her. "Open this."

"I thought we were going to wait to open presents until later—when we have the birthday cake."

"Just open it, Mom."

She tore into the wrapping like a little kid on Christmas and held up a blue and white baseball jersey with a large 51 printed on it. "Oh! Fifty-one! That's Ichiro's number! He's my favorite right fielder of all time!"

I smiled. "So why don't you wear that today?"

Mom was already folding the shirt and attempting to reinsert it into the torn wrapping paper. "I don't want to get mustard all over it, and you know I'll have to have a Major League Mariner Hot Dog with the works while we're at the ball park."

"But you don't have to spill mustard on your shirt. That's optional."

She stuck her tongue out at me.

"Just try it on, Mom."

She headed down the hallway to her bathroom. "At least you didn't get me a hat. I won't wear hats. Hats really mess up my hair."

I smiled. For the past decade, Mom and I had gone to Mariner games twice a year—on Mother's Day in May and on her birthday in August. It was a tradition I loved, and I eagerly looked forward to each game. She loved "her boys," and I loved spending quality time at the ballpark with the woman who had instilled a love of the sport of baseball in me at an early age.

"How's this?" said Mom, returning to the kitchen. She had on the shirt, along with a light summer windbreaker. A red windbreaker.

"Mother! You've got to be kidding!"

"Now you look here, young lady..." She squinted her eyes, put her hands on her hips and dramatically stomped her foot.

"The shirt is blue and white, the jacket is red. Red, white, and blue are America's colors. Baseball is the all-American sport. You've always known how patriotic I am, so quit complaining, and get in the car. I want to get there in time to watch batting practice!"

There was no arguing with logic like that, so I picked up my car keys and we headed out the door.

God bless my mother; God bless the USA.

—Jan Bono—

39

Chicken Soup for the Soul

The Wrong Bag

Every survival kit should include a sense of humor.
~Author Unknown

I stumbled to the kitchen. It was way too early to be up after a long night writing. I filled the coffeepot with water and tilted the coffee bag over the filter. Nothing! I opened the bag wider and looked inside. Empty!

"Mom!" Lee called from the other room. "Mom?" I rummaged in the cabinets. There was another bag of coffee somewhere.

"Mom?" He walked into the kitchen. "Didn't you hear me calling you?"

"Yeah," I answered. "Whatever it is, just hang on a second. I'm trying to find some coffee." I checked the pantry. No coffee there either.

"This is important," Lee demanded. I paused and looked at him. "You have to make my lunch today. I'm going on a field trip to the courthouse." Oh, no! Was that today?

"Okay, I'll take care of it." I gave up the search for coffee and started looking for things to put in a bag lunch. We were out of lunchmeat so he got a PB&J sandwich minus the jelly because we were out of that too. There hadn't been time to go to the grocery store yet this week.

Ring! Ring! I snatched up the phone with one hand while searching for the Hostess cupcake hidden behind the canned veggies with the other. "Hello."

"I'm not going to be able to help decorate for Karen's bachelorette party tonight," my friend Amie said. "I have a job interview but I have all the decorations. Can you come by and get them before you take the kids to school?" Just great! As if I didn't already have enough to do. But I agreed. What else could I do?

I hung up and looked with longing at the cupcake in my hand. I'd hidden it away for a day like this, when things were crazy and I needed the comfort of chocolate. Sighing, I put it next to the sandwich I'd made for Lee. I didn't have any chips or anything to put in his lunch, so the least I could do was give him dessert.

Cody came running in. "Mom, I can't find my T-ball uniform."

"It's in the dryer." I looked over at my middle son, Rob, calmly eating his cereal. He was always so calm while the rest of us ran around like chickens with our heads cut off. I grabbed a Walmart bag from under the sink and handed it to him. "Would you grab Cody's uniform for me?"

I grabbed another Walmart bag and started packing Lee's lunch, glancing at the clock. We were running late and Cody and Lee hadn't eaten yet. I popped two waffles in the toaster; they could eat on the way. I rushed everyone out to the car and started to back up.

"Wait," Lee yelled. "I forgot my homework." I watched the minutes tick by while we waited for him to find it. He got back in and I pulled out of the driveway heading to Amie's.

"Don't forget Chelsea," Rob said from the back. Shoot! I forgot I was supposed to give the girl down the street a ride. I pulled back in and went the other way. We were really running late now. At least Amie was waiting outside with the decorations when we got to her house.

I was lost in thought, trying to figure out how I was going to do everything that needed to be done. Drop Chelsea and the older boys off at school, spend the day volunteering in Cody's classroom, pay bills at lunch, pick the boys up after school, take Cody to his T-ball game, drop the kids off at my mom's house, and decorate for Karen's party before it started at 7:00.

"Mom," Lee interrupted my thoughts. "You missed the school."

I turned around in the nearest driveway. "Sorry, guys. My mind isn't working very well today. I haven't had my coffee."

"You know coffee is a drug don't you?" Chelsea asked. "My class went on our field trip to the courthouse yesterday and the policeman told us all about drugs."

I pulled in the parking lot. "That may be," I answered, handing Lee his lunch. "But I could sure use some."

Thankfully, the staff lounge at Cody's school had coffee made. I sipped a cup and felt my mind begin to work again.

The morning passed without incident. At lunch, I ran out to drop off some bills and order a burger from McDonald's. While waiting in the drive-thru, I noticed the bag of decorations sitting on the floor. Curious to see what naughty items Amie had picked out for the bachelorette party, I opened it. The first thing I saw was the cupcake. Oh no! I had given Lee the wrong Walmart bag. I glanced at my watch. If I hurried, I might be able to make it before they started eating.

I pulled out of line and rushed to the courthouse. As I parked, I could see Lee's teacher getting the class settled on the courthouse lawn. I grabbed Lee's lunch and ran across the street. Where was he? There! I spotted him talking to a police officer and hurried over.

"My mom does drugs," Lee was saying. "But she ran out this morning and her mind isn't working right." He held his bag up. "That's why I got this instead of my lunch."

He turned the bag upside down and dumped assorted party supplies, many shaped like… man parts… on the ground at the officer's feet. I was standing there mortified, wondering if I could just slip away, when Lee saw me.

"There's my mom right there." I hurried to scoop the stuff off the ground under the watchful eyes of Lee's teacher and the policeman. I could feel my face burning as I mumbled something about a friend's bachelorette party and not having any coffee. I glanced around to see both the teacher and the police officer trying unsuccessfully not to laugh.

Later on I was able to appreciate the humor of the situation but not right then. I was too embarrassed. But I did learn a valuable lesson that day. Always double check the bags to make sure the right things go with the right people. And keep a spare bag of coffee in the pantry.

— Kimber Krochmal —

Chapter 4

Always There for Us

40

Never Too Old to Want My Mommy

*A mother's arms are made of tenderness and
children sleep soundly in them.*
~Victor Hugo

Dccember 16, 2009, was the worst day of my mother's life. It was the day I told her that her thirty-six-year-old daughter had stage III breast cancer. I will never forget the look of devastation in her tear-filled eyes as I told her. Seeing my mother sob uncontrollably broke my heart. It was one of the few times in my life that I saw my mother weak and vulnerable.

Since I had been diagnosed with advanced breast cancer, the doctors had a heavy-duty plan of attack to beat it, which would mean a double mastectomy, five months of chemotherapy, ovary obliteration, and five weeks of radiation. It also meant that a fiercely independent single girl who lived alone was in serious need of some help taking care of herself.

Thankfully, I was blessed with my own personal army of family, church, friends, and co-workers who had offered to help me out with whatever I might need, including meals and rides to doctors' appointments. But as grateful as I was, there really was only one person who I wanted by my side — my momma. My mother lived more than 300 miles away, but didn't even give it a second thought. She was going to be my primary caregiver, chauffeur, personal chef, nursemaid, communications liaison, counselor, and shoulder to cry on. No one else in the world could fill her shoes. It was a job that only she could do.

The night after my first chemotherapy treatment is forever imprinted in my memory. I was never so sick in my entire life. I couldn't even keep down a glass of water. And after hours spent in the bathroom, I weakly lifted myself into bed, weeping, "Please, God, take this away from me. Please make me feel better." At that moment, my mother crawled into bed with me, wrapped her entire body around me, and cried with me. Just like when I was a little girl, her arms enveloping me made it better.

Over the next six months, my mom traveled back and forth between two homes and two lives just to take care of her thirty-six-year-old little girl. She sat by my side for almost every chemo treatment and made me grilled cheese sandwiches in the middle of the night. She ran to the pharmacy when I was in severe pain and the video store when I wanted to be entertained. Basically, she put her life on hold to take care of me, her baby.

I think about what my mother sacrificed while I was going through such a tumultuous time in my life. She was attending to my every need, both physically and emotionally, but who was attending to her needs? Who heard her cry in the middle of the night when she sobbed for her daughter? I know what my mother would say if I asked her that question. She would say, "That's just what you do when you are a mother." And for that, I am eternally grateful.

— Tiffany Mannino —

41

Chicken Soup for the Soul

I Get Misty

A song will outlive all sermons in the memory.
~Henry Giles

My grandmother loved music and played the piano and the organ, and my mother played the piano as well. But she needed the sheet music for everything she played except for the song "Misty," which she knew by heart. It was a running joke in our family that every time we visited someone with a piano, at some point, my mother would sit down and laughingly ask, "Anybody wanna hear 'Misty'?"

My parents were married for forty-three years, taking up the RV lifestyle in their mid-fifties and traveling around the country. They settled in Longview, Texas, and bought a small house there. One night, my mother began to feel ill. She'd been plagued with respiratory problems most of her later life, and my father took her to the hospital. She was admitted for the night. The next morning, as my father was preparing to leave to visit her, the hospital called to tell him that my mother had passed away.

My father was shattered. I booked the next flight to Dallas, rented a car and headed to Longview.

Later that evening, I suggested we go out to dinner, if for no other reason than to get out of the house. He agreed, and off we went.

From the subdivision where my parents lived to the "restaurant row" of Longview was about a ten-minute drive. We ate dinner and tried to make conversation with each other. As we got in the car, I told my father that I wanted to make a stop at a convenience store to grab some diet soda. On the drive back, we began discussing the various things we needed to get done as far as a service, notifying out-of-town relatives, and other arrangements. As we talked and drove, I passed at least five or six different convenience stores, telling myself, "I'll stop at the next one."

Finally I came to an intersection that was also the turn-off to get to their subdivision. There was a store there, so I pulled in and got out, realizing that this was my last opportunity to grab some soda.

I opened the door and walked in, and as I did, I heard music coming from a radio behind the counter.

It was Johnny Mathis singing "Misty."

I froze. And then I smiled, realizing that it was my mother reaching out to me one more time, asking if I wanted to hear "Misty."

— Greg Moore —

The Jacket

A grandma is warm hugs and sweet memories.
She remembers all of your accomplishments and
forgets all of your mistakes.
~Barbara Cage

When I was a child, our family would go to my grandparents' every Sunday night for dinner. We'd walk in the door, and the first thing to greet us would be the wonderful aroma of roast beef cooking in the oven.

But what always made the visits extra special was dessert. My grandmother would always scoop ice cream for my sister and me, smother it with chocolate sauce, and top it with a maraschino cherry. Then she'd look around slyly as if someone might be lurking. If the coast was clear, she'd always put an extra cherry on mine. (I don't remember if she did the same for my sister, but I'm guessing she did.)

She was the stereotypical grandmother — caring and doting, spoiling her grandchildren, always willing to help out my mom. But there was her other side. She took no sass from two daughters, nor from her sons-in-law, and definitely not from her grandchildren. She had no qualms about doing "the right thing," no matter the consequences or embarrassment she might inflict. That leads me to another kind of grandmother memories.

It was a beautiful fall day in 1968, a Saturday. I was eleven years old and on my way out the door to see a movie with some friends.

Always There for Us | 129

"Take your jacket. It's chilly outside," my mom called from the kitchen.

"Okay!" I yelled back and raced out the door. I could see my friends already at the corner waiting for the bus to take us downtown.

Yeah, it was a little chilly outside, but certainly not enough to warrant a jacket. Cool eleven-year-old boys did not wear jackets unless the temperature dipped into the low forties. Really cool boys didn't wear jackets until the temp hit freezing. It didn't matter if our skin turned blue and goose bumps covered our arms. It just showed how tough we really were. Besides, it had to be about fifty degrees that day, and the sun was out. Not even close to jacket weather. So, out the door I went, sans jacket.

As I trotted down the driveway, my grandmother pulled up in a white car. I stopped to give her a quick peck on the cheek and a "hello."

"What do you think of my new car?" Her voice was full of pride.

"Looks great." I barely noticed, more concerned about being with my friends.

"Shouldn't you be wearing a jacket?"

I shouldn't have said what I did, but my friends were waving frantically, signaling the bus was in sight.

"Mom said it was okay." I took off running toward the bus stop.

Best-case scenario: Mom and Grandma would never mention it to each other, and I'd get away with it. Worst-case scenario: My mom would find out I didn't take my jacket, and I'd get grounded. But what could I do? The bus was on the way.

The bus picked us up, and we took our seats in the back, like we always did, as far away from the adults as we could.

Not six blocks away from where we boarded, the driver stopped to pick up another passenger. As the bus started to roll, it came to a sudden stop, blaring the horn as the passengers lurched forward. The horn stopped, and the door opened. Up the steps climbed my grandmother. The bus went silent as this small, elderly lady tromped to the back of the bus, locking me in a death glare. When the passengers saw whom she was scowling at, all eyes turned toward me. How could anyone not notice my face turn a bright shade of red?

She never said a word as she stood in front of me, her arm extended, my jacket dangling from her fist. Sheepishly, I took the jacket. Still without a word, my grandmother turned around and exited the bus.

As soon as the doors closed, everyone on the bus, friends and strangers alike, erupted in laughter. I felt about two inches tall, and wished I was so I could hide. Still beet red, I looked out the window to see a shiny white car back away from where it had blocked the bus. The bus continued on its route, my friends teasing me relentlessly, and smiles flashed on all the passengers' faces. I'm sure they all had a great story to tell when they got home.

I came home that afternoon, and my mother never said a word about sending Grandma after me. For my part, I thought it best to keep my mouth shut, too. For the rest of the day, we pretended that nothing happened. I was able to put the incident behind me. But the following evening was dinner at the grandparents'. How should I act? She had made me a laughingstock — something my friends would never let me forget.

It turns out nothing happened. My grandmother never said a word. And when it was time for dessert, there was an extra maraschino cherry on top of my ice cream. All was forgiven.

— David Fingerman —

Double Exposure

A mother's love runs deep and its
power knows no limit.
~Author Unknown

The last time my mother was at our house was Thanksgiving Day. She had been diagnosed with advanced stage cancer two months earlier, and she was already showing signs of weakness. So instead of the usual "Thanksgiving at Grandma's house," we decided to have it at ours.

By the time everyone arrived, the house smelled of turkey and stuffing, and the tables looked festive and inviting. It was a good day for my mom and dad, with a house full of children and grandchildren. We ate and laughed about times growing up. Then, while the kids played, we put the football game on TV and played pinochle with my dad.

It was nice for us to see my mom dressed up and out of their house for a change. She spent most of that day sitting in the comfortable rocker in the living room. We took lots of pictures that Thanksgiving.

After that day, Mom's condition worsened quickly. She died two weeks later, just before Christmas. It was the first of many holidays and special occasions without Mom there to celebrate with us.

Time lessened the grief, but we still missed her very much. She and my dad had always been there for their grandchildren's birthdays, school events and special times in their lives, and my dad still came. One of those special occasions arrived the following spring.

Our youngest daughter made her First Holy Communion, which

is a special celebration in our church. I got out the white dress and veil that my mother had bought for me when I made my First Communion. I washed it and hung it out to dry. The lace sparkled in the sun. I replaced the yellowed ribbon and sewed a new white slip. How sad, I thought, that Mom would not be here to see her granddaughter on this day. Sarah was especially close to her grandma and grandpa. She had spent a lot of time with them before she started school, since they babysat her when I returned to work. It would be the only First Communion of our six children that my mom would miss.

We had lots of family over that day and, as usual, we took lots of pictures with family and friends. I was anxious to see the pictures, and quickly took them in to be developed. This was back before digital cameras, when you had to load the film into the camera, and then take the film to the drugstore to have the pictures developed.

When I picked up the photos I opened the folder, and for a moment my heart almost stopped. Right on top was a picture of Sarah in her communion dress sitting on the arm of the rocker, and next to her, sitting in that comfortable rocker, was my mother! The picture was a little fuzzy, but there was no mistake — it was Sarah and her grandma, on the day that she made her First Communion.

When I got over my initial shock and looked through the rest of the pictures, I realized that the photos had been double-exposed — communion pictures taken on top of Thanksgiving pictures. In the time that had passed there were holidays and birthdays when I had taken other pictures. But somehow I had missed taking in this one roll of film from Thanksgiving. And I had re-used that roll of undeveloped film on that day, thinking it was a new roll of film.

What were the odds! But that day in May, my daughter's picture was taken sitting next to her grandma. It was as if my mother was sending a message from heaven saying, "See, I haven't missed anything! I've been right here beside you all the time."

— Peggy Archer —

44

Turning to Mom

Because I feel that, in the Heavens above, the angels,
whispering to one another, can find, among their
burning terms of love, none so devotional
as that of "Mother."
~Edgar Allen Poe

I was finding lots of things as I looked through the old cedar chest. Ornaments that I made in elementary school—could that really be fifty years ago? Cards I had received and stashed away, cards Mom had received and stashed away before me. That chest held two intertwined lifetimes of memories. Finally my eye caught the glint of the coil-bound notebook that I had been searching for. I knew the pages contained the comforting words I needed.

It had been a long and strange day, and I was seeking comfort. Earlier that day, I completed the final tests in a long litany of pokes, prods, and X-rays. Now I needed something to calm me as I waited for the verdict. I felt alone—abandoned, even. I needed the loving assurance that only a mother can give, and that was why I was poring through that chest.

Mom had faced similar moments as she journeyed down her own cancer path decades earlier. I had experienced her journey by her side, and then laid her to rest.

What I was seeking now were *her* thoughts as she waited for "the news." That's what I knew she had tried to write about in this notebook that I had bought for her. Peeling back the cover now, I was eager to learn from her wisdom and was immediately struck by the dearth of words. So few pages had been filled — and two of them were in my own handwriting. This surely wouldn't be enough to hold onto. But then I began to read...

> *Dear Mom,*
> *This isn't anything fancy, but this type of scribbler is just what I use for my journal. I think your idea for writing your experiences/thoughts/revelations down is a really good one. It will likely help you a lot and, who knows, it may end up helping other people. But I think you should do it for yourself first — writing can be very therapeutic.*

I looked up from the notebook, struck that the person "it may end up helping" turned out to be me. I didn't think of this at the time I had purchased it, of course, but this simple notebook and the few pages that had been used were a gift. To myself.

I turned the page to reveal my mother's entries.

> *August 8, 1995*
> *I finally got started to write. 2 weeks ago today July 25 I had surgery removing my left breast — let's go back to June 26 at doctor's for annual check-up. Whole world changed. Found lump in my breast and she explained it was very suspicious and she made appointment for many tests. She asked how I was? I said, "You tell me." Things moving very fast now and surgery is in a few days. She said I was taking it very calmly. It was then I realized the same calm (my guardian angel?) that I got when Bob's diagnosis was revealed. She said about steps I'd go through anger, denial, etc. I had remembered this from Bob's experience, too, and left it in God's hands. With my doctor's warning and God's guidance, I was calm.*

There it was. That calm that enveloped her in that moment remained until her end. That's what I remember most about that long-ago time, and what I craved to feel now. With her few simple words, that's what she was providing. When was the last time I had put God first? My daughter, my obligations to family and friends, deadlines and commitments, busyness of life — that's what fueled my days. But heeding this guidance from heaven, that's what was needed here for me right now. Her journal continued to describe the logistics of the next few weeks, the appointments and tests, and her continual reminder to herself of her "heavenly guidance."

> *Told my kids and what a shock it was for them. They are trying to take it in stride, I can see, but I'm sure they remember this happening with their Dad nine years ago. At this time I prepare myself for the worst. If it was my time, I had lived so much longer than Bob, had raised four children who were well-established, had seven grandchildren and I had a lot to be thankful for. I'm not afraid to die, because of all the people I love who have gone before me. Very conscious of suffering I might go through, but also know that God wouldn't give me anything I couldn't handle.*

And that was it. A few paragraphs that, in this cellar on this day so many years after she wrote them, felt to me as though she was holding my hand. I sat quietly with her words, feeling reminded of my own gifts. I, too, loved my life and felt grateful. I calmly looked down to read the short final passage, in my own handwriting:

> *Thank you for living as long as you did. Thank you for loving as well as you did. Thank you for teaching all that you did. Thank you.*

A heavenly conversation with my mother. A message of comfort, delivered to myself through the years. My mother had spoken to me, at my own long-ago behest, and her voice was never more clear.

And just then the phone rang and I turned to look calmly in its direction. I was surrounded by angels and I felt strong.

— Sandy Kelly —

45

The Inside Story

I was 32 when I started cooking; up until then,
I just ate.
~Julia Child

I stared at the chicken section in the grocery store, trying to figure out why there were so many options. There were legs, thighs, whole organic chickens, split breasts, breasts with skins, skinless breasts, fryer chickens and roaster chickens. The choices seemed endless. At least I knew I wanted to make a whole chicken. But which one? Should it be the fryer or the roaster?

I had never cooked a chicken before in my life. I had just moved into my new home with the man of my dreams and I had a baby on the way. The tears started stinging my eyes. My only option was to pick up my cell phone and call my mom. I told her where I was and what my great dilemma was. There was a familiar sound on the other end of the phone. Still staring at the chicken choices in front of me I sighed, "Mom, are you laughing at me?"

I believe she hiccupped and erupted into another fit of hysterics. At that point I hung up. Yes, I hung up on my mother. Here I was, young and ambitious, willing to showcase my love for my family through food, and the chicken was defeating me. And all my mother could do was laugh at me? I almost stormed out of the grocery store and ordered pizza for dinner.

Instead, I called her back, "Are you done yet?"

Gasping for breath she replied, "Yes," and then started laughing again.

I stood in front of all that chicken while my mom tried to catch her breath and I struggled with the great chicken debate.

"You... should... get... a... roaster..." she replied between gasps of breath.

"Thank you, Mom," I said, with an attitude that said I wasn't playing around, and hung up.

I grabbed my roaster chicken, paid for my other groceries and went home. I took the chicken out, grabbed a pan, gathered some spices and was getting ready to cook that bad boy up when my phone rang.

"Yes?" I said.

It was my mom again. She had taken control of herself.

"Are you cooking the chicken?" she asked.

"Yes," I said.

"Did you take the innards out?" she said softly.

"The what?" I pulled the phone away from my ear and stared at it like she could see me.

When I put the phone back to my ear she was saying, "...inside the chicken. You have to take that stuff out."

I looked at the chicken. I saw the little opening where its head used to be. "I'm not sticking my hand in that."

She snickered into the phone, "Oh yes you are, if you're cooking that chicken and not trying to kill anyone. You need to take the plastic bag with the innards out before you cook it."

I believe at that point I made a sound that was something akin to, "blechhhgrossill-ick-ick-ick!"

My mom's voice went soft in my ear. "I'll tell you a story while you take the insides of the chicken out."

"Okay, I'm listening," I said while having an internal conflict about sticking my hand inside the chicken.

"I didn't always know how to cook." I could hear the smile and whimsy in her voice. "And, I can still remember the first meatloaf I tried to cook for your father. I was so young. All I wanted to do was make a home-cooked meal for my family. So I gathered all my ingredients, mixed up that meat, added eggs, breadcrumbs, seasoning and then I flattened it as I put it in the pan."

"Why?" I might not have been the best cook around but I had never heard of flattening a meatloaf.

"Well, my dear, I thought that my meatloaf would rise in the oven just like bread rises. It turns out, it doesn't."

"You didn't!"

"I did. I'll never forget that meatloaf. Just like you'll never forget your chicken. Did you get the insides out?"

I had not noticed but I was holding a dripping bag filled with neck, liver and who knows what else in my free hand. I had just plunged my hand right in, grabbed that bag and pulled it out while my mom told me her story.

"Yes, I got it," I said into the phone.

"Just throw them away for now. I'll tell you how to use them on your next chicken," she said with a slight hitch in her voice. I think she was about to laugh again.

"Thanks, Mom," I said, and suddenly I was reassured that it was okay. It didn't matter if my chicken didn't come out perfect or if my mother's meatloaf never rose. It only mattered that I wanted to do something for my family and was making the effort to do it. That was the whole concept of food and love that my mother had taught me growing up.

"Don't forget to give the chicken a good butter massage before putting your spices on it," she said and hung up.

"What?" Wasn't sticking my hand inside it enough? Now I had to give the bird a spa treatment before eating it. I was never going to cook a chicken again. Never. Ever.

It has been ten years since my first chicken. I've grown quite experienced in the art of cooking a chicken. I have cooked hundreds of chickens over the years — some fryers, some roasters, each one better than the last. I'm no longer grossed out about sticking my hand inside a bird or having to feel it up before cooking it to a tender juicy crisp. And, I know that one day I'm going to have to tell my son the story of the first chicken I tried to cook for his father when he calls me up to complain that my future daughter-in-law doesn't know the difference between halibut and flounder. I may have to tell him about Grandma's meatloaf too.

—Linda St.Cyr—

46

Chicken Soup for the Soul.

Mom Comes to Play

*The day I decided that my life was magical,
there was magic all around me.*
~Author Unknown

As a child and teen, I was fascinated with dreams — I even made a presentation to my high school English class about dream symbols — but I didn't pay serious attention to dreams until after my mother's unexpected death at age sixty-nine. I say "unexpected," but somehow I knew it was coming. At the very moment I got the news, I was staring at a book, *Life After Death*, by Deepak Chopra. It was on my desk at work.

When my mother passed, it reawakened my childhood hobby from twenty years earlier. I started journaling my dreams and began to read more books about death, such as Sylvia Browne's *Visits from the Afterlife*.

Like most thirty-five-year-old women, my life was still ridiculously busy. There was no time for spiritual quests. A week after my mother died we closed on a bigger house in the suburbs, and barely three months after we moved in I became pregnant with our second child. It was a lot of change at once, and there wasn't much time to grieve her loss.

One night, about a month after we moved into our new house, I found myself roaming around in a stupor, unable to find anything. This house felt too big! I began to sob uncontrollably.

Then it hit me: My mother was really gone, and I was moving on without her. I couldn't bear the thought. She would never get to see my new house, never know that I was having another baby. I would have no memories with my mom in this house, the one where I would raise my children.

I felt guilty. How could I enjoy all this without her? My mother was dead; I shouldn't be allowed to be happy. I didn't think I deserved this nice house, this family, or this life.

I curled up on the rocking chair in the corner of our huge bedroom, sobbing and wailing, the sound muffled only by my husband blow-drying my three-year-old daughter's hair after her bath.

That same night my mother came to me in an incredible dream that changed everything.

She was at the foot of my bed. She ripped the covers off, grabbed my hands and pulled me right out. I giggled, "Mom! What are you doing?" I was so happy to see her.

She led me to the big open space in our bedroom and started dancing around with me in a circle. She was so joyful and playful!

Then my sister, my daughter and my husband were all there too, holding hands and dancing in a circle, all of us laughing and happy.

Next, the scene moved to the closet in my daughter's room, where my mother and I talked for a long time. She looked very young and pretty, like in her teens. Her voice was high-pitched, as if it came from somewhere else. I asked her if she liked being on the other side, and she said she did. It seemed like we talked for an hour in there. I felt so incredibly happy to see her and to be able to ask her all those questions.

The last thing I remember was being back in my bed. She deliberately put my hand into my husband's hand — and then I woke up.

I felt such a deep sense of peace after the dream; it was like nothing I'd ever felt before. I immediately woke my husband to tell him about my extraordinary experience.

It was as if my mother came to tell me to enjoy all these wonderful things in my life. She was still with me. She was fine. She wanted me to give my love to my husband and children now. The dream lifted the spell of depression I didn't even know I was under.

Little did I know that my mother was also showing me all the wonderful moments to come in our large master bedroom, all the many times that I'd be dancing with my children in a circle, filling that big empty space with laughter, play, and joy, appreciating its size.

It's been six years since her passing, and Mom doesn't visit me in my dreams very often now. But I know that if I ever truly need her, she will be there for me.

All I need to do is focus my thoughts and the energy that I put out into the universe — even my tears — and I have direct access to her.

— Sharon Pastore —

47

Straight Talk from Mom

Happiness is not defined by any circumstance,
condition, or person. You need not tie your happiness
to anything. The choice to be happy is always
yours to make.
~Dr. Anil Kumar Sinha

I t was November 25th, the day before Thanksgiving, and I unloaded my senior year angst in a heartfelt letter to the universe, detailing my unhappiness and how everyone in my family thought I was a grouch.

"I'm never happy anymore," I bemoaned. "Basically, that's the whole problem. All my happiness is temporary. I can be happy for one day or so — maybe I've had an elevating talk with someone or a really fine weekend with my boyfriend — but the feeling just doesn't last. In fact, within a short time I can hardly even remember being happy and feeling good."

For all its highs, my final year of high school was extremely conflicted. Excitement at the thought of leaving home mixed with a fear of failure and intense sadness at the thought of leaving my safe and loving family, possibly forever.

After dumping my conflicted thoughts in blue ink on lined school paper, I folded the missive, shoved it out of sight under my dresser, and got back on the treadmill of schoolwork, piano and organ lessons, a part-time job, and endless college applications.

Thanksgiving came and went, followed by Christmas and New Year's, as my forgotten letter gathered dust under my dresser. Then, one January day, I came home from school to find my letter lying in full view on top of my dresser. Pulse racing, I unfolded it and an additional sheet of lined paper folded around my one-page missive. My page was written in blue ink. But my mother had added her own words in flowing red pencil, completing the front and back of my sheet of paper and extending onto a second sheet.

Mom started out by assuring me that no one in my family viewed me as harshly as I viewed myself, and added that we all have occasional periods of grouchiness. But Mom's amazing outlook on the subject of happiness was what really caught my attention.

"Happiness isn't something you can grasp. It is mostly anticipation of a future event or recollection of a past one. Sometimes, present happiness is found in many small ways every day — the joy of feeling needed, the pleasure of helping someone, the gratification of creating something, the satisfaction of a job well done — fleeting moments to be sure, but woven together they blend into a state of happiness that is more constant and longer lasting than a highly elated happiness of shorter length.

"Wendy, everyone learns to recognize all the forms of happiness as they go along in life if they only look around them and outside of themselves. Even then, there will be a few November 25ths to reckon with. Keep the faith!"

No doubt worried that I might interpret her discovery and subsequent outreach as a breach of the Teenager's Bedroom Privacy Act, Mom added a whimsical P.S. that made me smile then and still makes me smile today.

"Dressers need to be dusted under every so often, even by me."

I don't remember what I said to my mother after reading her uplifting response, but I know we discussed the subject in greater detail. And in the many years since, I've found her sage advice to be spot on. Happiness — that precious fuel that drives our daily lives — isn't something tangible that is handed out to us. It's a purposeful choice we make when we decide to seek and find happiness every day in the crazy world around us. As Mom so kindly and clearly pointed out, happiness abounds in the small things, whether past treasures, present moments, or anticipated futures. The key is to learn to recognize happiness in its many forms, to watch for it continually, savor it fully, and remember it always.

My mother gave me a piece of advice that resonates as surely and purely today as it did back then. Woven together, a lifetime of happy moments creates a tapestry of contentment, peace and joy that swaddles us like a cozy blanket when times are tough. Happiness is out there waiting for us even on our darkest days if we only leave our hearts open... and keep the faith.

— Wendy Hobday Haugh —

A Place of Love

Home makes the man.
~Samuel Smiles

Home. The word kept running through my mind as we drove along the dusty road deeper into the country. All around us oak tress drooped in the sweltering sun. I peered through the dust at the little farmhouse we were nearing. It stood alone at the end of the road, looking more tired than I felt. I swallowed a knot of fear in my throat.

My mom had moved us to California in search of a better job. We lived close to the beach and I woke up each morning to the smell of salt in the air. It had been great, but then my mom's company closed and we had to go back to Texas. I was okay with that, happy to be going home, settling into the city again and returning to my old school.

But my mom told us that the cost of moving had eaten up all our savings, and she still hadn't found a job. That meant we couldn't afford to rent an apartment in the city, so we had to stay with someone until we saved enough money to get our own home. Then she told us the real shocker. We'd be living in the country with our grandmother, whom we'd never met before.

Stepping onto the creaky porch, I put my suitcase down and looked at her. She was a tiny woman with white curly hair. She smiled when she saw us and began speaking, but it was all in Spanish so I couldn't understand her. My mom smiled back and said, "Your grandma says welcome home."

As I opened the screen door and went inside, I couldn't imagine this place being our home. The farmhouse was the only home within miles of anything. It was a dilapidated four-room shack that smelled of dust and mildew. Everything in the house was old, including our grandmother. We'd never met her before because we lived far away in the city. I didn't know how to feel about her.

My mom carried my youngest brother inside and put him on Grandma's bed. Grandma stood beside him and stroked his head, singing to him. Although I couldn't understand what she was saying, my brother seemed to like the song. She turned and gave each of us a hug. Her arms were thin and bony, and when she moved she moved slowly. I was afraid she'd break.

That night we lay on blankets on the cold wooden floor. I heard all kinds of noises I'd never heard in the city. Strange birds called out in the darkness. Crickets and frogs chirped and croaked. I heard sounds in the wall that I guessed were mice. I shivered under the blankets and moved closer to my brother. This was in no way the place I'd hoped to come home to.

That first week we all got a crash course in farm living. You get up early on the farm, and I mean early. Grandma showed my brother and me how to gather eggs from the chicken coops behind the kitchen porch. I got pecked by more than one angry hen. Mom and my sister helped Grandma in the kitchen, and as I stood throwing feed at a horde of clucking, scratching chickens, I shivered and wished I was anywhere but here.

Grandma showed us how to care for her kitchen garden. My hands got raw pulling weeds and hauling buckets of water to the screened-in garden. We finally got a break after lunch, and my brother, sister and I wandered around. We found a turtle in the grass, and built a house for it from scrap wood. When we showed it to Grandma she smiled and nodded. I was actually happy as I sat down to a great tasting chicken dinner that night. That is, until my sister leaned over and whispered, "This isn't chicken. Grandma took our turtle and fried it. Grandma told Mom it was nice of us to catch dinner."

Life went on like that. Since Grandma had no tub or shower, she,

Mom, and my sister bathed in a big iron tub inside. When it was our turn, my brother and I had to take the tub outside and bathe under the trees while the chickens and goats looked on. When winter came we got to experience cold like we never had before.

But something funny happened along the way. I got really good at taking care of chickens and goats, and the vegetables my brother and I got from the garden that fall made everyone happy. Grandma showed us how to do a hundred different things with just our hands and some simple tools. Even though we couldn't talk to each other, smiling and hugging went a long way to showing how we felt.

Then one summer day, Mom told us she had found a job in the city and rented an apartment. We were going to leave for our new home the next day. That night, as we lay on our blankets and tapped on the wall to scare the mice away, I thought about all that had happened, and about the grandma I had come to know and love.

The next day, we said our goodbyes. I hugged Grandma tightly, feeling her small but strong arms hug me back. As we drove away from the farmhouse, I realized something. The place you live isn't really what makes any house a home; it's the people with whom you share it. Smiling and waving at the woman who had welcomed us with love and caring, I knew that no matter where I went there would always be a place for me here, a place that truly was, now and forever, my home.

—John P. Buentello—

At Maddy's Side

*To us, family means putting your arms around each
other and being there.*
~Barbara Bush

"I can't do that!" I told my sister-in-law Jeanne. My beloved mother-in-law, Maddy, at age ninety-one, had suddenly slipped from needing frequent visitors to needing full-time help, including someone to walk her to the bathroom in the middle of the night. Now she needed someone, this very night. Because there was no time to buy any kind of bed alarm or monitor, what was needed was someone to arrive that night and actually crawl into bed with her, to be there to hear if she tried to get up alone. I could not imagine doing that. It was so private, so personal, so intimate. What if I didn't hear her get up? What if she fell when I was in charge? What if she was as scared as I would be if someone had crawled into bed next to me in the middle of the night?

I called my own sister to discuss the situation. "I can't do that!" I complained.

"Well," she said, "you actually can." And she left it at that.

I thought it over. I thought about all the things Maddy had done for me in the nearly three decades that I'd been married to her son. She had accepted me at first sight. She had supported me when I was the first mother in the family to work outside of the home. She had always treated me like gold.

And then I remembered the closets.

When my husband and I bought our first house, many years ago, we bought a true fixer-upper, and we had one month to make it livable before we moved in. Every surface needed to be cleaned, repainted, re-wallpapered, or re-carpeted. My father-in-law Johnny had recently retired, so he and Maddy quietly adopted our house as their project. Every day that month, while my husband and I were at work, Maddy and Johnny found a job that needed to be done in our new house, and they did it. Each evening, when we arrived to work on the house ourselves, something new would magically be different. One day, we found the trim painted. Another day, we found the ceilings washed. Once, we discovered the tall weeds outside had been cut back.

But one evening we arrived and could not figure out what Maddy and Johnny had tackled that day. We could tell they had been there, but what had they done? We worked all evening before we figured it out. They had painted the inside of every single closet! Who would think of such a touch? What considerate people! We were delighted.

Johnny's been gone for ten years, and Maddy has been a big part of my life, supporting me through good times and bad. And now, when Maddy needed me, I thought about all the things she had done for me since the closets.

I called my sister-in-law back. "Of course, I'll be there tonight!" I told her.

I arrived late that night as a caretaker was leaving, put on my pajamas, and quietly crawled into Maddy's bed. A few hours later, she woke up and started to get up for the bathroom. I rushed to the other side of the bed to take her hand. She was surprised, mostly because I stepped on her foot! But other than that, she was just fine with having someone suddenly show up in her bedroom in the middle of the night.

"Who's that?" Maddy asked.

"It's me, Jane, your favorite!" I told her. I like to think that, anyway.

"Oh, hi!" she said brightly. "It's nice to see you!" And she took my hand and off we went.

In the months since that night, my husband and I have spent many days and nights at Maddy's house, taking turns with his brothers and sisters and professional help, making sure that someone is always at Maddy's side. Sometimes, it fits in well with our lives. Sometimes, it doesn't, but we do it anyway. During those times, I just think about the closets. She was there for me then, and I'm here for her now.

—Jane Brzozowski—

50

Crazy Always Finds a Way

*Within our family there was no such thing as a person
who did not matter. Second cousins
thrice removed mattered.*
~Shirley Abbott

Mom had always told her four kids to make sure no
friend spent a holiday alone. So one year, at our pre-
holiday meeting over the dining room table, we added
up the number of "lonely" guests. We'd invited more
than eighty strangers to Mom's Thanksgiving! Mom started crying,
envisioning the Mount Everest of potatoes she'd need to peel.

We jumped in to help. We were going to make this happen together,
as a family, and relieve Mom of as much responsibility as she wanted
to relinquish. So, item by item, we asked Mom what she wanted to
avoid. First? Washing dishes all day. The china and silver remained in
storage, and the paper and plastic headed home from the store. Then
we eliminated all in-house pots and pans; aluminum lined the kitchen
counters along with our garage-sale serving spoons. If a few utensils
got tossed with the trash, so what?

We talked Dad into cooking a pair of turkeys in the smoker, and my
brother said he would roast two more in his fraternity-house kitchen.
If our guests asked if they could bring something, we'd assign them an
item. My friends and my little brothers' guests would bring side dishes,

and the middle siblings would ask for desserts. And everyone should bring food picnic-style so there would be no heartbreak if dishes got lost.

We all pitched in for a pre-holiday housecleaning, led by my brother and sister. They were used to a standard for tidiness I could never meet, and quite frankly I've never let a messy house get in the way of a good time. When we were kids, my mother referred to my brother and me as Felix and Oscar. But I can do what I'm told!

Of course, Mom couldn't let Thanksgiving pass without whipping up a few of her favorite recipes. We kids told her, "Do what you want. If you change your mind, no one will ever know the difference."

On Game Day — I mean, Thanksgiving Day — we made iced tea and lemonade in five-gallon batches. We swore we wouldn't dump them on each other after our big victory. I was in the restaurant business at the time, so I got some industrial-sized garbage bags and borrowed trash cans. My brother borrowed chairs and tables from his frat, and we covered them with disposable tablecloths.

We stationed serving lines in three locations in the house, including the garage. We made a pact that we wouldn't *ask* guests for labor, but we wouldn't turn it down either.

When our guests began to arrive, some asked if they could help. *Phew!* We worked those friends of ours into friends of Mom and Dad in no time at all. I suspect few houses experienced the genuine laughter and good cheer the Howe house did that Thanksgiving. It seemed like everyone was making new friends, and there wasn't anywhere else they wanted to be on a fall Thursday afternoon.

Hours after the last guest left, my family plopped down at the table and swore we'd never, ever do that again.

The next year, we invited only sixty.

Occasionally, I'll hear from old friends who were with us that Thanksgiving, even after all these years. They still think we were crazy to try anything like that, but my family and I have found that crazies adapt and overcome — with big hearts and welcoming smiles… and paper plates.

— Mark A. Howe —

51

Thanks, Mom

Death ends a life, not a relationship.
~Jack Lemmon

One Sunday afternoon during a visit at my parents' house, my mother led me into her bedroom. "Suzanne, I have something I want to give you." She pulled open her top dresser drawer, lifted out a small box, and handed it to me.

"What is this, Mom?" I asked and tugged at the lid. The interior, lined by royal-blue velvet, held a gold wedding band. A continuous leaf pattern had been etched on the surface. I glanced at her and smiled. "Really?"

"This ring belonged to your grandmother, given to her by Grandpa in honor of their 50th anniversary. She bequeathed it to me when she passed away. Try it on and see if it fits."

"But, Mom, don't you want to wear it? There's no hurry to give it to me."

"I want to be sure you have this. I made a promise to my mother to pass it down to you."

I slipped off my diamond wedding ring and slid on the shiny band. It fit my finger perfectly. Butterflies fluttered inside my chest as I admired the new piece of jewelry. My thoughts couldn't make sense of the gift, but it held a very special meaning for me. The family connection brought tears to my eyes.

"It does fit me well," I said and smiled.

"The ring's too tight on me. I'm so glad you're able to wear it in her memory. Take a look inside. He had their initials engraved in there, too."

I slid it off, squinted and saw the tiny letters inscribed in the gold.

"How unique. Thank you very much, Mom." We hugged.

Three months later, we buried my mother at age sixty-eight. She had found out she had pancreatic cancer in May, and there was nothing the doctors could do. At her funeral, I reminisced about the day she gave me that ring. She had already known her fate. She was a brave soul.

Since the moment I'd put on that ring, I'd never taken it off. It meant so much to me, and I now wore it in memory of my mother *and* grandmother.

A year later, I decided to color my gray hair. I had to remove the ring to put on the rubber gloves. That next morning, I couldn't find my precious ring anywhere. I retraced my steps. Had I set it on the bathroom sink or tossed it on my dresser? I searched each place thoroughly. I couldn't find it.

I berated myself. That ring stood for so much. How could I have been so careless?

Six months later, I still hadn't found Grandma's wedding band. How could it have just disappeared? I vowed to keep looking.

One night at 2:00 a.m., when I was sound asleep, I heard my mother's voice in a dream. She said, "Suzanne, move the dresser." My eyes opened wide, and I bolted to a sitting position. I'd know her voice anywhere. Chills traveled through me. I searched the corners of my dark bedroom. *What had just happened? Was it really her?*

Nothing was amiss. My husband snored away on his side of our king-size bed. I dropped back to my pillow. First thing tomorrow, I'd check the floor beneath the triple dresser.

After morning coffee, I borrowed a wooden yardstick from my husband's tool rack. I squeezed my body into a tight corner beside my dresser and stared. Total blackness greeted me. I rose and grabbed a flashlight, returned and peered in again. In the illuminated area, I saw a glint of something metal. I stood and crammed that yardstick in as far as I could. Then I swept the carpet toward me. Dust bunnies came out. No ring.

I swiped again and dragged out a lost earring—one of a pair that had recently been misplaced when I was in a hurry to insert it. *Was that what she meant?* I sighed. Thinking positive, I gave it one more try and raked the floor even harder. A gold item flashed as it rolled by. My heart did flip-flops. I knelt and scooped it up.

My grandmother's ring.

I'd found it. Immediately, I slipped the band back on. Joy flowed through me. I glanced up to where my mother resides now. And after she spoke to me in that dream, I know she watches over me. Thanks, Mom.

— Suzanne Baginskie —

The Answer

*I know no blessing so small as to be reasonably
expected without prayer, nor any so great
but may be attained by it.*
~Robert South

After years of trying to start a family, and the loss of several babies, my parents were elated to learn there was a six-day-old baby girl waiting for them! My mother had an arthritic condition, and because of this they had just about given up hope of ever being able to adopt.

The year was 1941, and Pearl Harbor had just been bombed. Within two short years, my father enlisted in the U.S. Navy and left his little family for training camp in Idaho. A few weeks later, at the age of twenty-nine, he collapsed after a forced march and died of a heart attack. Letters addressed to his "little angel girl" were all I had to remember him by.

My early memories are of my mother crying and going away to the hospital. I vividly recall being awakened in the middle of a cold December night and rushed to her bedside. She told me to be a "good girl for Grandma," waved goodbye, and later that day joined my father.

At the age of two, I was an orphan. I went to live with my paternal grandmother. I remember missing my parents so very much. Photo after photo, in a timeworn album, showed the proud new parents holding me. The looks on their faces radiated love. As a small child, I knelt in front of a large crucifix that hung on the wall in my grandmother's bedroom. I promised to be a "good girl" and begged God to give my parents back to me. "If I can't have both of them, then please, just give me one!"

My pain lessened with the passing of time.

One day when I was about twelve years of age, my grandmother, who was illiterate, asked me to help her sort through some papers that had belonged to my parents. In doing so, I found my adoption records! To this day, no one knows how she acquired them. As I read the information, which included my birth mother's name, family history, and last known address, I knew that someday I would find her.

I married shortly after graduation and became a mother myself. I looked at my baby and thought how difficult it must have been to give birth and then have to give the baby away.

Several days before my twenty-first birthday, I decided to try to locate my birth mother. I called directory assistance and, using her maiden name, got the phone number of my maternal grandfather, still living at the same address listed on the adoption records.

My hands shook as I dialed the number. I told him I was a long lost friend of his daughter and asked for her phone number. I called the number, and when she answered, I said, "You don't know me, but I believe that twenty-one years ago you gave birth to me."

"I always knew that someday you would find me!" she exclaimed.

She wanted to know if I was given a good home and was devastated when she learned of my parents' deaths. Within an hour of our phone conversation, she was at my front door. Tears filled her eyes as she reached out and wrapped her arms around me. Her words echo in my memory to this day. "Oh, you're beautiful!"

We developed a special bond, and she became my best friend. We were blessed with years of sharing laughter and love. I could always depend on her to be there for me. When she passed away at the age of eighty, I sat looking at her for the last time. I remembered the prayer I had said as a child, when I begged God to give me back one of my parents. I realized at that moment that my prayer had been answered.

— Priscilla Miller —

The Visit

*In faith there is enough light for those who want to
believe and enough shadows to blind those who don't.*
~Blaise Pascal

It had been three years since I'd seen my mother. Nine months after my father's death, she had finally found the peace she sought. They'd been together sixty-two years. She tried to pick up the pieces of her life and move on, but she was lost without him. The phone call from the assisted living facility marked the end of her loneliness.

There were so many things I wanted to tell her — little things that wouldn't matter to anyone else, things only a mother and a daughter hold special between them. I'd pass a place we always liked to visit, and I'd want to call her to tell her about it. I'd forget she wasn't there.

Time has a way of healing the hurt. But I felt a gnawing ache, a conscious awareness that she was the only person who ever offered me unconditional love.

I was home alone one morning and doing laundry. With my arms full of clothes, I made my way from the utility room through the den toward my bedroom. As I entered the den, I stopped in my tracks. In front of me, in the recliner in the corner, sat my mother.

She looked up and smiled as I stared back at her. She wore light gray sweatpants and a matching sweatshirt. I noticed she wore the set of pearls she always loved — the same set that supposedly was hanging from a wall sconce in my bedroom. Her new glasses, the kind with clear frames, were barely noticeable, and her hair matched her outfit.

Mom and I shared a brief moment of eye contact, and then she was gone. I felt her presence in the room as I said, "I love you, Mom."

I slowly walked past the recliner and into the bedroom. I glanced at the wall sconce and saw her pearls. I had placed them there just before her service. I threw the clothes on the bed, but I couldn't let the feeling go. I walked back into the den and sat down in the recliner Mom had just vacated.

"Where did you go?" I asked as my eyes took in every corner, every chair, and every inch of space in the room.

My gaze fell upon something beside me on the floor — my study Bible.

I didn't use that Bible often — only when I needed clarification of some of life's questions. It contained three different translations of the Good Book, and it was extremely heavy. I couldn't remember the last time I'd used it, or any other Bible as a matter of fact. With my life in shambles from my recent divorce, I had let my Christian upbringing fall by the wayside as I wandered aimlessly, day by day, trying to figure out what had gone wrong. Two years worth of feeling sorry for myself and blaming everyone else had taken its toll on my faith and my ability to allow God to direct my path. However, the study Bible lay open before me and without hesitation I picked it up.

It was opened to the book of Ecclesiastes, the third chapter — my mother's favorite. She'd read it to me many times during my childhood, and it carried through to my adulthood as one of my most well loved chapters. She liked the poetic flow of the words "to everything there is a season, a time for every purpose under heaven: a time to be born, and a time to die..."

I knew I had not opened that Bible; in fact the cover was dusty.

"What are you trying to tell me, Mom?" I asked as I again searched the room.

The only reply I heard was one she always would say when an answer was obvious: "You figure it out — you're a smart person."

She'd come back for a reason, and that was to deliver a message. I reread the familiar words: "a time to cry and a time to laugh; a time to grieve and a time to dance."

"It's time to get on with it, huh, Mom?" I asked out loud.

I knew it was time to get my life together and get myself back in church. It was time to quit blaming myself and everyone else for past mistakes and move on. I smiled and tried to remember the last time I'd laughed out loud or danced, as the verses mentioned. It had been too long to remember. I reached down and closed the study Bible, then jumped out of the recliner and danced a little jig across the den floor. I laughed so loud that my cat ran behind the couch to hide. My faith in God and His ability to soothe my wounded soul was suddenly renewed and I felt like a new person.

There's definitely a season for all things. Mom was telling me to take life a day at a time and not get bogged down in things that don't matter. I needed to keep looking up and stay focused.

— Carol Huff —

54

Saved by "The Look"

I miss thee, my Mother! Thy image is still
The deepest impressed on my heart.
~Eliza Cook

Many of us remember the power of "The Look" with which our mothers showed disapproval. "The Look" could convey such a strong wordless message that it would stop us in our tracks. My own mother used "The Look" rarely, but effectively.

Even though I am far, far away from childhood and my mother died some years ago, I frequently remember her voice or see her face as I navigate through life. But I rarely think of "The Look" anymore. Thus it was a surprise when the image presented itself to me at an entirely unexpected moment.

On a summer afternoon, I was running late to an appointment. As I hurried across town, I looked at the gas gauge and saw the tank was almost empty. Not willing to risk running out of gas, I pulled into a service station. I leaped out of the car, slipped my credit card in the slot and began to fill up the tank. I looked west at the Rocky Mountains, and then glanced around, noticing that only one other car was there.

I had skipped lunch and suddenly realized I was hungry and thirsty. The more I thought about food, the more I wanted to run into the small station and buy some snacks. I argued with myself that I didn't have time, and my empty tummy was about to win the argument when I heard a voice I hadn't heard for a long, long time. I heard a loud "NO!" The power and strength of that word startled me. Still, I reached into the car for my purse when I heard it again, but this time I saw my mother's face with "The Look." With some confusion, I obediently dropped my purse back on the car seat and turned to replace the nozzle. How odd it felt to be chastised so strongly for simply wanting to buy a little snack!

As I replaced the gas cap I felt a rush of movement behind me and heard pounding feet as a man raced out of the station and into his car. With screeching tires he raced away as the cashier came staggering out of the door yelling, "Did you see him? Did you see that guy? He just pulled a gun on me and took all the money from the drawer!"

By the time he arrived at my car he was so shaken that he sank down to the ground. I tried to gather my wits.

"Just now?" I asked. "You were robbed at gunpoint JUST NOW?"

The cashier's hands were shaking, and he asked again, "Did you see him? I've got to call the manager and the police and if you saw him you could give a description."

But I couldn't describe the man who had been a blur as he ran to his car and drove off. I only had a vague recollection of the car. What I remembered was the vivid image of my mother that had appeared and the loud "NO!" All I knew was if I had gone into the station when I wanted to, I would have interrupted the robbery. I would have walked in on a man holding a gun right by the front door. He might have turned it on me. He might have panicked and shot me and the cashier. I sat beside the cashier on the dirty pavement, my hand on his trembling arm, and felt my heart thumping wildly at what might have been. I closed my eyes and gave silent thanks to God for His mercy and a mother whose care extended beyond the boundary of death to keep me safe in this life.

— Caroline S. McKinney —

Grand Moms

55

Lord Knows

Grandmother-grandchild relationships are simple.
Grandmas are short on criticism
and long on love.
~Author Unknown

In a way, my grandmother Victoria knew me better than myself. She recalls when I was around seven years old and wanted to be a pastor. A lifelong Pentecostal, my grandmother fully supported this career move. She even bought me a tiny blue suit so I could look good while reciting Bible verses in the living room. We called it my "pastor suit."

I loved and honored my grandma. I couldn't imagine disappointing her. When I came out at sixteen, the one person I knew I'd never tell was my grandmother. One, because she couldn't handle it, and two, because I couldn't handle losing her.

Victoria's righteous passion was well-known throughout Palmer, a small town in Alaska. You never quite knew what would stir her rage. Someone once asked why she kept playing the tambourine during slow songs at church, and she refused to look at the person again. When friends angered her, she cut them off. It didn't matter if the friendship had lasted ten or twenty years. I learned about these breakups through casual conversation, usually long after the rupture.

"Grandma," I'd ask her, "how's Philip doing these days?"

"Lord knows," she'd state.

This was code that their relationship was over, and so was the conversation.

During my first year of college, I knew I had to tell my grandmother. We couldn't have a real relationship unless she knew about me being gay and how instrumental it was in shaping me.

Spring was starting, and I was walking around the campus green, thinking of ways to tell her. I took a rest beneath a large oak tree. I thought of calling her landline on the mountain, but my heart started racing, and I felt like throwing up. If I couldn't think of the phone conversation without feeling dizzy, how would I act when it was time for me to tell her in real-time?

It hit me all at once that I'd send her a letter. My grandma was a prolific letter writer. In my first semester of college, she had already sent me seven letters. She preferred bulky, wide-ruled legal paper. She'd only write on one side of the paper and always with a red pen. She would fold the pages at least three times, shove the thick wad into an envelope, and seal it all up with tape.

I enjoyed these letters although I didn't finish all of them. Her cursive was wildly ornate. It took her a long time to write like this, and by page three she got impatient, and the words looped together in a blur I couldn't read. It didn't matter. I already knew her great themes: love of God, family, and being good to your teachers. She supported each theme with a new Bible verse.

I tore out three pages from a journal and started to write. On the first page, I told her about the motivated kids I was meeting and all the smart professors. On the second page, I said I loved her, and I was grateful for her help in raising me. And on the final page, I wrote, "It's because I love you that I feel the need to tell you I am gay. I've known this for a long time, and I want to tell you because I want to be honest and have no lies between us. I hope this doesn't change anything between us."

I tried to make everything light again by mentioning the spring weather and upcoming tennis try-outs. Then I folded the three pages like she did, three times, and squashed the pages into the back of my journal and walked to my next class.

I couldn't think clearly the next two days. I imagined Victoria sending me to a conversion camp. She might write back with all the Bible verses that supposedly hated gay people. Or knowing my preference for science, she might send me magazine clippings saying homosexuality made no evolutionary sense. The most probable reaction was also the worst: She would refuse to speak with me. When people asked how I was doing, she'd state drily, "Lord knows."

Eventually, I dropped the letter into a mailbox right outside my dorm. It was early in the morning, and with nothing else in the mailbox, I heard the letter hit the metal floor. For a brief moment, I wanted the letter back. But then I decided—I would rather have true rejection than false acceptance.

A few weeks later, I received a brown, flat envelope from Victoria. I weighed the package in my palms; it was light. The envelope had her familiar red script. *It couldn't be a bomb,* I thought. *And I'm pretty sure they still scan for anthrax. Right?*

I walked around the campus green again and sat beneath the oak tree where I had written the letter. My heart was pounding.

I ripped off the top binding like a Band-Aid. I tilted out the contents. My heart sank.

It was filled with photos. There I was on my fifth birthday with a bunch of cake on my face, smiling like crazy. There I was hitting a forehand at sixteen. There I was playing the trombone at thirteen. There were two dozen pictures with no explanation.

She no longer wanted to remember me. This was the first of a series of "Lord knows" statements regarding me.

I stuck my hand in the envelope again. My fingertips brushed a scrap of paper. I pulled it out. It was the size of a fortune-cookie scroll. In red coiled letters, it read: *"Yo te amo mucho, mucho."* I love you very, very much.

I laughed.

Under the oak tree, I flipped through more pictures. She saw me in each moment: spelling bees, band concerts, tennis tournaments. I shuffled them and felt her say, *I loved you in this moment, and this moment, and this moment, and I love you now.*

Tears swelled in my eyes. I had expected her to choose politics or religion, to find any reason to justify her disgust. But of all the things she could have said, she had chosen love.

—Matt Caprioli—

Granny Drives
a Hummer

*Regret of neglected opportunity is the worst hell
that a living soul can inhabit.*
~Rafael Sabatini

My boss's eyes were wide and questioning. "You're quitting to move to Argentina?"

"I have this novel I've been writing, and I just can't seem to find the time to finish it here in New York. I've been trying for a few years now." It was seven, to be exact.

I knew that I sounded like a lunatic — which is why I was even more surprised when he responded, "That's great, Rach. I'm excited for you."

Afterward, as I walked to the subway from the Urgent Care Center where I worked as a Physician Assistant, I wondered if I had made the right decision. People normally did this kind of thing after a bad breakup, or a near-death experience, or maybe after they lost their jobs. But to walk away from a six-figure salary at the age of thirty-one to "write a novel" seemed crazy, even to me. That being said, I'd been saving up money and could afford at least a three-month sabbatical.

In college, I had majored in Spanish Literature and hoped that one day I would write stories like the ones we read in class. But I'd always loved working directly with people, too. So after years of volunteering in my local ER and Health Department, I decided to apply to Physician Assistant school. I took everything from Organic Chemistry to the GRE, got accepted into my state college's Masters of Physician Assistant Studies program, and from there moved to New York to work at a top hospital.

I had also started writing. I was more than a hundred pages into my novel when I stopped. Doubts filled my head, and I told myself that no one would want to read my work. So the unfinished story had sat on my computer, untouched, for more than two years. But I had also written a couple of short stories that managed to make their way into publications, giving me a glimmer of hope — faint, barely visible, but present. I knew that if I didn't take a few months off to focus on finishing my novel, it wasn't going to happen. I also asked myself, *Even if it never got published, would my time in Argentina still be worth it?*

I wondered what my family would say when I told them about my plan to move, especially my grandmother. She was a nurse and had played a huge part in my decision to go into healthcare. Magee, as my siblings and I called her, had worked hard her whole life to provide for her family, and hadn't been able to travel outside the United States until she was in her seventies.

I thought back to 2007, the year I'd spent living with my family right after college, paying off student loans. I stayed with my parents, but my grandparents' house was in the neighborhood, and so I'd passed many an evening at their home.

Magee was turning seventy-four that November. "Please don't buy me anything for my birthday this year," she'd requested of us. She was a minimalist and preferred to keep her house clutter-free.

This worked out for me as I was making $8.10 an hour as a nurse tech at our local hospital. I decided to give her an experience gift instead, but struggled with what we should do.

As her birthday drew near, I got more and more anxious about it. I thought about dance classes (my granny loved her Zumba), a trip to a nearby city for lunch, or seeing a play together. Nothing seemed unique, though.

Then one day, as we were watching TV, waiting for supper to finish on the stove, a Hummer commercial came on.

Almost as if to herself, she said, "I've always thought it'd be fun to drive one of those things."

I looked over at her and smiled. Finally, I had my answer.

When her birthday arrived a week later, I told her I was taking her out for lunch, but secretly I had a pit stop to make first.

When I pulled up at a car dealership, she looked around, confused. "Are we here?"

I smiled and pointed over to the far corner of the lot where the Hummers were.

She gasped. "No. I couldn't!"

But I knew she could. She'd always been the active type who didn't let life's speed bumps slow her down. Besides, she was a terrific driver. As we ambled over to the Hummers, though, I could tell she was afraid. Even I had to admit they were much bigger in person than on TV.

Magee waited by one as I went inside the building to talk to the car salesman. I explained that it was my grandmother's birthday, and would he be so kind as to let her test drive one of the Hummers on the lot?

A spark lit in his eye, and he grinned. "C'mon!"

He helped my grandma in and sat in the passenger seat as I climbed in the back.

Before starting up the car, I could see my granny hesitate. She took a deep breath, winked at me in the rearview mirror, and turned on the ignition.

For the next fifteen minutes, we drove around some of Tallahassee's most beautiful back roads. The sun streamed through the branches of the overhanging canopy trees and threw mosaic-like shadows across the road. I cracked open the window and felt the cool breeze blow my hair back away from my face. Magee beamed, moving the steering wheel with ease as the car salesman told her about the Hummer's finest features.

When we got back to the lot, she handed over the keys, giggling like a schoolgirl. "That's the most fun I've had in a long time!"

The salesman passed Magee his business card and told her to call if she had any further questions, but I sensed that he knew this was a one-time thing. He wished her a happy birthday and even obliged us by taking a photo of Granny and me in front of the Hummer.

"What did ya think, Magee?" I said as we walked back over to my little beat-up Camry.

"To be honest, I was scared half to death! But I knew if I didn't do it, I'd regret it."

I nodded and hugged her.

All these years later, those words have stuck with me. Sometimes, life gives us opportunities that will never happen again. And, sometimes, we have to create them.

As I took a seat inside the subway car and we pulled away from the platform, I knew I was making the right decision. Whether or not my novel ever got published, the time spent in Argentina experiencing new things would still be worth it. Like Granny, I needed to grab onto the steering wheel and risk the ride of a lifetime.

— Rachel Elizabeth Printy —

57

Flying Fish

*A grandparent is old on the outside
but young on the inside.*
~Author Unknown

When I grew up in rural Kansas, we took Christmas dinner seriously. My grandmother began losing her mind in earnest about a week before the holiday. She would drag out the good dishes that had been purchased weekly at the local grocery store over what seemed to be years. I can remember when she would come home with a new component for the set and make my grandfather place it in the china hutch after she moved every single piece at least twice to find just the right spot for it. I will never forget the time he dropped the new sugar bowl and broke it into two pieces right before her eyes. We won't even discuss what words came from my five-foot-tall grandmother.

She cooked for days—homemade mincemeat pie, fudge and divinity, and the most mouthwatering cloverleaf yeast rolls. There was rarely anything my family could agree on, but everyone loved the taste of those rolls. If there were just one left in the basket, several people would be eyeing it. More than once, my cousin Brian got a fork in the hand for being too slow to grab the roll.

During the most memorable holiday season of my childhood, we had fried fish as well as ham for Christmas dinner. My grandfather would fish for crappie and filet them with no bones. We had freezers full of it, and I grew up spoiled by the harvest from our gardens and from hunting and fishing. We ate what my grandpa provided and were the better for it. Those crappie were special to us. Gran would dip them in a beer/pancake batter and fry them in an old, iron pot with a basket. It was and still is the most delicious fish I have ever eaten.

We ate well that year, until no one could move or eat one more morsel — and then the fight started. I cannot tell you what it was about, but the grand finale of it found my grandmother wearing a piece of fried crappie on her forehead. There was a moment of shocked silence as the fish began a slow descent down her nose and finally to her lap.

The family held a collective breath, not sure what would happen. My grandparents were the stern, silent type. In fact, I was positive there was no humor in them that I could see. My cousins, my father and I very carefully pushed back from the table. It was one of those moments that lasted a hundred years, and we were all at her mercy.

Gran raised a hand, wiped a smear of homemade tartar sauce from her forehead and looked at it. I could feel the laughter bubbling up inside me, and I fought to control it. My cousin Michelle pinched me on the leg, hoping to stop me from committing the ultimate act of childhood idiocy. I thought for a moment that my young life would be over when I heard my father making a noise like a cat coughing up a hairball. We all turned to see him, red-faced and struggling to maintain his composure, but it was clear he would be the first to snap.

All eyes went back to my grandmother, smeared with tartar sauce and stone-faced. My father continued to fight the laughter, and looks bounced between the eighteen adults and six kids around the table, like a tennis match.

Finally, Gran drew in a breath. We all held ours. She lifted the fish from her lap, where it had ended its slide, looked at it and then looked at my father. Then she said, "Oh, to hell with it," and lobbed the fish across the table at him, where it landed on his shirt with a plop. The moment hung there in stunned silence, and then the food began to fly.

I think it took us most of the afternoon to clean up the mess that followed, but it was, in my memory, the best Christmas ever.

After she passed, with most of us kids being adults and starting families of our own, we talked about it and decided to have one more holiday meal together. We gathered at my grandfather's and did all the old traditions. We got out the china and the table, and my aunty tried her hand at the cloverleaf rolls. As we sat together one last time as a family, my cousin Brian gave the blessing, and in a quiet voice he thanked the Creator for flying fish.

—Cj Cole—

58

She Altered My Attitude

Attitude is a little thing that makes a big difference.
~Winston Churchill

My ninety-year-old grandmother rested quietly in her hospital bed after a visit from her heart surgeon. He explained that she needed a quadruple bypass and she clung to the only good news he delivered: she had the body of a seventy-year-old.

Grandma's vanity required that she still dye her hair and the brown curls framed her porcelain face, her warm eyes, and her thin-lipped smile as she asked, "What would you do?"

My grandfather had died nearly thirty years earlier and Grandma had independently made decisions ever since. I knew she'd made up her mind before she'd even asked, but she liked me to feel included in her life especially after my mother passed away.

"I'd have the surgery," I said.

She nodded and then softly said, "I don't want to go home and wait to die. Besides, I'll be fine."

She was right. A few days later, a post-op nurse allowed me to visit Grandma in the recovery room after her surgery, a rather unusual privilege in hindsight. I was relieved Grandma had survived the operation but had been strangely confident that she would. Surprisingly, she lay naked and unconscious on the gurney, not yet cleaned up or bandaged. She had yellow iodine smeared all over her upper body between her elongated breasts and I was impressed that her enormous incision was stitched together as perfectly as any seam she'd ever sewn.

The sight of her chest rising and falling was comforting, but if Grandma had been awake she would have been embarrassed for me to see her naked. I held her hand and pondered the point at which my body would look like her medically speaking "seventy-year-old" one and worried that given my stressful job, it would be by the time I was forty instead of ninety.

About a year after my Grandma's successful surgery, my partner Ann and I invited her to our house for barbecued ribs. It was one of her favorite meals. I thought she'd enjoy a diversion from the usual mashed potatoes and gravy fare served daily at her assisted living apartment.

That particular Thursday night, both Ann and I got stuck at work. We got home only minutes before Grandma arrived, which killed any hope of serving her normal early dinner. I bought some time by offering to show her my nearby office while Ann got dinner going.

I helped Grandma carefully lower herself into my sports car and then I drove the short distance to my company's headquarters. She almost gasped as I turned down the tree-lined driveway that framed the roadway to the front of the building. Her face was full of wonder, like it always was, and her bright eyes took in everything around her.

"It's so beautiful," she said. "It looks like a park."

I'd never really thought of the grounds that way. My mind was usually distracted by the latest project delay or staff crisis. I drove to the private driveway at the back of the building and used my security card to enter the underground garage. The automatic door slowly opened and I parked my car in my assigned spot and started her tour.

Grandma was impressed with everything: the pristine underground garage, the sheer number of cubicles that stretched as far as the eye could see, the variety of logo-wear for sale at the company store, and the smell of food wafting from the full-service dining room.

As we stepped into the cafeteria I asked, "Given your diabetes, should we grab something here to hold you over until we get home?"

She looked at the herbed chicken dinner, the salad, soup, and sandwich bars and said, "I don't want to spoil my appetite, but do they serve such extravagant meals every night?"

Again, through her eyes I'd taken the quality and convenience of our cafeteria for granted, but the aromas made me want to head home for our own dinner.

"Just one more stop on the tour, Grandma. I want to show you where I sit."

We walked to my office and we both plopped down in chairs around my small conference table. She stroked the mahogany and said, "This is really nice." Then she pointed across my office to the chair behind my desk and asked, "Who sits there?"

Grandmother had always gotten a glazed look on her face whenever I explained what I did for a living, but it seemed she thought I worked at the conference table while "my boss" sat in the big chair behind the desk. Knowing she had been impressed with even that, I giggled as I said, "Well, Grandma... I do... this entire office is mine. I usually sit there at the computer and use this table for meetings with my staff."

Her eyes flashed with astonishment and she looked around my office with a new appreciation. Her response struck me. She'd attended teacher's college — or normal school as she called it — but when she got pregnant with my father she gave up her career. The opportunities for women had expanded far beyond those available to my grandmother: teacher, nurse, secretary, or homemaker.

She went over and sat down in my desk chair. She spun the chair around and then, one by one, she stared at the photographs of Canyonlands, Zion, and Yosemite National Parks that I'd taken while on vacations.

I pointed to one picture on the wall entitled "Attitude." It had a rainbow stretched above a roaring mountain stream and William James' words embossed at the bottom.

"I bought it with your Christmas money last year."

She looked at the picture, drew in a deep breath and then read the words out loud, "The greatest discovery of any generation is that a human being can alter his life by altering his attitudes."

She said, "I like all your pictures, but I think that one's my favorite."

"Me too, Grandma. Are you ready to go home and eat?"

She nodded. As we left my office she stopped outside the door and looked back. She gestured towards my nameplate and said, "I didn't notice that when we walked in."

She touched the letters of my last name... of her last name... and then she looped her arm through mine, patted my wrist, and said, "You've certainly done very well for yourself. I'm so proud of you."

When we got back to my house, Grandma patiently waited for us to serve dinner. It was almost eight when we finally sat down for our meal. Grandma attempted to eat her plate of ribs, but the pork was tough as bricks. When she finished eating what she could, she wiped her mouth with her napkin and unwittingly summed up her philosophy of life: "That barbecue sauce sure was tasty!"

My employer's headquarters, my office, and even my job never looked as wonderful as they did, that day, through my grandmother's eyes — her glistening grey eyes that always sparkled with possibility and only lingered on the good, especially when she looked at me.

— Kris Flaa —

59

No Longer a Thief

Nobody can do for little children what grandparents
do. Grandparents sort of sprinkle stardust over the
lives of little children.
~Alex Haley

My grandma was now a tiny version of herself, but even on days when she was trapped deep within the fog of dementia, the best parts of Grandma were still there. She may not have known our names, and she mistook her son for her precious husband whom she mourned terribly, but she was a sweet, happy lady always bringing smiles to the staff and fellow residents where she lived.

We were all experiencing a great loss — she was right in front of us, yet, she wasn't. She was lost in the recesses of her mind, her memories jumbled, faces and names confused. I wanted desperately for my preschool daughter to know my grandma. The tricky part was that my daughter experiences autism. How would I bridge the gap between loved one and stranger, seventy-something and five-year-old, a person who experiences dementia and a person who experiences autism?

I knew that when we introduced the two, my daughter would need to stay busy. I never take her anywhere without a well-packed activity bag. I also thought that my grandma might enjoy participating in the fun, so I packed for two.

The bag had treasured favorites like beads, pipe cleaners, crayons, paints, Play-Doh and other activities. From the moment my beloved grandma set eyes on my daughter she was enchanted by her every move. I stood back and watched my grandma beam. She wasn't quite sure who this little girl was, but she loved her all the same.

We found a table and set up our activities. Grandma eagerly participated, and though she was slower and her response times delayed, she gave every activity a try. But most of all she loved just being with her great-granddaughter and absorbing her youth and innocence.

I watched the two people I loved dearly and took mental snapshots of these precious moments. I watched as Grandma's worn hands brushed my daughter's hands, who was just beginning her life, and I watched as Grandma held on as long as my daughter would allow.

The irony of their social dance did not escape my notice. It didn't matter that my daughter couldn't make eye contact with Grandma, and it wasn't important to my daughter that my Grandma couldn't remember her name. For this moment in time, they were secret friends in a pretend tree house giggling and creating and just enjoying each other's presence. It didn't matter that they were scores of years apart in age, or that their social skills were terribly lacking; they had found common ground in shared activities and being friends. The absence of details and specifics that had built walls between so many others and had caused them to fall away, were the very glue that made this new, beautiful friendship work.

The absence of judgment and expectation was freeing for these two friends. They could make up stories, or speak in echolalia and neither one of them was offended, impatient, or annoyed. It became part of the dialogue.

The staff marveled, and everyone who watched this exchange, from nurses to other family to visitors, were charmed and touched to witness this precious new friendship bloom. While the friendship was nurtured and grew deeper it became increasingly more difficult with each visit to continue with the same activities. The hugs lasted longer, photos were taken, and the two friends were oblivious to what the rest of us knew was coming.

When Grandma passed away on a cold January day, I lost a beloved mentor and icon, a once strong and confident woman who taught me so much by her example and faith, and someone who loved me in the worst of times. But I also experienced my five-year-old daughter's loss of one of the most precious friendships she will ever experience — a friendship based on charm and whimsy, no expectations or judgment, and freedom to be exactly who God made her (and my grandma) to be.

Often, autism and dementia are viewed as thieves — faceless villains who steal and destroy. But in this story, autism and dementia were not the enemy; they were stepping stones to a beautiful and rare friendship.

—Amy L. Stout—

60

Fade to Black

Love is like dew that falls on both nettles and lilies.
~Swedish Proverb

She can't remember the last time she saw him, though it was only three years ago. It was on July 3rd, a hot, moonless summer night, and she'd spent the final moments holding his hand, alternately speaking to him in hushed tones and singing "Let Me Call You Sweetheart" ever so softly into his ear, her cheek meeting his where it lay on the stiff hospital pillow.

But she can tell you how they met, in vivid Technicolor detail: about the pouring rain that day some seventy years ago when her big brother brought him to the house, a drowned rat by all appearances. But even so, she couldn't take her eyes off his; the way they twinkled and danced! Just one look, and before she knew it she was following him into happily ever after.

She can't remember the name of the nice lady who fed her lunch yesterday and breakfast this morning; the one who cajoles her into taking "just one more bite"; the one who brings the Styrofoam cup of too-sweet lemonade to her lips to wash it down; the one who is a mere child herself, but inevitably crows about what a "good girl" she's been to eat so much of the pureed food that passes as a meal these days.

She will ask you, though, about your babies, and even about Ms. Stinky-Son, her great-grandson's not-so-favorite kindergarten teacher. She'll ask if "that woman" ever gave him back his truck, recalling an incident long forgotten by the parties involved. Her voice is animated as she stands ready to defend the shaggy-haired five-year-old with the tear-stained face of a decade or more ago, standing before her mind's eye in a twisted version of the here and now.

She can't remember why she doesn't see you every day, or, perhaps more aptly put, that she doesn't. Where has everybody gone? Why is she in this awful godforsaken place? She hates it here, she says, without saying a word, but still, you can read the indictment on her face. She wants to go home. Can't you take her there? Sit on the big flagstone back porch and gaze across the river, have a glass of tea and talk about remember when? The pleading that goes unsaid is enough to break a heart in two, jagged edges still piercing and pinching long after the visit is over.

She won't remember that you've been here, almost as quickly as you go. Tomorrow, today will be just yesterday, those short-term memories the first attacked by the cruel, unforgiving scourge that wipes the surface of her mind clean each night.

But I'll remember.

"I have to go, Grandma. I'll be back soon."

Her face turns, seeking mine.

"I love you," I say, nearly choking on the emotion welling up.

Her cloudy eyes find mine, and lock there in a long, present moment.

"I love you, sweetie," she states with all the authority of the grand-mother I've always known. "And don't you ever forget it."

— Jennifer Waggener —

61

The Wink

We light candles in testament that faith
makes miracles possible.
~Nachum Braverman

Every year at Hanukkah Grandma Sally lit her menorah from the wrong end. Every year my dad, her son, blew out the incorrect candle and lit the right one before the blessings and the dinner began. And every time he did that Grandma Sally chastised him affectionately for not leaving well enough alone.

That was the signal for me to begin reciting a scaled-down version of the Hanukkah Story, making sure to include an explanation as to why the holiday began with the lighting of the candle on the far right.

As I recited, Grandma Sally would wave her hand dismissively from side-to-side always with an accompanying "tsk-tsk" to show her disapproval for the exactness of this candle-lighting tradition.

Sometimes I was convinced that Grandma Sally had gone slightly senile and that accounted for her confusion, but when I brought that up to my dad in her defense, he countered by telling me she was sharper than our finest holiday cutlery.

I knew Grandma Sally adored my dad so I could not imagine her intentionally trying to upset him by knowingly lighting the wrong candle.

I also knew that she knew Jewish customs and law as well as any rabbi. So what accounted for this aberrational Hanukkah behavior?

After many years of candle-lighting chaos I finally asked Grandma Sally (out of earshot of my dad) what was behind her apparent rebellion.

"When Grandpa Joe passed away I wanted to stop celebrating Hanukkah. To me, the world had grown dim. But your father was adamant that we celebrate the holiday for your benefit, and because you were my first-born grandchild I honored his wishes. That first Hanukkah I unpacked the menorah Grandpa Joe had used ever since he was a little boy. He would always cup my hand in his and we would light the menorah together as a perfect team. I couldn't light it without his hand around mine so I bought a new menorah, the kind with orange bulbs rather than candles.

"That first year, right before you came over for the first night of Hanukkah, I tested all the lights to be sure they worked. Every bulb lit up except the one farthest to the left. I tightened it, then loosened it, then re-tightened it and then tried all the other bulbs on the menorah in its place. It stubbornly would not light so I figured the socket was bad and I would return it to the store in the morning.

"After you left that evening I switched off the menorah and went to bed. I had trouble sleeping so I curled up in my favorite cozy corner by the fireplace and started looking through one of our photo albums. I came to a beautiful picture of Grandpa Joe and me lighting the menorah many years before you were even born. As I went to turn the page I noticed a light flickering by the window. When I moved the curtain aside, the little orange menorah bulb farthest to the left was blinking on and off. It only blinked long enough for me to notice it and long enough for me to smile. When I turned the menorah back on and tightened all the bulbs in place every one lit up brightly except the one farthest to the left. Each year since then when I light the candles on our menorah I honor Grandpa Joe by starting on the left. It's my special wink to him. I know that God would understand and I hope that every rabbi would find it in his heart to do the same."

Grandma Sally has not celebrated with us for a very long time (at least in the traditional way that is). But, I certainly feel her hand cupped around mine every Hanukkah when I light the first night's candle (the one farthest from the left).

— Lisa Leshaw —

62

Grandmother's Skirt

Grandmas hold our tiny hands for just a little while,
but our hearts forever.
~Author Unknown

My heart broke a little when I hung my grandmother's skirt in my closet this Christmas. It's a red and green plaid skirt that sits perfectly on my hips and floats at my knees, a "traveling pants" sort of miracle being that I'm six feet tall and my grandmother was five feet tall on her tallest days.

The skirt is one of two items I took from her closet when she passed away. The other was a bland oatmeal sweater that smelled like her. I kept that sweater on for days after she died, breathing in her smell even as I lay in bed nights, listening to the sounds that felt all wrong in her house.

But the skirt went unworn.

The first Christmas season after she died, I couldn't put it on without crying and so it hung at the back of my closet, its red and green merriment lost in a dark corner. The second Christmas season after she died, I was able to wear the skirt with only the slightest quiver in my bottom lip when I looked in the mirror.

I paired my grandmother's skirt with a black jacket zigzagged with zippers and tall, black boots with the skinniest of heels. For good measure I added my favorite leather studded bracelet. I remembered my grandmother wearing the skirt, so proper in her heels and pantyhose and a red sweater on top. She would've laughed and shaken her head at her modest skirt paired with my hints of edginess.

A thousand times I wanted to send her a photo. I wanted our pictures to stand next to each other, each of us wearing this magical skirt, her red lipsticked mouth smiling next to my own pale grin.

I'm not fashionable or trendy in any sense of those words. I'm gangly and awkward and when I can find pants that don't look like I'm readying for a flood, that's a fashion win in my book.

When I stepped out in my grandmother's skirt, it was a whole new experience. Compliments were showered upon me.

"I love that skirt."

"That is a fantastic skirt!"

"You look radiant in that skirt. It really brings out the color in your cheeks."

Needless to say, I felt great in that skirt, so great that I carefully put it in my clothing rotation as often as possible. I wore the skirt when I went to see *It's a Wonderful Life*. I wore it to three Christmas parties. I wore it to the Christmas sing-a-long on the last day of school.

So, as I carefully put away my grandmother's skirt that Christmas Day, I smiled, because somehow, in spite of her passing, my grandmother still manages to give incredible gifts.

In her skirt I felt vibrant. I felt confident. I felt beautiful. The most magical gift of my grandmother's skirt is that long after I took it off and put it back in the closet, those feelings remained.

— Alicia McCauley —

63

Just a Dream Away

My grandmother is my angel on earth.
~Catherine Pulsifer

I was sitting on a wood bench in a garden filled with daisies, which were my grandmother's favorite flower. The sun was shining and felt warm on my skin. The air had a faint smell of sandalwood and vanilla. It was the unmistakable aroma of my grandmother's favorite perfume. She had passed away several years before, and I still missed her terribly.

All of a sudden I could hear her voice. It started off faint, like a whisper, and continued to grow louder and louder. "Wake up, you need to put him in his crib." She just kept saying it over and over, getting more and more frantic. Was she here? Her presence seemed so real.

The sunny sky turned dark and lightning began to shoot all around me. All of a sudden, I felt two frail hands grab my shoulders and shake me violently. I heard my grandmother's voice again: "Please wake up; you need to put him in his crib. There is not much time."

I woke up in a cold sweat. There were tears streaming down my face. It took me a moment to collect myself and figure out where I was. The room was dark, except for the glow of the television. I could hear the rain hitting the roof. I had fallen asleep watching cartoons on the couch again. I looked over at the recliner and saw my one-year-old sleeping peacefully, curled up under his favorite blanket. The thunder boomed outside and I decided that the sounds of the storm must have been responsible for my nightmare. I crawled off of the couch and went to get a glass of water.

As I entered the kitchen the lights started to flicker. I heard another loud burst of thunder and my electricity turned off completely. All of a sudden, my grandmother's words echoed through my mind. "You need to put him in his crib. There is not much time."

I walked back into the living room and went over to the recliner. I scooped my little man up into my arms. He nuzzled his head into my chest as I cradled him closer. I walked slowly to his room, navigating through the dark hallway, trying hard not to wake him. He smelled like lavender baby lotion. His eyelids fluttered and he smiled as he slept. I laid him in the crib, covered him with a blanket, and kissed him on his forehead. I whispered, "I love you more than pigs love slop." This was an old saying my grandfather had always told us. I stood there in the dark staring at him. I brushed my hand across his forehead and kissed him one more time.

As I was leaving his room, the entire house shook. There was a loud crash followed by the sound of wind and rushing water. My heart started pounding so fast I thought it was going to jump right out of my chest. I quickly looked back over to the crib. My son was still sleeping peacefully. I ran into the hallway. The wind was ripping through the house. I could feel the temperature dropping. When I reached the living room I saw a sight that brought me to my knees. A giant tree limb was sticking into the house through the bay window. It had landed right on the recliner that my son had been sleeping on moments before. There was broken glass everywhere. The wind and rain poured through the broken window. I ran over and tried to move the tree limb. I tried to push it back outside, but it was thick and heavy. I began shaking and crying hysterically. The reality of the situation hit me like a ton of bricks. If my son had still been lying on that recliner, his little body would have been crushed under the immense weight of the tree limb.

When the storm ended and the sun came back out, we inspected the tree. A bolt of lightning had hit it and severed the limb, which sent it flying through my bay window. The force and impact were enough to do severe damage to the house and ruin several pieces of furniture.

All of that could be repaired or replaced. I felt immensely grateful that my son was sleeping soundly in his crib when the branch came crashing in. I believe that my grandmother came to me in my dream that night, to save her great-grandson's life.

— Tiffany O'Connor —

64

That Darn Cat

It is impossible to keep a straight face
in the presence of one or more kittens.
~Cynthia E. Varnado

"Brace yourself," my brother warned as he hung up the phone. "Grandma is coming."

Don't get me wrong. We loved our grandma but when we heard that she and Gramps were coming for Christmas, we had mixed emotions. Gramps, a big, jovial fellow was always making us laugh. But Grandma, although tiny in stature, could be a grouch! She didn't mince words. "Nice girls don't wear tight dungarees." Now I wouldn't be able to wear my new jeans. "Only fools spend money on movies." There went our plans to see *A Magic Christmas.*

My brother and I quipped in unison: "When Grandma speaks, everyone cringes." Mom was not amused and warned us to be respectful.

Then we remembered Grandma's number one rule: "No pets in the house." Milot, our beloved cat would have to be banished to the basement. The basement wasn't heated. We glanced sadly at the gray and white Maine Coon, pregnant with her first litter. She was comfortably curled up on the counter in the kitchen — for now.

Mom had taken great pains to make everything perfect for the holidays. A bright, berry wreath hung on the front door. Live poinsettias adorned the windows. The vanilla fragrance and the soft light of scented candles created a calming effect. She smoothed out the festive red and green fabrics concealing the foldout tables and reminded us, "Mind your manners, don't talk with your mouth full, and use your napkin."

"What's a napkin?" half-joked my older brother, Dee.

The house was glowing. And so was Mom.

It was the first time all the relatives were coming to our new home. "Ooohs" and "ahhhs" were heard as each one entered. The grandparents were the last to arrive. We heard Gramps' old Chevy come to a screeching halt. I ran to the door as my brother removed the cat from the room. I gave Gramps a big kiss and turned to hug Grandma. She held me at arms' length, scrutinizing my face and blurted, "Too much rouge!" She meant "blush."

"Oh, Mama," Gramps jumped in protectively. "It's the cold that's making her cheeks so rosy."

My brother carried their overnight bag into the spare bedroom. They were staying a couple of days.

As Grandma's gaze took in the elaborate decorations, a "Humph!" escaped her lips. "Nothing better to do with your money, Mrs. Millionaire?" In the true essence of goodwill, Mom tactfully ignored the dig and welcomed her parents affectionately.

Everyone gathered in the tiny quarters. We spent a while catching up. Aunt Katherine got promoted. Adele announced her engagement. All good news except Grandma's arthritis was acting up.

Eventually, we took our places for the feast. Traditional American fare was tastefully arranged all around. There were even delicious side dishes from our grandparents' old country. The turkey took center stage. The parties at each table joined hands as the youngest, Cousin Mille, said her well-rehearsed grace. Things went without a hitch until she got to amen. Then an unexpected snicker arose from the kids' section, followed by increasingly louder chuckles and giggles. Soon boisterous laughter was in full swing. With a low moan coming from deep within, Milot, the cat was moving in slow motion, dragging Grandma's size 44 Double D bra behind her.

Mom's face was ashen. Grandma's mouth was open wide. Her complexion had taken on the color of the pickled beets on the platter in front of her. The laughter had come to an abrupt halt. An ominous silence ensued. My brother snatched the cat—which refused to let go of the brassiere—and whisked her out of sight. Mom threw us a harsh look and Grandma scolded, "An animal belongs in the yard; not in the house." Gramps grabbed a shot of Schnapps and practically shoved it under Grandma's nose: "Here, Mama. This will help your cold." Grandma slugged it down. And then another.

The Schnapps seemed to help because gradually the corners of Grandma's mouth turned up. She confessed, "That darn cat! She made me smile." Before long, we were all smiling and chatting, gladly putting the cat-and-bra incident out of our thoughts. The rest of the meal went smoothly. The supper was a huge success.

When all the dishes had been cleared, we gathered around the brightly lit tree and followed our custom of Christmas caroling. Aunts, uncles, cousins, brothers and sisters put aside any differences of the previous months. A feeling of contentment, gratitude and love enveloped us in a warmth not unlike a bear hug. For a few hours, harmony and accord prevailed; at least in spirit if not in our musical attempts.

Sometime later Mom noticed that Grandma was absent from this pleasurable and rare gathering. "Go find her," she urged.

I wandered toward the guest room. The door was slightly ajar. Without opening it further I peeked inside. Grandma was sitting in a recliner, her head bent over something. I looked closer. Milot, the cat was snuggled happily on her lap. Grandma's face wore a blissful expression. Her weathered hands gently stroked the cat's chin and behind her ears. "Pretty Milot. Whose kitty are you? Are you Granny's little darling? Yes, you are," Grandma purred. I don't know whose purr was louder.

Busted!

I sneaked away without being seen.

In February, when Milot had her litter, Grandma timidly asked for one of the kittens. She and Christmas spent the next seventeen years living together in peaceful contentment. And Grandma's disposition improved immensely.

—Eva Carter—

65

Love on the Menu

Grandmother — a wonderful mother
with lots of practice.
~Author Unknown

"Mom! We've arrived!" I called, as I pushed open the screen door. After eight hours in the car, my husband, our six-month-old son and I had at last driven down the long driveway to my parents' home by the lake. The cool breeze from the shore and the shade of the tall pine trees offered relief from the heat of the summer day.

"Welcome!" my mother cried as she emerged from the kitchen and reached out to hold Timmy. "It's been three months since we've seen this little guy!"

Several months earlier, my husband and I had taken Timmy to visit my parents' home in Massachusetts. On that occasion, my brother and his wife had flown in from California with their new baby boy. The cousins met for the first time at Gramma's house. My mother had made grand preparations as two sets of inexperienced parents descended on her home with portable cribs, diaper bags, and baby toys. On the refrigerator door, she had written the words, "Welcome Andy & Timmy!" and she had used kitchen magnets to create a scene of diapers drying on a long laundry line.

Could two boys be more different? Andy was slender, Timmy was chunky. Andy whimpered gently while Timmy used his voice at full throttle to let the world know his needs. Both boys were teething and drooling, so Gramma produced frozen juice bars to soothe their gums. Now on this second trip to her home, Timmy already sported eight new teeth!

"Are you hungry?" Gramma asked Timmy as he squirmed in her arms, anxious to get on the floor and explore this new world.

"Thanks, but he can wait, Mom," I replied. "I just nursed him in the car. I brought some Cheerios and rice cereal with us for him."

I had only recently introduced Timmy to "real" food. The parenting magazines had warned me about introducing new foods one at a time, about avoiding foods like eggs and peanuts that might cause allergic reactions, about grinding the food carefully. I soon realized that my mother had not read those magazines.

When I got up after a brief nap, I found Timmy seated with my mother at the dining room table. Timmy was happily licking peanut butter off his fingers.

"He was hungry so I made him a little sandwich. I hope that was okay?"

"Er, fine," I replied. After all, what could I say? Short of pumping his stomach, there was nothing I could do. Trying to add authority to my words, I added, "Doctors say that peanut products could cause him to develop allergies later."

"Oh, he seems to be just fine. Children are very resilient. They survive an amazing variety of parenting styles."

Over the next days Timmy's menu expanded rapidly. Bananas, ham salad (never mind all the preservatives and nitrates), egg salad, honey, spaghetti and meat sauce. He gummed them all with gusto. My mother handed him the food and he figured out a way to get it down. Seeing the special bond forming between these two people I loved, I learned to relax and enjoy my son as much as he enjoyed stuffing his mouth.

Twenty-five years later Tim still has no sign of allergies. Gramma may not have followed doctor's orders, but she was right about one thing: Grandchildren are very resilient creatures.

— Emily Parke Chase —

Christmas Comfort

A grandmother is a safe haven.
~Suzette Haden Elgin

My mother had passed away in October and I was bereft. Our fifteen-year-old daughter Jessica was despondent, too. Her Mimi had been her world.

We had run away to out-of-town relatives for Thanksgiving, and now we faced our first Christmas without my mother. To make it more painful, Jess's birthday was Christmas Eve. My husband suggested we escape to New York. What could be more festive than the holiday lights and Broadway shows?

We had gone to the theatre that night, had enjoyed a late supper afterward, and had returned to the hotel exhausted. Our room had a wonderfully inviting king size bed, which the three of us shared. Robert fell onto his side and was deep into dreams before Jess and I had washed our faces. I crawled into the middle with Jess to my right. She had been unusually quiet and I knew she was missing her grandmother when I heard her whisper, "Mom, would you please 'tickle-scratch' my back?"

"Sure, sweetheart." My mother had been the world's best back-scratcher. She had the lightest touch and the greatest endurance anyone could ever imagine. How many nights had that gentle hand lulled me to sleep, her fingers barely sweeping over my skin from shoulder to shoulder and across my neck? Unfortunately for Jess, I had inherited neither the instinct nor the patience to do it the way Mama had done.

But I would try.

Jess turned her back to me, and, as I lifted my arm toward her shoulder, the atmosphere in the room seemed to change. It became cooler — not unpleasantly so, but cooler and different. Where it had been completely dark the minute before, there was now a soft glow around us, and then, something, or someone, took my hand and guided it over and around my daughter's back. It was as if my hand had become the object on a Ouija board. I did nothing. My delicate movements were totally involuntary and foreign to me. My own hand was weightless and tireless. I had no control over where or how to touch her — or when to stop. Eventually, my hand moved to the top of her left shoulder and patted it twice. With that, the session ended, and the darkness returned.

I brought my hand back to myself and pondered what had just transpired. A few moments later, I thought I heard Jess sniffle.

"Are you still awake, honey?"

"Uh huh. Mom, Mimi was here, wasn't she?"

"It seemed that way. Why do you say so?"

"Somehow the room felt different, strange. And the way you scratched me felt just like her. You never have done it for so long. And then the signal that you were through."

"Signal?"

"You tapped me twice on the shoulder. That's what she always did when she was finished."

"I don't remember her doing that. Hmm, I guess that really was Mimi letting us know she is still with us and she is okay." With that Jess hugged me and fell fast asleep.

We could not have had a better Christmas present.

— Grace Givens —

She Knew

*We should all have one person who
knows how to bless us despite the evidence.
Grandmother was that person to me.*
~Phyllis Theroux

The house was filled with people: my father-in-law, my husband's sisters and their spouses, our nieces and nephews. The tree with its colorful decorations was surrounded by piles of presents. We had enjoyed a delicious Christmas dinner and now it was time for the gift exchange. My father-in-law was busy handing out the gifts. Rachel, our fourteen-month-old daughter, sat on my lap, excited by all the bright wrappings, bows and activity. Gifts were being unwrapped, paper was flying, and laughter filled the room.

My father-in-law handed me a gift. "For Rachel from her grandma" he said to me. I quietly took the gift and looked at my husband Marvin with a puzzled expression. It had been almost three years since his mother had passed away. Rachel, with our help, tore the paper off the big box. Inside the box was a beautiful blond curly-haired doll with blue eyes. She wore a pink gingham dress with a white apron. In her arms she held a baby doll that wore a matching pink romper. Marvin removed the doll from the box for Rachel. As we admired the doll, we noticed a knob on the back of the doll. I carefully turned the knob. The doll started to sway back and forth, the motion causing her to rock the baby doll in her arms. A lullaby accompanied the movement. Rachel looked at the doll with wide eyes and reached her arms out to take it.

I was still puzzled. When my mother-in-law passed away, Marvin and I had been married for eight years. Those years were filled with infertility treatments, adoption agency interviews and paperwork. At the time it had seemed that we were no closer to having a baby to call our own than we had ever been.

Now almost three years later we had our precious daughter. I wondered about the story behind the gift of the doll. Thinking of my mother-in-law's love for shopping I thought that perhaps she had bought the doll and stored it away for one of her other granddaughters. After all, she had already had twelve granddaughters among her twenty grandchildren. Rachel's grandpa must have found the doll in the back of a closet and selected it for her.

As the Christmas celebration continued, Marvin's sister Barbara shared with me that she had been shopping with her mother when the doll was bought. Barbara had asked her mother whom she was buying the doll for. Barbara was surprised when Mom replied that it was for Marvin and Donna's daughter. "But Mom" she said, "Donna and Marvin don't have a daughter, and even if they have a baby it could be a boy." Mom insisted on the purchase and Barbara knew that it was better not to argue with her mom.

Later Luella, another of my husband's sisters, told me her story. One day she had been helping her mom clean out a closet. Finding the doll, she had asked her mother whom the doll was intended for. Again the reply was that the doll was for Marvin and Donna's daughter. Luella, not wanting to press the issue, carefully put the doll back in the closet for safekeeping. I now understood that this doll was for Rachel, a special doll picked out for her, before she was born, before we even knew if she was ever to be.

Once home I thought about putting the doll away, safe from little hands, a keepsake for her to have when she was older. But then I decided that it was more important for Rachel to have the doll now. Over the years, the white apron tore, the doll's hair was messed up and her leg even fell off. In time I came to realize that the real gift was my mother-in-law's faith, her belief that one day her son Marvin and his wife Donna would have a daughter to love and raise. Even if Grandma was not there to share in the joy, her future granddaughter would have a precious gift from her grandmother.

—Donna Welk Goering—

Honorary Moms

Excellent Stock

When you are sorrowful look again in your heart,
and you shall see that in truth you are weeping for
that which has been your delight.
~Kahlil Gibran

My husband is Scottish. Not "American of Scottish descent" Scottish, but "born and raised over there and talks with an accent" Scottish. So, after we were engaged, we planned a trip to Scotland to introduce me to his family. Now, I am a native Texan, and I can sometimes, on the rare occasion, when extremely provoked, use some interesting vocabulary words. On the plane, my well-intentioned fiancé gave me a rundown of all the words I wasn't to use in front of his mother. "Even though nice girls say those words in America," he added—looking as if he were trying to convince himself I was truly a nice girl and worthy of meeting his Mum—"nice girls in Scotland don't."

I remember biting my tongue. I loved this man, and I would not scream obscenities at his mother when we met, no matter how tempting he had just made it seem.

When I met her, a five-foot-two, ash-blond sixty-year-old, she asked how I felt after my trip. I very carefully considered my vocabulary, and replied with one of the new Scottish words I had often heard my husband use.

"Well, Liz, I'm happy to be here, but I'm totally knackered."

My husband turned bright red. My mother-in-law raised one

eyebrow and very politely offered to make me a cup of tea. My brother-in-law wasted no time telling me that the cute expression I had just used meant exhausted, yes. But exhausted as in "weary from too much conjugal bliss."

Ah, first impressions.

Those early years were not smooth sailing for Liz and me. She was the epitome of Scottish womanhood. "If Napoleon had had a Scottish wife," my father-in-law said, "we'd all be speaking French now." It was true. Liz was frighteningly competent, and at twenty-four, I knew I was nowhere near her league. She could do it all — cook brandy snaps from memory, whip up a four-course meal every night, sing in the local operatic society, serve as headmistress of the primary school, raise three ambitious and intelligent sons to adulthood, and keep an immaculately clean household.

On the other hand, I was a Texas girl, a child of divorced parents, who swore, drank margaritas, cleaned only when the toilets got too disgusting, and could cook any recipe as long as it started with a can of cream of mushroom soup.

We grew closer when I gave birth to my son, her first grandchild. Even though she had knitted a closet-full of tiny pink wool sweaters (as if the gender of my baby could be determined by how many pink winter garments she sent), she loved my red-faced, colicky boy and spent a month with us after his birth. She filled my freezer that month. The first day home from the hospital, I wandered blearily downstairs around ten a.m. to find her in my kitchen with a casserole, a giant pot of ratatouille, and a sponge cake already made. She did this every day for a month — cooked two or three meals in double batches, and froze enough dinners that I didn't turn on the stove for three months after she left.

I remember sitting on a kitchen chair, watching while she made stock. "First stock is best," she told me, meticulously picking the last pieces of meat from a roasted chicken and placing them in a bowl. "But during the war, we made first, second, and sometimes third stock." She broke the bones down, and added onion, carrots, garlic, salt and pepper. I had never seen stock made before; I thought it came in cans.

As I watched, she turned the scraps I had always thrown away into the most delicious soups and stews, sharing stories from her life as she worked. I was in awe of her.

As we were the possessors of the sole grandchild, my in-laws came to stay with us, for a month at a time, every nine months or so. We made each other crazy. We learned not to let it show.

When I was pregnant with my second — another boy who could have worn a different hand-knitted pink sweater every day for two weeks — we found out that Liz had cancer. Not breast cancer, or skin cancer, or one of those kinds of cancers that people recover from and live for decades longer. She had ovarian cancer — they call it the silent killer — and it was in stage four. I didn't know what stage four meant then. After about ten minutes on the Internet, I discovered it usually meant "hopeless."

She wouldn't talk about it, and never acknowledged how bad it was. She died when my second son was eight months old, after a long visit two months before. I remember the day I reached into my freezer, three months after the funeral, finding a shepherd's pie she had made and frozen, knowing that was the last dish anyone would ever eat that she had cooked.

It was delicious, of course, but we all cried through dinner.

When Liz was alive, I would call my sister to vent. "She unpacked my linen closet this morning, and ironed all the sheets," I would shout into the phone. "What the heck is that about?" My sister was always appropriately sympathetic.

"What a witch," she would murmur, "to iron your clothes for you without even asking. How rude."

Now, with a closet full of linens that have more wrinkles than a thousand grandmothers, I regret those complaints. I miss Liz, and wish I could have her back, so she could see her grandsons learning to walk, to read, to ride their bikes. So I could thank her again for all those meals, and the stories. So I could show her that she was one of my life's great blessings.

I am a mother of boys, like she was, and I hope someday to be a mother-in-law. I pray I will be like Liz, teaching my sons' brides how to put together a meal, how to hold a colicky baby, how to fold a fitted sheet, and biting my tongue when they do it all wrong. I have learned a hard truth: the mother-in-law you feared and loved can disappear, in a heartbeat, in a day, leaving you with a heart full of longing.

But if you are very lucky, like me, you may realize you have something of her left to pass down. A skill to teach your own daughters-in-law. A recipe for making the best out of what you have — for holding on to every bit of goodness you can — like the one I learned from my magnificent mother-in-law: the secret to making truly excellent stock.

How to Make Liz's Excellent Stock

After a turkey or chicken dinner, place in a large soup pot the remaining bones, skin, and any small bits of meat. Add a chopped onion, a teaspoonful or so of salt, a dash of pepper, some sliced carrots, celery, a bay leaf, and a clove of garlic if you like. (Liz would use whatever sad, withering vegetables I had in the fridge. Of course, she never commented negatively on the state of the veggies, only smiled and said they were "perfect for stock.")

Add enough water to cover it all and bring to a boil. Immediately turn the heat to low; simmer for two hours. Strain the liquid into a large bowl and refrigerate for four hours or more. Skim the fat off the top. Use the remaining stock as a base in soups, or to replace canned broth in any recipe.

— Nikki Loftin —

The Code Reader

*One of the basic needs of every human being is the
need to be loved, to have our wishes and feelings taken
seriously, to be validated as people who matter.*
~Rabbi Harold S. Kushner

I was twelve when life overwhelmed my mother and she signed
herself into a psychiatric facility. We lived in rural Northern
California where my dad worked as a logger. He left the house
before dawn and returned after dark. The oldest of five children, I did my best to help my elderly grandmother care for my three
younger brothers and sister. Money was tight, but we always ate well,
had clean clothes and a warm bed to sleep in.

In those days, my mother's condition was called a "nervous break-
down." I was just old enough to know she was in trouble, but not old
enough to know where I fit into what "drove her crazy" or what might
make her better. I wrote cheerful letters, hoping to boost her spirits
and remind her how much she was missed. We loved her and hoped
she would be home soon. Of course, we all promised to behave and
not upset her.

No matter how much I tried to concentrate at school, my mind
wandered and my grades slipped. My heart ached with confusion and
uncertainty. Years later, I would learn the "problems at home" that I
thought were invisible to a certain teacher were actually obvious to her.

Gladys Hue, the local high-school public-speaking teacher, also
worked in the elementary schools as a speech therapist. She was tall,

about fifty, with a blond pageboy and dancing blue eyes. The day she walked into my sixth grade classroom to screen children for her special program, Mrs. Hue, dressed in a pastel blue dress, reminded me of the golden-haired angel we always placed atop our Christmas tree.

She explained she was there to listen to each of us and, just like a hearing test, see who might need a little extra help with their words. In the company of a few colorful puppets, she commenced a student-by-student series of private interviews. By the time she got to me, I had perfected a heretofore nonexistent stutter.

When I sat down at the small table in the back of the room with Mrs. Hue, I became the center of her attention and sputtered out my name: "Ja-Ja-Jackie." Her smile never faded as she asked several questions and listened intently to my now faltering pattern of speech. Not once did I sense judgment or suspicion. To the contrary, I felt important — like I used to feel with my mother. But most of all, deception aside, I felt like I was being heard.

For all the things I was about to learn from Mrs. Hue, the most profound remains the realization that a child's inability to express her feelings is not a reflection of how deeply she feels. Fledgling humans that they are, children often communicate, for lack of a better term, in code. Gladys Hue was a code reader, and on that day she saw a freckle-faced girl with curly hair reaching for what we all long for — to feel valued and understood.

For a brief few weeks, Mrs. Hue's speech-therapy class filled the void left by my mother. There were about ten students. Some had lisps; some substituted the letter "w" or "y" for the "r" sound; and others, like me, stuttered. We practiced enunciation with puppets, performed dramatic narrative sentences with dress-up hats, and sang with the accompaniment of tambourines and triangles. Miraculously, my stutter vanished within a few days!

Years later, I confessed to Mrs. Hue that I really hadn't had a stutter. The ever-present twinkle in her eye brightened as she revealed she had known the truth all along. To my surprise, she added, "You know, you needed me as much as I needed you." She went on to explain she didn't have the heart to deny me something I so clearly wanted and secretly used me as a "diction model" for the other students.

Mom was home by the end of summer, and our family set about the business of trying to regain our stride. Unfortunately, turmoil in one form or another persisted. Headstrong and prone to help the most helpless, Mom took on a new role as a mental-health advocate, and our home became a local group-therapy hub. By the time I started high school, my parents were on their way to a divorce, and I again sought refuge in a class taught by Gladys Hue.

Popular opinion holds that most people are more afraid of public speaking than death. Perhaps if more people had a teacher like Mrs. Hue, that ratio would shift significantly. "Tell them what you're going to tell them," she taught us. "Then tell them, and then tell them what you told them." This was her hallmark message to those of us who dragged our feet to stand behind the podium in her classroom, grateful the structure hid trembling knees and provided a handhold for sweating palms.

Religiously, she counted how many times speakers said "uh" to help us better string together words and thoughts. Her critique on organization and content balanced the positive and negative. "Jackie, this is a wonderful idea," she once said to me about a speech on world peace, "but reading it is like trying to swim through a muddy pond." Because her praise mattered so much to me, I did what any aspiring young public speaker would do: I broke into tears and ran to the library.

Eventually, through trial and error, I earned my way onto Mrs. Hue's competitive forensic-speech team. The challenge was fraught with fear and doubt, but her unwavering faith in me, her magical ability to see potential where I saw none, kept me striving. I even achieved the highest honor of any of her students as a California state finalist in the 1968 Annual Lion's Club Student Speaker Contest.

Shortly before I delivered my speech, Mrs. Hue, known for her stylish elegance, removed the sparkling earrings she wore. "Now that you're a young lady," she said, handing them to me, "we're going to doll you up."

I placed second that day, but had so far exceeded my own expectations that I came to realize the greater prize was having been one of

Gladys Hue's students. More than teaching, she embraced and inspired, nudging some, prodding others, tirelessly challenging each of us to wrangle our fears and fully engage our imaginations.

I last visited Mrs. Hue shortly before she passed away in 2010 at the age of ninety-five. I recall marveling at how little the years had diminished the graceful flick of her hand as she spoke or the all-knowing light in her eyes. I told her, "I owe so much to you." She shrugged, alluding to a philosophy she shared with many teachers—she had simply opened doors for her students. It was up to us to walk through them. Her attempt at humility soon melted into a twinkling of delight and pride, and once again, decades later, student and teacher needed each other. I needed her to know as much as she needed to hear how deeply valued she was as a code-reading educator who changed my life.

—Jackie Boor—

70

Can You Hear Me Now?

Give up all hope of peace so long as your
mother-in-law is alive.
~Juvenal

My mother-in-law was from the "old country." Her knowledge of modern technology was, to be polite, limited. Very limited. Just about nonexistent. She was perfectly capable of understanding how to use these newfangled devices, but she had no interest in learning. She was content with the old ways. They had worked for her for years, so please don't try to show her any new contraptions, even if they would make her life easier. Her mind was made up, and she knew she was right.

She did love watching television and didn't ever want to miss her special shows, so she mastered the on-and-off switch and channel-selector dial very quickly. But forget about teaching her to use the remote control. We tried so that she wouldn't have to get up each time she wanted to change the channel. It was a lost cause.

My family and I were into technology. We had computers, cell phones, fancy TVs—all the latest things. And, oh my goodness, we even had a machine that answered our phone and recorded messages for us when we were out. What a novel idea! We told my mother-in-law about the answering machine, showed it to her and explained how it worked. Over and over. We played the greeting for her that I had recorded. It was such a pleasant greeting. Good luck with that! She just looked confused. The concept didn't register. She couldn't figure it out.

My mother-in-law would call our house and, if we were out, my voice would greet her and ask her to leave a message. That was the first problem. She wasn't absolutely delighted with me in the first place because I had married her son. Truth be told, she wouldn't have thought anyone was good enough for him, so I tried not to take her attitude too personally. But now she liked me even less. She felt that I was being very rude and insulting to her when I answered the phone but wouldn't talk. And why did I tell her to leave a message? Why didn't I just talk to her?

Here's something else about my mother-in-law that is important to understand: When she would call at night and we were not home — and if we had forgotten to tell her we wouldn't be home — that meant something was terribly wrong. She knew we were all dead. In a ditch. Or we were in the hospital having major surgery and were not expected to live. Or we were lost in the mountains without food or water, and we were going to freeze to death. Couldn't we just be out to dinner, or at a party with friends, or at a movie? No way.

So when she would call and get our answering machine, she would freak out. And how did we know this? We would listen to her messages when we got home.

"Hello, Barbara. I want to tell you that Aunt Rose called." (Long pause.)

"Barbara? Hello? Can you hear me?" (Longer pause.)

"Barbara! Don't you care? Talk to me. Well!"

And then she'd hang up and call right back.

"Hello? HELLO?? HELLO! Barbara? BAR-BAR-A!! I know you are there. I can hear your voice. Why don't you talk to me? Well!"

When my name turned into three syllables, I knew I was in trouble.

The best part is when she would decide that our number was not working correctly and have the operator try to call. Wow, would she get mad. Poor operator. When we would come home and listen to our messages, we could hear the entire conversation.

"Madam, there is nothing wrong with this number."

"Then why can't I talk to them?"

"I'm sorry, Madam. I don't think they are at home."

"Then why does my daughter-in-law answer the phone? She's there."

"Ma'am, that's their answering machine. It's a tape. It's just her voice."

"What do you mean? A tape? Why is her voice on a tape? I know she's there."

"Ma'am, they have a machine that answers the phone when they're not home."

"How is that possible? I know they are there, and they're just not talking."

"LISTEN, LADY. Leave them a message. There is nothing I can do."

"Well, you have some nerve talking to an old lady like that!"

You get the picture. There was just no way for her to grasp the concept and understand this type of technology. When we would get home, listen to our messages and call her back, she would tell us there was something wrong with our phone, and that she had to call the operator to help her. Then she would berate the operator for not doing her job and not being able to get her call through to us because she knew we were there. Of course, she knew I was there because I had answered the phone!

My mother-in-law is no longer with us. She never, ever did understand the concept of an answering machine, and we stopped trying to explain it to her. She never, ever completely forgave me for marrying her son either, but she and I did eventually make our own kind of peace. And now every time I hear my own voice on my answering-machine tape, I remember those messages she would leave, and it makes me smile.

— Barbara LoMonaco —

71

Just When I Needed It

Give yourself entirely to those around you. Be generous
with your blessings. A kind gesture can reach a wound
that only compassion can heal.
~Steve Maraboli, Life, the Truth, and Being Free

"Look, Mommy, look!" Jimmy had a hopeful smile. He was holding a plastic package filled with green army men. "Can I buy these, please?" I returned his sweet smile and told him that he could put his treasure in the shopping cart along with the food and other necessities that we were buying. I watched as all three of my children—Steven, age eleven; Ana, age eight; and Jimmy, age five—chose a few small items to keep them occupied in the car during our long ride from Georgia to New Hampshire.

My heart ached, even as they happily picked out their new toys and activity books. This trip was monumental, and I was both excited and terrified. After divorcing my husband of sixteen years, I was taking the children back home to my family.

The children were happily chattering about their new toys as we stood in the checkout line. As I watched our purchases add up on the register, I started to get nervous. It was obvious that the running total I had been calculating as we shopped was wrong. We would have to put back all the children's toys and activity books.

Tears were clouding my eyes as I told the children I wouldn't be able to treat them after all. They didn't say a word, but their crestfallen faces broke my heart. Ana ran her hand down her pony's mane one last time before she removed it from the conveyor belt. My children were losing their father, their friends, their home, and even their cat.

Suddenly, a petite woman with dark brown hair and two young children of her own stepped in front of me. Because of my tears, I was barely able to see the forty dollars she placed in my hand. When I realized what she was offering, I started to protest, but she put her hands over mine and said, "I've been in your shoes before. Please buy those things for your children."

At that moment, I felt her sincerity and it comforted me deeply. I cried once more, but this time it was tears of relief. I hadn't realized how much strain and loneliness I had been feeling, and how worried I was about the children's loss. This woman may have been human, but, to me, she was an angel.

All I could do was thank her over and over. After I paid the cashier, I tried to give this generous woman the change, but she refused to take it. Her kindness overwhelmed me.

That good-hearted woman had no idea that she changed my life that day. From that point forward, I hoped for the chance to do the same for someone else one day when I could.

Then one day the children and I were shopping in Walmart. We found ourselves in line behind a mom whose infant was sleeping in a car seat in her shopping cart. She was in the same pickle I had been in: she had more items than cash and she was struggling to choose what to buy. My heart went out to her and I knew I wanted to help. When I saw that one thing she had to give up was a bag of red apples, something so simple and nourishing, I didn't waste a moment.

Steven was ahead of me in line, so I asked him to tap her gently on the arm. When she turned I said, "If you will allow me, I'd really be happy to pay for your order."

She stared at me for a moment in disbelief. Then her eyes widened and she replied, "All of it?"

I smiled and answered, "Yes, because a few years ago I was in need and someone did the same for me. Please let me do this for you."

Still looking shocked, she thanked me and added her discarded things back onto the conveyor belt. I could see the weight lift from her shoulders and it brought me such joy. After it was paid for and bagged, the young mother gave us a big smile and another heartfelt thank-you. She left the store with a spring in her step that day. My children and I had quite a bit of springiness, too, along with a strong desire to continue paying it forward.

—Jennifer Zink—

72

Mrs. Usher

*You save an old man and you save a unit; but you save
a boy and you save a multiplication table.*
~Rodney "Gipsy" Smith

I was twelve years old when I was released from reform school in Florida. I was locked up in the juvenile hall because I refused to ever return to the orphanage where I'd spent most of my life. I was never going to return there, even if I had to spend the rest of my life locked in a small cell. I'd flatly refused to even walk out the front door of the juvenile hall to help them clean up the streets, for fear they would take me back to that awful orphanage.

It was a Wednesday morning when a man named Burt, who worked for the court, came into my cage-like cell and asked if I wanted to go somewhere special for Thanksgiving dinner. I told him that I did not want to go outside the juvenile shelter. I liked Burt because he was a nice man. Burt kept on and on about that dinner and how a kid should not be locked up on Thanksgiving, so I finally told him that I would go.

Later that afternoon, an older woman named Mrs. Usher came to the shelter. She talked with me for about ten minutes and said she wanted to take me to her house for Thanksgiving. She said no child should be locked up in a cage. Before we left, I made her promise she would bring me back the next day. She and I walked out together and drove to her home.

As we walked into the house, I was surprised at what I saw. It was really small, not like the big dormitory house that I lived in at the orphanage. You could sleep thirty or forty people in our house at the orphanage.

I was really surprised when I went to their bathroom. I saw right away that they were not rich at all. They only had one toilet and one sink in their bathroom; they were really poor, and they did not even know it.

Wednesday afternoon and evening were very difficult for me. I wanted so badly just to get out of there and be back in my cage. There must have been fifty people going in and out of that house, getting ready for the big Thanksgiving dinner the next day. I was really scared. I didn't like people very much, especially grown people. They can do some really bad things to you when you're a kid. I never moved out of the chair, until almost all those people were gone later that afternoon.

Mrs. Usher came into the living room and asked if I wanted to have a Coke in the small bottle. I told her "thank you," but that I did not care for anything. I wanted that Coke really bad, but was just too scared to take it. Late that night when everyone was asleep, I snuck into the kitchen really slow and quiet-like, and took a cold Coca-Cola out of the refrigerator. I drank it real fast, in about five seconds, and hid the bottle cap behind the refrigerator. After that, I pressed the cold bottle against my stomach so it would be warm like the other ones. Then I put it in the carton so no one would ever know I drank it.

The next day was almost as unbearable for me. I would have rather died than have gone through that big dinner. All those strange people were laughing, joking, and making all kinds of noise. I have never been so embarrassed and so scared in all my life, and that is the God's honest truth. I hardly ate anything that day, even though I had never seen so much food in all my life. I sure was glad when it was finally over.

Later that night after everyone else had gone to bed, Mrs. Usher took me out onto her front porch. I really didn't want to go out. I knew that I would be asked a bunch of dumb questions, questions that I could not possibly answer. I just wanted to be left alone until I was returned to the juvenile shelter the next morning. Nevertheless,

I got up and walked out onto the porch.

We talked for hours and hours. She was a real nice lady. I had never once sat and talked with anyone before that in my whole life. It was my first "nice and slow time," as she called it, and I really liked it.

I will never forget her kindness and her warm smile. But what I could not understand was why she did all of this for me. Why would anyone be kind to me? So I always kept one eye on her all the time.

Mrs. Usher got up from her chair and went into the kitchen. When she returned, she brought a small bottle of Coke for each of us. She smiled and handed one to me. I will never forget that either. That was the best Coke I ever drank in my whole entire life.

The next morning, we ate some breakfast together. Then she told me to go into the bedroom and get my things so she could take me back to the juvenile hall like she promised. When I was in the bedroom, I heard her in the hallway talking on the telephone to the authorities. She asked them why I was being sent back to the reform school. She wanted to know what I did that was so bad that I had to be sent back there. They told her that I did nothing wrong, but they had nowhere else to put me. I heard her get very mad at them and say, "I'm not going to bring him back to the juvenile hall to be locked up again like an animal!"

God knows I loved that woman for saying that!

It was the most wonderful thing anyone ever did for me as a child. That, of all the things in my life, is the one thing that made me want to become somebody someday. That one little sentence which came out of her mouth was the small and only light guiding my life for the next forty-five years.

I stayed with Mrs. Usher for several weeks, then left to go out on my own at the age of thirteen. I told her, "I have to make it on my own now 'cause I'm a man."

I continued to see the Usher family on and off for the next twenty or thirty years, until their deaths. I know they would have adopted me, but when it was discussed, I told Mrs. Usher that it was too late for me. She placed her hands over her face and cried.

I just wish I could have shown her how much I really loved her before she died, but I didn't know how to show love. I didn't even know what love meant or what it felt like.

So I tell her now, on quiet nights on porch swings, "Mom, now that you are in heaven, I hope you know how much I love and respect you. I hope you know how much you added to the life of one lonely, little boy who nobody else in the world wanted. I love you, Mom."

—Roger Dean Kiser—

73

In Security

The greatest happiness of life is the conviction that
we are loved; loved for ourselves, or rather,
loved in spite of ourselves.
~Victor Hugo

We had been married for nine months, and I was still learning the ways of my in-laws. It was my first Christmas away from my family and our familiar traditions, and my heart ached for home.

My in-laws are lovely people, in every sense of the word. Their home belongs in a magazine, with hardwood floors and chic country-home decor. My mother-in-law is always perfectly dressed for every affair and my father-in-law is a beloved pastor of the largest church in their town. I felt even more insecure because my brother-in-law had married his high school sweetheart so they had known her for years. I was the new person — a short geeky science nerd who had never been out in the country.

My husband told me not to worry so much. Everyone would like me. But I still felt out of place. I didn't know all the people they knew and I didn't understand their insider jokes. I couldn't even learn the family games quickly enough, and I felt as though every misstep I made was being recorded in their minds whether they were conscious of it or not.

On Christmas morning, I called my family to wish them a happy Christmas morning, I told them I loved them, hung up and started to cry. I felt like a failure in every way: a failure as a daughter-in-law and a failure as a daughter to my parents by not being with them on the most special holiday of the year.

I crept downstairs, trying to blend in with the perfectly decorated walls. They were all gathered at the table eating… fresh cinnamon rolls. Just like at my parents'. With real cream-cheese frosting. And there was a plate waiting for me.

"Happy Christmas morning, hon!" said my father-in-law.

"Your stocking is over here," said my mother-in-law.

My mother-in-law had put out stockings sometime during the night. She had handmade every one herself. And there was mine, with my name stitched across the top in red thread, with a little heart woven beside it.

My insecurity disappeared. I finally felt loved. But I suddenly realized it wasn't the first time — they had loved me the whole time. I looked up at my mother-in-law, and I saw in her eyes the same hope I had: that I would love and accept them back.

The best present I received that year was the other half of my family, and I've been reminded of my good fortune every single Christmas since.

—Nan Rockey—

Putting Up

Keep your eyes wide open before marriage,
half-shut afterwards.
~Benjamin Franklin

Our neighbor across the street hosted a small birthday party for her eighty-nine-year-old mother and called a few of the ladies on our street to celebrate with her. Her friends were long gone by this age, and for undisclosed reasons, the few extended family members were estranged. So, armed with a few pretty packages, my friends and I happily attended.

Upon first glance, Mary looked like the quintessential silver-haired, sweater-wearing grandmother. Short curls framed her wrinkled face, which lit up in a broad smile when she saw us. Her sweet, high-pitched voice was reminiscent of a tiny, magical fairy with a tinkling laugh. It was always a joy to be with her. As she sat in her rocker, her fingers nimbly twisting and tangling yarn into yet another afghan, she shocked us with stories of how she rebelled against her parents' wishes and traveled to dangerous places around the world at a time when young women were expected to settle down and have kids. After she married, she rode on the back of her husband's motorcycle until she got one of her own.

When she spoke of her husband, her eyes moistened. He had passed away more than a decade earlier, but she still talked about him all the time. At the party, we sang the birthday song, and she blew out the candles. "George would be ninety-five if he were alive today," she said. We all marveled with our mouths full of buttercream.

"Yes," she continued. "We were married for fifty years." Fifty years. If we had marveled before, we positively gushed over this major accomplishment. Most of us had been married for only ten or fifteen years and had contemplated divorce at one time or another. I was going through a rough patch with my own husband at the time.

Being married for fifty years seemed inconceivable. I couldn't resist asking this sage wife how she had managed to stay married so long. "Mary," I whispered. "What is your secret for a long and happy marriage?" I didn't want just a long marriage. I wanted a happy one, too, and her marriage had been both.

The old woman looked at me for a long time. Finally, she quietly put down her cake plate, leaned forward out of her rocking chair and, with a bony hand, beckoned me closer.

"To be married for as long as I was," she whispered, "you have to put up with a lot of crap." And then she fell back into her chair. It took me a while to process what she had said, and then I began to giggle. Oh, the simple truth! As I shared her words of wisdom with the rest of the party, everyone laughed and laughed as Mary sat there with her eyes twinkling.

"I need to cross-stitch that and hang it over my fireplace!" one of the ladies exclaimed. As seemingly crass as the words might sound at first, they really put things into perspective. In our grandmothers' day, the phrase "putting up" meant either of two things: 1) They stored their food through canning, pickling or drying. 2) They endured or suffered in silence during situations that they didn't particularly like. It is true that when we're married — or in any type of interpersonal relationship, for that matter — we will not like everything about the other person, and most definitely will not like everything that happens or everything he does or says. But is that a good reason to end a relationship? Is it divorce-worthy?

Those words have stuck with me ever since. When we really love someone, do we put strings on our love? Do we require perfection from the other person in order to deserve their love? I do not like everything about my husband, and I can assure you that he doesn't like everything about me. But we put up with that sort of stuff because we love each other. Love outweighs the petty annoyances, the maddening frustrations, and even the bitter disappointments. Love does not require perfection, and to be married for a long time like Mary, we have to put up with some things we don't like.

It was the best marital advice I'd ever heard. Now, I have a happy and long marriage, too. We've been married for over thirty-three years, and if we live long enough, I know that we'll make it to fifty years like Mary. Because as you put up with some of the less-than-perfect stuff, your marriage undergoes a deep and meaningful transformation, and suddenly you discover what unconditional love is all about. And it may not be easy, but it is so worth it.

—Lori Phillips—

My Angel-in-Law

*The guardian angels of life sometimes fly so high
as to be beyond our sight, but they are always
looking down upon us.*
~Jean Paul Richter

The psychic medium paced the studio, his shaggy white hair flowing behind him. He pursed his lips, listening to an internal dialogue that forty hopeful people could not hear. We were all there for essentially the same reason — to connect with a lost loved one.

He paused, his eyes closed, and then offered clues to the audience as to whom he was channeling. We were instructed to raise our hands if the details resonated with any of us. He gravitated toward different sides of the room as if by radar, divulging additional details until he could single out the person whose loved one was communicating from the other side. The room was full of mourners looking for solace, and a glimpse into what world, if any, their loved ones now inhabited. At least I know I was.

While I believed in the power of psychics, many in the room did not. They wore cynical scowls, and the medium encouraged their doubt. He welcomed skeptics, and hoped to prove his genuine gift by providing specific information that no one else could know. He acknowledged that his industry was full of charlatans, preying on believers who'd pay any fee for a message, an image, or some hope. It was easy enough to fool them. Most anyone could proffer vague

Honorary Moms | 227

details that desperate people would interpret as personal. Who didn't know someone who'd had a heart attack, walked with a limp, or had passed in a tragic accident? Grief made people gullible.

I'd been to this medium's group readings on other occasions. I'd lost a brother, both sets of grandparents, and several friends. After my brother died suddenly, I sought answers through psychic reading in order to make sense of the loss. This particular psychic had "read" my brother with such clarity that I hoped to re-experience some of the comfort, spiritual nourishment, and peace I'd previously felt. I knew I might not get a personal reading this time, as there were only so many he could squeeze into the allotted two hours.

What I never imagined was that I would hear from someone I'd never met.

My mind flashed to three years earlier, as I lay in the recovery room, struggling to breathe against an invisible weight on my chest. While I'd been told that the transfer surgery to implant three fertilized embryos had been textbook easy, I nonetheless knew something was wrong. In that moment, I couldn't think about the years I'd struggled with infertility, the multiple failures, the pills and shots, and the crushing monthly disappointment. I just needed to breathe.

My body had hyper-stimulated from the fertility drugs, producing twenty-three eggs in a single month, and it would take a while to recover from such a taxing feat. Awash in hormones, continuously breathless and tremendously uncomfortable, I was on bed rest for a month. That rest gave me the opportunity to think, obsess, and pray. I hoped to become pregnant and I yearned to recapture who I'd been before the infertility. My happy, busy life had been invaded by the pain and frustration of infertility, and it was all consuming.

I gradually recovered from the hyper-stimulation and learned that I was carrying twin boys. It was a high-risk pregnancy that eventually returned me to bed rest because the boys were positioned very low and they needed more time to develop their lungs before they could safely be born.

Again, with hours to fill the day, I read through baby rearing books and name books. We'd intended to name Twin A after our grandfathers, and Twin B was to be named after my husband's mother, who had died when he was ten years old. I often stared at pictures of my husband as a little boy with his mom, and could feel their profound sadness while she grew sicker and succumbed to a diabetes-related illness. I'd already formed a bond with my unborn boys and could not fathom a separation like my husband endured with his own mother. I wished that I had known my mother-in-law, and that she could be a part of the miracle that was taking place. I was pleased to honor her memory with our child's name.

When I delivered two healthy five-and-a-half pound boys we were overjoyed. Unfortunately, that joy was tempered by the temporary paralysis that I experienced in both legs, lasting for six weeks after their birth. I could not pick up my babies when they cried; I could not walk to them and watch them sleep in their matching bassinets. I was dependent on others to bring the boys to me, and I worried that our bond would be hampered by my temporary disability.

I never considered that I wouldn't recover; I simply had to. My babies needed me, and we had a life to lead that did not involve my using a wheelchair, walker, or cane. Despite my new-mother fatigue, I had physical therapy each day until I was able to walk without assistance. Sheer determination to be the mother I wanted to be for my babies helped me regain the use of my legs.

I recovered and was happily raising my twins when my brother passed. His death cloaked me in a depression that only the toddlers could lift me from. The psychic had helped me before. I was there again to see if my brother's spirit was still around me.

The group reading was almost over when I heard the psychic mention that he was communicating with a woman who had been a teacher and was diabetic. I, along with several other people raised my hand. He approached my general vicinity, throwing more details, until there were only a couple hopeful hands raised.

"Who has the twins?" he asked.

My spine tingled as I called out that I did. He approached me and asked if I knew someone who'd been scalded in the bathtub. I held my breath. That particular incident was very traumatic for my husband. He witnessed his mother, who'd lost sensation in her foot, unknowingly step into the blistering water. It was the beginning of her decline.

"Yes, that was my mother-in-law," I whispered.

He nodded, looking up.

"She wants you to know that she watched over you when you were pregnant and afterward with your legs."

It was in that moment that I realized she did know me, and loved me. She was a part of our lives in her own way, and I was enormously grateful.

I'd finally met my mother-in-law.

— Shanna Silva —

76

Thank You for Your Service

One of the deep secrets of life is that all that is really worth the doing is what we do for others.
~Lewis Carroll

"Thank you for your service." After more than twenty years of active duty in the military, I still blush at this comment. It's always nice to hear, but it makes me feel awkward. I don't think my enlistment is some amazing thing worth special attention.

In high school, I worked on comics instead of homework. My above-average grades could have netted the scholarship I needed, but classmates with better scores beat me out. With little money and few options, the recruiter's pitch and the thought of a stable paycheck sounded pretty good.

Even so, I deeply appreciate the occasional free cup of coffee, surprise discount on dinner, or simple expression of gratitude.

I never expect it or demand it. I chose this life with a decent understanding of what it entailed. And my wife, who also served, chose to marry into the military with first-hand knowledge of what that meant. We walked into it with eyes wide open.

My kids, on the other hand, were drafted into this life at birth. They've spent the majority of their lives in a foreign country that is more home to them than the United States whose uniform their dad puts on each day. My brother-in-law calls them his Japanese niece and nephews, despite their blond hair and pale skin.

They endure the transitions and challenges of military family life with patience and resilience, but it takes a toll. They've lost touch with friends in our moves across the world. Even when we stay in one place for a few years, other families get orders and friends move away.

Although modern technology makes communication instantaneous and easy, our time overseas still separates us from family on both sides. My kids have grandparents, aunts, uncles, and cousins they see every few years at best. Such is the price they pay for a decision they never made.

But sometimes we find, or create, "family" in unexpected places.

A few years ago, we moved to Nebraska and settled into the Omaha community. My children made some friends in the neighborhood with practiced ease and speed born of years of temporary but meaningful connections. My wife and I also sought out places to connect.

Shortly before the move, I committed to "this whole writing thing" I'd toyed around with over the years. I realized that being in the States meant access to writing groups and seminars. With a quick Google search and an e-mail I found the monthly critique group I'd attend for the next two and a half years.

My wife and I met with published authors and amateur writers who welcomed us and helped us learn the craft. A kind widow nicknamed "the lion-hearted" Kat hosted the group and provided the relentless yet constructive criticism the rest of us seemed too timid or kind to give. Her warm and inviting home became a peaceful refuge we looked forward to each month. We encouraged one another, developed friendships and watched each other's skills improve.

With Christmas approaching, the group made plans for a casual gathering that included our families. I showed up at our host's house with my wife and four kids, and found out that, for various reasons, no one else could attend that night. So the planned party became Kat and the Williamsons instead.

With a two-year-old, a seven-year-old, a middle-school boy and a teenage girl, Kat had her hands full. But we played silly games, the old-fashioned sort that involved talking face-to-face, telling jokes and stories, and interacting with people instead of electronic devices. Then Kat brought out thoughtful Christmas gifts for the kids to enjoy, along with a fruit-filled Jell-O dish for dessert.

That night, we left with stomachs and hearts filled with cheer.

Later that week, I got an e-mail from Kat, thanking me for coming and especially for bringing the children.

"I didn't think about your four kids when you and Jami came to critique group each month. Seeing them in the house made me realize they are far away from family just like you are. And I thought about how long it's been since the laughter of little children echoed in this house. I know I can't replace family, and I wouldn't want to try, but I thought, 'Well, maybe I can be a surrogate grandma to those kids.' So I'd like to have you all back for your son's birthday next month, and then have you visit every month after that."

Kat saw it as supporting the troops in general while ministering to a specific family's needs. And she made good on her invitation. For the next year and a half, we regularly visited and shared our celebrations, birthdays, holidays, and everyday lives with this wonderful woman who saw my kids and said, "I could do something special for them."

Kat's hospitality and love blessed not just me but my entire family, especially those "drafted" in. So, while I'm sure she doesn't need to hear it, I'll say it anyway: To Kat, and to the many people across America (and with our troops overseas) who reach out in similar ways to touch the lives of military members and families, thank you for your service. It matters more than words can say.

— David M. Williamson —

77

Love Is the Answer

Be completely humble and gentle;
Be patient, bearing with one another in love.
~Ephesians 4:2

My mother-in-law, whom I called Grandma for twenty-five years, was a true Southern mom. Cooking was a gift she gave her family daily. The meals were routine — sausage gravy with biscuits, fried chicken, salmon patties, and chicken-fried steak. If you wanted fried potatoes or any of the above at midnight, she would make them with a smile on her face. The moment her feet hit the floor, the bacon and eggs hit the pan. This was her routine every morning, despite the fact that she lived alone for forty years. Widowed at age forty-five, she chose never to date again. There was only one love in her life — her husband of twenty-four years and the father of her two sons.

Unfortunately, Alzheimer's disease stole Grandma's independence. When she was no longer able to live alone, my husband and I agreed to ask her to stay with us. We made this decision with some misgivings, as we realized our own freedom would be limited. But Grandma's freedom had been taken from her forever by Alzheimer's.

When Grandma came to live with us, my husband and I decided to keep her bacon and egg routine going. On the first morning, my feet hit the floor early and into the kitchen I went. The bacon had just started to sizzle, the wonderful aroma filling the air, when I heard a voice from behind. "Good morning, Nancy, I'm here!"

Looking up, my eyes met Grandma's. And looking back at me were eyes as black as black could be. She had gone to bed with white, sparse eyebrows, and now she had eyebrows like Groucho Marx. Apparently she had done her make-up with a hidden Marks-A-Lot marker rather than Maybelline, to create lasting color around her eyes.

Of course, I didn't say a word about it. Reassurance and security are things my mother-in-law needs daily. Jingle bells, secured to her walker, alert us to her wanderings. Some nights we awaken to every light on in the house as she jingles her way into our bedroom. Peering in, she sweetly asks, "Are you there?"

We gently reassure her and she returns to bed. Sometimes a kiss and tucking-in is all she needs. Other nights my husband must awaken fully and talk with her to calm her.

Grandma takes full responsibility for her dog, Happy. We no longer count the number of times we answer her question, "Where's Happy? Happy can't get out, can he?" One night I heard her feeding Happy at 3 a.m. The next morning, I found birdseed in his dish. She has lived with us almost two years now, yet often looks at us quizzically and says, "I had a nice time, but Happy and I need to get home."

There are times I become frustrated — when her clothes are dirty, or her Depends need changing, yet she remains unaware. It's then my eyes go to the photographs on her bedroom wall and my impatience softens. I see a beautiful young wife, vacationing with her husband in Colorado, wearing a starched blouse and a skirt, with hose and pumps. That lady is still in there. On good days we still see her.

Grandma occupies her time doing word searches, looking after Happy, watching movies with me or Rangers baseball with her son. On good days she cannot get enough to eat and whatever I cook is met with, "This is my favorite." We are blessed, as she is easy to please and remains in good spirits (most of the time). After all, we all have our moments, don't we?

Well-meaning friends and family members are the first to ask about our new roles as caregivers. We tell them we have learned a lot over the past two years. We have put into practice the words of wisdom I learned as a nurse and a flight attendant: "Put on your own oxygen mask before assisting others."

As caregivers, we take time out to pursue what we enjoy. We visit with family and find sitters to stay with Grandma. We enjoy gardening, reading, writing, walking our dog, Zoey, or simply going out for coffee. We commit to taking care of ourselves.

It has been a challenge to grasp Grandma's hand and walk confidently with her through these last pages of her life. We keep our eyes open to see the blessings she brings into our days and the wisdom she shares along the way. After all, there are still things she can teach us… like who knew a Marks-A-Lot would give far more lasting color than Maybelline?

As each day closes, Grandma sits on her bed, reading and rereading cards sent by her sons, granddaughters, grandsons, and daughters-in-law. Looking up as I say goodnight, she whispers, "Remember, love is the answer."

— Nancy King Barnes —

78

It's Just Your Turn

No matter who we are, no matter how successful,
no matter what our situation, compassion is something
we all need to receive and give.
~Catherine Pulsifer

I had assured my husband that I could attend my first doctor visit after the birth our child, Robert, on my own. I knew he was worried he had already taken too much time off work. Besides, I was confident I could handle it. I had stocked the diaper bag and included extra supplies in the car just in case. I had even worked out the timing so I could stick to Robert's schedule by feeding him in the parking lot before my appointment. That way he would be ready for a nap when I needed to head in. My plan went smoothly and I was feeling pretty good when I walked into the office.

I was informed at check-in that the doctor had been out earlier that morning for a delivery and was running late. No problem, I thought. I found a spot in the crowded waiting room off in the back corner where I could set my things and my now sleeping baby.

All was well for about fifteen minutes. Then, Robert woke up very upset. A dirty diaper, I thought. I gathered up supplies and trekked to the bathroom down the hall. Once there, I realized that wasn't the problem. I went back to the waiting room with Robert still crying. Maybe his tummy was bothering him? After ten minutes of pacing the room and patting his back he was still not happy. Could he possibly be hungry again? Nervous about breastfeeding for the first time in public,

I gave it a shot. No good. It actually seemed to make him angrier. I couldn't figure out what was wrong and how to fix it. I considered leaving, but assumed they would call us back soon.

Over the next hour, I repeated the process again and again. Changing the diaper. Pacing the waiting room. Patting his back. Trying to feed him. Changed, paced, patted, and fed. I was exhausted and flustered and near tears. I knew we were disturbing the rest of the women in the waiting room but I had no idea how to fix the situation.

Feeling a bit hopeless, I went to the front desk to inquire about rescheduling. I was willing now to call this whole visit a bust. I was assured that I would be called in just a few minutes. Turning back to the waiting room I got a full view of the others there. All had impatient looks on their faces and I was overwhelmed with embarrassment. Robert was still fussing and had been nearly the entire time we were there. What kind of mother was I if I couldn't get my infant to settle down?

Nervously, I began pacing and patting again. An older woman who had been quietly reading a book caught my eye. "I am so sorry," I blurted out. "I'm not sure what is wrong."

The woman's face softened as she laid her book on her lap. "Oh, sweetie," she said. "Please don't worry about it." Looking around the room, she added, "We have all been there. It's just your turn."

It was one of the kindest things anyone has ever said to me. Perhaps, too, one of the wisest observations on parenting. With her simple words, she had assured me that my current crisis would pass. Sure enough, it did. Moments after, I was called back to the exam room. Twenty minutes later I was headed home with a happily sleeping baby in his car seat.

After seven years and two more kids, that phrase remains a maxim of mine. Toddler throwing a fit in the aisle at Costco? "It will pass. It's just your turn." Kid having trouble at school? Take a deep breath. You can figure out a solution. "It's just your turn." Visit to the emergency room? You can handle this. "It's just your turn."

We tend to only hear about the best parts of people's lives. What they post on social media or say at a play date are the stories they choose to tell. It doesn't always reflect their real challenges and if it does, like my story above, it is told after the fact when some resolution has been reached. When you are smack dab in the middle of the drama it can be hard to imagine getting out of it and tempting to assume that everyone else has it easier than you.

The truth I learned that day from one woman's kind words is that every tough situation will eventually come to an end. Every problem has a solution if you give yourself time to figure it out. Challenges aren't a mark of bad parenting so much as they are part of life. Accepting that "it's just your turn" and approaching those challenges with a positive attitude is what matters. And, maybe too, remembering that some kind words to someone who is struggling can make a real difference.

— Elizabeth Moursund —

Mom Can Make Anything

79

Note to Self

The only real mistake is the one from which
we learn nothing.
~John Powell

There was a noticeable shift in our routine the evening my mom sketched stationery. My mother, a lover of schedules, sent me to bed at the usual time of 9:30 but instead of turning in as she normally did, she remained in the living room.

When I didn't hear the tinny voice of a news anchor through the TV or the familiar swoosh of water streaming from the kitchen faucet, I wondered what kept my mother up past her bedtime. I found her hunched beneath our sole lamp, sketching. When I asked what she was drawing, my mother covered the page with her arms and ordered me back to bed.

A wave of resentment rose in my belly. Hadn't I begged my mother for pastels? And what about the construction paper she had denied me only a week ago? "Unless you intend to eat it for lunch, put it back," she'd said. Yet, here she was drawing in a pad that had to cost at least as much as the construction paper.

"It's not fair," I said before stomping my feet all the way to my bedroom.

That night, as I lay in bed gazing out the window, past the rooftops where chimneys puffed white smoke that swirled against the sapphire sky, I cursed my life. Why couldn't I be like the other kids at school who owned scratch-and-sniff stickers, and who ate Twinkies and Moon Pies at lunch? I fell asleep that evening believing I was the unluckiest girl in the world.

The next morning, the bags under my mother's eyes were darker and puffier than usual, and she yawned twice while stirring the pot of oatmeal. "Drink your juice," she said, pointing at the kitchen table.

"I don't want any," I said, still sullen from the night before.

"There are plenty of kids who don't have juice. You do, so drink up."

My mother often reminded me that there were many people less fortunate than us, people who didn't have beds to sleep in, or food in their fridge. But that morning, I didn't want to hear it. I covered my ears with my hands and thought, "So give those people my juice. I don't want it."

She sprinkled a spoonful of brown sugar on top of each bowl of oatmeal and carried them to the table. "I suppose you don't want any of this either," she said. That's when I noticed that a stack of paper sat next to my juice glass. I stepped closer and saw a perfect reproduction of Minnie Mouse on the top sheet. I glanced quickly at Mother, who stared at the oatmeal in her bowl, but the slight pink of her cheeks told me that she had made the drawing. When I fanned the sheets, Tinkerbelle, Papa Smurf, Winnie the Pooh and Charlie Brown leaped to life.

A month earlier, when my teacher Mrs. Hunter announced our class would complete a pen-pal project, I'd asked my mother to buy me stationery. At the drugstore, we learned that a pack of ten cost close to seven dollars. "You'll have to use regular paper," my mother said. But now I realized she had stayed up much of the night to spare me the ordinary.

Later that morning my classmates displayed their sheets of stationery while I blanketed my desk in my mother's drawings. "That's awesome," Sandi, the girl who sat next to me, said, pointing at my mother's sketch of Smurfette. "Wanna trade?"

For a second, I thought about swapping the drawing for one of Sandi's pink sheets of paper embossed with Strawberry Shortcake, but then I thought of my mother hunched beneath our lamp. I shook my head. "My mom made these for me," I said proudly.

"Cool," said Sandi. "My mom can't even draw a stick figure."

As I wrote letters to children in Ghana, Vietnam, Nicaragua, and Korea, I imagined their smiles as they opened the envelopes containing my mother's stationery, and for the first time, I realized that I was the luckiest girl in the world.

— Alicia Rosen —

80

Tin Can Christmas

You give but little when you give of your possessions.
It is when you give of yourself that you truly give.
~Kahlil Gibran

When I was eight years old, my father moved our family from New Jersey to Massachusetts to start a business in the town where he'd grown up. At first, my brothers and I were unhappy about the move because it meant leaving our friends and classmates. The relocation was especially hard on my mother, as it placed her hours away from her mother and sisters for the first time in her life.

Once landed in our new home, my brothers and I occupied ourselves with making friends, tackling schoolwork, and playing with cousins we'd never met before. It was harder for Mom, though, to meet new people. On top of that, we were short on funds while my dad worked to launch his business.

As fall turned into winter and money remained tight, my parents were arguing more than ever and Dad was scrambling to work odd jobs while he got his business off the ground. Gifts were not really in the budget that year, and Mom's spirits grew as gray as the skies.

On top of all this stress and sadness, we discovered that most of our Christmas tree ornaments had broken during the move from New Jersey.

My mother, ever resourceful, took an unexpected action. On a mild day in early December, my brother and I came home from school to find Mom in the back yard, assembling an impromptu crafts station on the picnic table. "We lost our Christmas ornaments," she proclaimed, "so we're going to make our own." Mom had gathered spray paint, sequins, and glitter to adorn the unlikeliest of decorations: tin can lids. She'd spent the past week removing and saving the lids after meals, and that day she eagerly waited for us kids to arrive before cutting them with tin snips into stars, bells, angels, and trees.

My brothers and I got to choose our shapes and decorate them as we laughed, sang carols, told tales about our new teachers and classmates, and basked in Mom's renewed cheer. That December afternoon at the picnic table was more memorable than most Christmas mornings full of shiny paper and expensive gifts.

To this day, my brothers and I speak fondly of our "tin can Christmas" as we point out the few surviving ornaments on our parents' tree. Primitive, yet crafted with love and hope, they are more precious than most of the glittery, store-bought new ones.

I recall that ornament-making party in the back yard as a glowing example of my mother's creativity, resilience, and ability to bring love and light to our days no matter how dark her own were. Struggling with three kids, financial hardship, persistent migraines, part-time jobs, and a business to co-manage, Mom didn't have much time or space to explore her passions during my childhood. But she was usually up for fun, and sometimes went out of her way to create it.

The magic of that particular Christmas came directly through my loving mother, who could turn tin cans into angels, and darkness into light.

— Kim Childs —

81

Cooking with Mom

A recipe has no soul. You, as the cook,
must bring soul to the recipe.
~Thomas Keller

I'm four years old. Mom is always busy working, but she pulls down the big heavy mixing bowls and chooses the huge yellow one. It's a baking kind of day. She gets out the amber jar full of flour and lets me pack the brown sugar. My favorite part is when it all slides into the bowl in the shape of the little, copper measuring cup. She shows me how to carefully separate the eggshell so no pieces fall in. We make the best chocolate chip cookies. We eat a few chips together while we're mixing them, and she makes half with no nuts just for me.

She teaches me that sugar is a wet ingredient and how to multiply fractions and that if you pull the mixer out of the batter before you turn it off, batter splatters everywhere.

I'm six. Mom gets me up in the middle of every night and carries me to the car. It's time to make the donuts. She lays me in a lawn chair in the back of the donut shop and covers me with her jacket before she gets to work with Dad. There, under her jacket and in the midst of all that hustle and bustle, I feel completely safe, secure and loved. I get up and try to talk customers into playing *Candy Land* with me before I catch the bus for school. I get to take donut holes for snack time. I'm everyone's favorite snack-bringer.

I learn about friends and eighties music and that the way to anyone's heart is through his or her stomach.

I'm seven. Mom teaches me to scramble an egg and how to be careful with the gas when I light the burner. How to keep stirring so the eggs won't stick and burn on the bottom. And not to use metal in a Teflon pan.

I learn to get up before my mom to make my own hot breakfast and watch the news, cause that's what grown-ups do. And I learn that when I fall asleep in my chair, Mom will pick up my dishes and clean whatever mess I left in the kitchen without ever saying a word to me about it.

I'm ten. Mom takes me to the grocery store every day to get the ingredients for endless casseroles, meat loaves and fried chicken. I complain a lot. I learn about budgets, Green Stamps, and that all that stuff tastes better than I would ever let on.

I'm eighteen. I make my first solo fried chicken, mashed potatoes and gravy, all from scratch of course, and I start a fire in the kitchen. My date offers to help from the living room, but I save the chicken and he's none the wiser about the fire.

I learn that no matter how old and wise I get, my mom is never more than a phone call away when I realize I'm out of my depth. And, later, that they actually make mixes for things like mashed potatoes and gravy, but that that would be cheating and it probably wouldn't taste as good anyway.

I'm twenty-eight. For my birthday, I ask my mom to finally show me the trick to her famous pies for which there is no recipe. She shows me how to mix the ingredients for the crust, just as her mother showed her. She tells me that we'll pre-bake these for cream pies but that you don't do that for custard-style pies. We whip egg yolks and double-boil pudding for hours.

I learn that, regardless how detailed your notes, nothing can replace practice and an inherent knack, and that using my great-grandmother's rolling pin, my maternal grandmother's recipes and my paternal grandmother's pie pan while cooking with my mom creates a feeling of connection I can't explain.

I'm thirty. I finally pin my mom down on her homemade dressing and giblet gravy. Like the pies, she learned from her mother, and there is no recipe. She can't tell me any specific measurements, but she can go on forever with that dreamy look in her eyes about how special it was for her mother to impart to her these same skills.

I learn that I really can pull together an entire holiday meal.

I'm thirty-one. I'm standing in my mother's kitchen with her and my sister, my memories so thick I can hardly breathe. I'm helping her weed through a lifetime of collected utensils and appliances for their imminent downsize. Throw that away, sell this, keep that. Yes, sell all the new-fangled, modern plastic stuff. But I will never part with those multi-colored glass mixing bowls, the copper measuring cups, the old pie plates and baking dishes and cookie jars from my childhood in the kitchen. With my mom.

I learn that sooner or later, we all have to let go of the things, because the memories are now a part of who we are. But I also learn why my mom was always so happy in the kitchen. With her mom.

And now, no matter what happens, I've learned that my mom will always be with me in mine.

— Kimberly Noe —

I've Got That Tupper Feeling

All women become like their mothers. That is their
tragedy. No man does. That's his.
~Oscar Wilde

While other kids my age were listening to Disney songs, the songs I knew by heart were Tupperware jingles. My mom was a "Tupperware Lady" throughout my childhood. As a child, I often despised Tupperware and what it represented. Having a mother who sold Tupperware meant she was gone most weeknights holding parties. She drove a wood-paneled station wagon, sang corny Tupperware jingles and talked Tupperware and food freshness — all the time. While other kids were picking out cool themed lunchboxes or were able to carry a brown bag that could be thrown away to allow for more playground time, I was given the Tupperware lunchbox complete with sandwich holder and mini cup. That cup, as I remember, barely held a sip of juice. I hated that lunchbox!

Our meals were created from recipes she learned in the Tupperware training classes or newsletters. We were the guinea pigs... testing the recipes prior to the parties so she could demonstrate the containers. Casseroles with cream soup or Jell-O molds were a constant menu item. Homemade play dough was made from kitchen ingredients and ended up an ugly color because the food coloring ran together. As each holiday rolled around there was always the kooky themed recipe such as Dinner in a Pumpkin.

As my teen years approached, I made some crazy affirmations: I vowed I would never cook with cream soup, never drive a station wagon and never, ever have a piece of Tupperware in my house. The years passed quickly and I believed I was on the path to keeping my vows.

Then... I moved out, bought a house of my own, got married and started a family. Before I knew it I was cooking meals with cream soup and had multiple cupboards containing Tupperware and matching lids. As if all of this was not bad enough, when my son's first Halloween rolled around, I didn't even think twice. I started shopping for the ingredients for Dinner in a Pumpkin!

As an adult working to help support my family I realized that my mom being gone at night and holding Tupperware parties was not necessarily something she wanted to do, but rather something she had to do to help support her family. Sure it seemed to me she loved her job and all things Tupperware, but selling Tupperware afforded my sisters and me ballet lessons, softball, family vacations, birthday parties and the latest fashions. Through food containers, recipes to demonstrate them, and many nights out earning a living, she showed us how much she loved us.

I think back now to my childhood and all the things Tupperware made possible for us and I am grateful that my mom worked so hard. As a busy mom myself, many of my recipes have cream soup in them, but my favorite recipe comes around once a year when, to my son's horror, I can hollow out the pumpkin and sing, "I've got that Tupper Feeling."

Beef Dinner in a Pumpkin

2 lb. lean hamburger
1 (8-12") diameter fresh pumpkin
3 garlic cloves, minced
1 medium onion, chopped
12 small mushrooms, sliced

1 medium bell pepper
1 1/4 cup uncooked rice
1 1/4 teaspoons salt
1/2 teaspoon pepper
5 tablespoons butter
1 can stewed tomatoes
2 cups beef broth
1/4 cup grated Cheddar or Longhorn cheese
Parsley sprigs
8 to 12 cherry tomatoes

Wash the pumpkin and cut the top stem out to create a lid. Scoop out the seeds and stringy fibers.

Melt two tablespoons of the butter. Take a plastic sandwich bag and dip it into the melted butter to grease the inside of the pumpkin. Turn the pumpkin on its side and sprinkle inside with 1/2 teaspoon salt.

Sauté onion, mushrooms, bell pepper, and garlic in the remaining 3 tablespoons butter.

Add the 2 pounds lean hamburger, brown, and drain.

Then add the rice and stir until thoroughly mixed.

Add the remaining salt and pepper, the stewed tomatoes, and the beef broth and bring to a boil. Boil for 2 minutes then fill the pumpkin with this mixture.

Replace the pumpkin lid and place the pumpkin in a shallow greased baking pan. Bake approximately 1 to 1 1/2 hours at 350 degrees. Pumpkin is ready when tender and should remain firm enough to hold the filling without danger of collapsing.

If necessary, more beef broth can be added.

When baked, remove from the oven, lift lid and sprinkle inside with the 1/4 cup cheese.

Return pumpkin to oven without lid until cheese is melted. Remove from oven, replace lid and garnish around the bottom of the pumpkin with fresh parsley and cherry tomatoes. Serve from the pumpkin, scraping some of the pulp into each serving.

—D'ette Corona—

The Barbie

Mother love is the fuel that enables
a normal human being to do the impossible.
~Marion C. Garretty

Hanukkah came early to our family in 1963. My mother, nine months pregnant with her fourth child declared we would celebrate the festival of lights right now, tonight. She knew that in all likelihood she would be in the hospital when the first day of Hanukkah arrived and she didn't want us to miss out.

Back then Hanukkah wasn't a big deal. We all knew the story of how a small group of Jews led by Judah Maccabee had fought the Romans. Even though he was badly outnumbered, Judah and his followers had won the battle and were able to once again practice their religion. They needed enough oil to burn for eight days to make the temple holy again, but they had only enough oil to burn for one day. A miracle happened and the oil burned for eight days. That night, as we lit the first candle, we all thought of the story and of course of the present we would get to celebrate the first night of Hanukkah.

I was seven and the oldest. I couldn't tell you what my brother and sister got but I can tell you every detail of my gift. It was my first Barbie, and she was beautiful! She had long blonde hair, perfect features and a red bathing suit. Ever so carefully I took her out of the box, knowing I was the luckiest girl in the world. I had a Barbie! Then, as I surveyed my new friend it occurred to me, she had no other clothes! Wasn't

Mom Can Make Anything | 253

the whole point of having a Barbie doll being able to dress her up?

My mother sensed my growing disappointment. What could she do? She understood, but with all the preparations for the new baby it hadn't occurred to her that Barbie needed a wardrobe. She promised me she would sew an outfit for Barbie, and it would be ready when I got up in the morning. I went to bed excited and looking forward to playing with my Hanukkah gift.

The next morning I woke early and ran downstairs looking for my mother. The house was quiet. I peeked in my parents' room, and there was Barbie sitting in the middle of the dresser and wearing the most beautiful dress I had ever seen! The material was a blue print, not unlike the drapes my mother had recently made for the basement windows.

My brother, now awake due to the racket I had been making, came running into my parents' room as well. He noticed that my dad was sound asleep in bed but my mother was nowhere to be found. We both jumped on the bed and then on Dad.

"Where's Mom?" we demanded.

"She's in the hospital," a groggy Dad shared with us.

We jumped on him again. "Did she have the baby?"

"Yes," he replied, "soon after we got there."

"What did she have?"

"A baby girl! Now let me sleep!" he replied.

I found out later that Mom hadn't quite finished making Barbie's dress when she went into labour. She knew how disappointed I would be, so she somehow managed to finish the dress before heading to the hospital. Of course the self-centered seven-year-old who spent the day playing with her new Barbie had no idea of the determination and love her mom had shown. It wasn't until I had children of my own that I thought back to the day of my sister's birth.

Mom always commented that when you have children you don't divide your love between them — you multiply it. She had shown me this truth so well that night. Even though all of her energy should have been focused on bringing her new baby daughter into the world, she made sure her three other children did not miss the first night of Hanukkah and were taken care of in every way. And of course she gave us the best Hanukkah present ever, my sister Marla.

— Cindy Armeland Clemens —

My Mother's Recipe Box

Let your tears come. Let them water your soul.
~Eileen Mayhew

My husband reached it for me. It was on the highest of our kitchen cabinet shelves, the one that remains out of sight/out of mind. My mother's no-nonsense green metal recipe box had been stashed there three years ago, after her death at 97. And there it had stayed.

So many of the other objects in her household had been carefully sorted out, distributed to family members, donated to charity. But this box — this humble, ancient box, remained with me, untouched. I couldn't have explained to anyone exactly why.

Somehow, that afternoon, I was ready.

My first thought, as I touched the box and pried open its lid, was a guilty one. Why hadn't I seen to it that Mom had a prettier recipe file? Why hadn't I found a cheerful one for her, something sweet in floral or gingham?

Guilt is a handmaiden of sorrow, and I'd had plenty of both since the December day three years ago when we stood at my mother's grave and said a last goodbye.

There had been those awful wrenching times when I'd reached for the phone at dusk for our usual pre-dinner conversation, and forgotten that the number I was calling was "...no longer in service," as that awful, disembodied announcement reminded me.

There had been the presence of that empty chair at the table for family milestones, the proof that we were no longer going to be graced by the sweet face of our matriarch, beaming because family was her taproot, her greatest source of joy.

And there had surely been those moments when I thought my heart would break from missing the tiny blond woman who had loved all of us so unconditionally, and had asked so little in return.

But opening that recipe box… that was a long-overdue marker on the journey to healing.

Mom was a legendary cook. The sort who didn't actually need a recipe to guide her. Instinct was her best teacher, and somehow, she could make a meatloaf taste like filet mignon, or raise a simple roasted chicken to lofty heights.

But over the years, Mom had fortunately reduced some of her recipes to writing. "Someday, you may want these," she had said prophetically.

"Someday" had come.

Sitting at the kitchen counter, I began my search for remembered pleasures… for the taste of my childhood, at least figuratively.

As I scanned the categories — main dishes, side dishes, holiday foods, cakes, cookies — there was Mom's familiar scrawl. Her loopy letters, the "t's" left uncrossed in her haste, the crowded script — all came rushing back. It had been so long since I'd seen that familiar handwriting, now that her anniversary and birthday cards signed "With all my love," no longer arrived in our mailbox.

Mom had no patience for fad diets. So I sifted through detailed instructions for making a rich lasagna, a brisket swimming in gravy, for meatballs and spaghetti with her own "secret" sauce ingredient — brown sugar.

There were recipes for everything from a simple egg salad with pimentos to a noodle pudding that she had learned from her own mother.

Mom's parents — my maternal grandparents — were Eastern European immigrants, part of that vast wave that had arrived on these shores in the early years of the 20th century. And in this golden land, food—lots of it—was their solace. It soothed the loneliness, bewilderment and fear of lives forever changed.

So much of my own history and heritage was in that green metal recipe box.

I spent one long afternoon with it, smiling, remembering, and yes, weeping. So much of Mom came flooding back. Decades later, I was back in her kitchen—and it was so clearly HER kitchen in the days when fathers seldom strayed into the inner sanctum. I was smelling her amazing pot roast, her sour cream/apple coffee cake, her split pea soup.

And I was wishing—how I was wishing—that she was back, too, in her aqua cobbler's apron with the white ruffle.

"Do NOT overcook, Sally," I found on one recipe card for pot roast. It made me laugh out loud, because that was, after all, my high culinary crime. And Mom knew it.

Hours later, when I'd rummaged through the last of the recipe cards and newspaper clippings stuffed in the back, I felt a kind of peace I hadn't in too long. It was the sense that somehow Mom was in my life again.

She was peering over my shoulder, checking, re-checking, scolding, advising, and yes, teaching. She was handing down her traditions in the most loving way—through food as love.

Mom-food. The best of all possible cuisines.

And I carefully, deliberately placed that green metal box with its stubborn lid on the kitchen counter. Front and center.

Exactly where it belongs.

— Sally Schwartz Friedman —

85

Hand-Stitched Love

From home to home, and heart to heart, from one
place to another. The warmth and joy of Christmas,
brings us closer to each other.
~Emily Matthews

S natches of holiday music hit me from all sides as I walked through the mall. It was two weeks before Christmas, and I wasn't sure how I was going to make it. Try as I might, I hadn't been able to figure out a way to make my meagre budget as a second-year grad student yield up the cash for a trip home. The distance from Halifax, Nova Scotia, to my parents' house in Simcoe, Ontario, might as well have been measured in light years rather than kilometres. For the first time in my life, I wasn't going to spend Christmas at home with my family.

I was going to have to cope, that was all. But privately, when I allowed myself to admit it, I realized the whirlwind of part-time work, research, sports and social activities I had plunged myself into couldn't make up for the bare, honest fact that I was homesick.

About a week before Christmas, I received a notice to pick up a parcel from the post office. When I arrived to claim my prize, a box of gratifyingly large proportions, wrapped in brown paper and bound with twine, was thrust into my arms.

I scurried home to my apartment, placed the box on the kitchen table, and painstakingly undid the knots in the twine. A pair of scissors would have done the job more quickly, but I wanted to savour the moment.

Finally, the string fell aside and I stripped away the paper wrapped around the cardboard box. I opened the flaps to reveal a bulky cloth object. When I unfolded it, I gasped in surprise when I realized it was a quilt, lovingly crafted by my mother. But it was not the normal patchwork kind. No, this one was definitely different.

On a green background my mother had recreated, with a combination of sewing and embroidery, an image of home. There was our house, right down to the three white front pillars and the number 80 on the middle post. There was the redbud tree, with clouds of purple blossoms painstakingly hand-embroidered, and a tartan blanket spread below it like the one on which my mother and I would lie during lazy summer afternoons to read our books.

There was more: boldly orange tiger lilies at the base of a big pine tree; green shrubs with flowers embroidered on them; and the grey shed that housed the lawn mower and assorted garden implements. A badminton net was represented by a broad strip of lace spanning the space between two brown fabric posts, a croquet course serpentined across the yard and an image of Tiny, our Toy Terrier, was embroidered beside the blanket.

I pictured my mother bent over her handiwork on the dining room table at home, her brow furrowed as she concentrated on her work, her bent fingers holding the needle while her hands moved steadily as she made the painstaking, tiny stitches. How many hours of work this must have taken!

This quilt was more than material, batting, and thread; there was love sewn into it as well. As I wrapped it around me, I felt a warmth that was more than physical.

So what if I wouldn't be home this Christmas? Home had come to me. More than that, I realized now that home and the love that resided there would always be a part of me, no matter where I went. And in that moment, I knew that this Christmas, and all the Christmases I might have to spend away, would be okay after all.

— Lisa Timpf —

86

The Best Gift of All

Any mother could perform the jobs of several
air traffic controllers with ease.
~Lisa Alther

arry was seven and I was five and we were obsessed with dinosaurs. When we saw the plastic dinosaur models at the toy store, we wanted them more than anything else.

I wrote a letter to Santa, asking him to please, please bring me a Stegosaurus model kit. Larry wrote a similar letter, asking for a Tyrannosaurus Rex model. We both wrote in our letters that we had worked awful hard to be good that year, which we had, and if Santa could just see his way to bringing each of us a dinosaur model kit, we wouldn't ask for anything else.

When my mom read our letters, she looked at us and asked, "Are you sure you're both old enough for a model kit? Those things can be hard to put together."

"We can do it!" I told her, envisioning how I would snap a few pieces together, put a dab of glue here and there, and voila, my Stegosaurus would be staring at me with all the prehistoric coolness only a gift like that could bring.

"Not a problem!" my brother Larry said, probably imagining how ferocious and mighty his easily put together Tyrannosaurus would look once he spent five minutes or so slapping it together. The smile on his face grew even wider than before.

"If you think you can really do it," she said, looking unsure. "I'm sure Santa would be glad to bring you model kits for Christmas."

"Dinosaur model kits," my brother said. He showed her an ad we'd cut out of the toy store's catalog.

"Stegosaurus and Tyrannosaurus Rex," I added, pointing to pictures of the specific kits.

Mom looked at the pictures. "There sure are lots of little bitty pieces," she said softly.

"It'll be easy!" I said confidently.

Well, Christmas Eve came, and my brother, sister and I went off to sleep, although I didn't do much sleeping. Somewhere around 5:00 a.m., Larry and I slipped out of bed and crept downstairs to find that Santa had come and gone, and under the tree were two big presents for my brother and me!

I tore the wrapping paper off mine and jumped for joy. My model Stegosaurus! Santa had brought me the toy I had wanted more than anything. My brother got his Tyrannosaurus Rex, too. We danced around the living room, then ran to the kitchen table and opened up our model kits… and stared at what looked like a million pieces of plastic. There was a big, fat manual that had instructions on how to put the model together. It might as well have been a manual on how to fly to the moon. My brother and I sighed at the same time.

Still, we were excited and we set about twisting and bending the pieces out of their plastic holders. When we were through, it seemed like there was even more pieces than before.

"You two are going to put those things together?" my sister asked, looking at the immense pile of plastic on the table. "You can't even match up your own socks."

"We can do it!" I said, grinning at my brother. I grabbed the tube of glue that Santa had been nice enough to include and had Larry read me the instructions from the manual.

Half a day later, all we had was a bunch of sticky pieces, some that were glued to the table, some to the instruction manual, and some to my brother and me. There was no sign of two ferocious, mighty dinosaurs.

And so, my brother and I did what any dynamic duo would do

when stymied by an impossible project: we began to cry. Larry and I cried our eyes out over the mess we had made and the pile of plastic sitting before us. Our mom dried our tears and handed us other presents to distract us, but we kept looking back at the pile of dinosaur parts and our eyes would well up again.

That Christmas night I felt as if a wonderful dream had turned into a nightmare. I don't know how long I lay there in my bed, dozing on and off, but somewhere in the middle of the night I heard a series of clicking sounds. I got up from bed and wandered into the living room, and this is what I saw: my mom was at the kitchen table, sorting through all the dozens of pieces, wiping off the old glue with a washcloth, and slowly gluing them together.

I stood and watched her patiently work, our secret elf who would make Christmas magic again. I couldn't keep my eyes open, and a part of me wondered if it was a dream. I wandered back to bed not knowing.

In the morning Larry and I sadly stumbled into the living room. We were prepared to toss the plastic mess in the trash and call it a failed experiment. We walked up to the kitchen table, looked for those heaps of sticky plastic parts, and we gasped. There, standing before us, was the most magnificent pair of model dinosaurs we had ever seen. My Stegosaurus and Larry's Tyrannosaurus Rex stood whole and proud and awesomely ferocious.

"Santa must have come back last night and fixed them for us!" Larry shouted, picking up his dinosaur and hugging it.

"That must have been what happened," Mom said, coming into the living room looking a little tired, but very happy.

I looked at my mom, and noticed that there was a small piece of plastic stuck to her pajamas. I ran up to her and hugged her tight, knowing that she had given us a truly wonderful gift: the gift of her time, her patience, and her boundless love. It was the best Christmas gift of all.

—John P. Buentello—

Mom Can Make Anything | 263

87

The Farewell Gift

What we do for ourselves dies with us. What we do for
others and the world remains and is immortal.
~Albert Pine

I t was only a backache... or so we thought. It would heal with time and rest, or maybe some pills. When it continued getting in the way of my mother-in-law Dee's favorite pastimes, especially her stitching and quilting projects, we decided more tests should be run. When the results came back, the news seemed impossible. The backache was cancer, and it was advanced.

Dee had always stitched and embroidered. She loved presenting handcrafted gifts to friends and family. Many weddings, births, and birthdays were commemorated with her beautiful pieces. When Kevin and I became engaged, she lovingly embroidered the Prayer of St. Francis on a wall hanging, knowing the prayer was dear to me. Dee's talents gave joy twice: first to her while she stitched and then to those who received.

Ready to try something new, Dee enrolled in quilting classes. She loved seeing the individual pieces come together into a work of art. She started small, making placemats, table runners, and tote bags. With the news of my pregnancy — Dee's first grandchild — came the excitement of creating a baby quilt. We didn't know whether it was a girl or boy, so the quilt would use a combination of blues and yellows, plaids and flowers, and the bumblebee theme we had selected for the nursery. She worked on it covertly, not even allowing us to see the fabrics. And then the back pain had begun, worsened, and finally became the devastating diagnosis of cancer.

As summer turned to fall, Dee's activity became more limited. Staying in one position too long was excruciating, and she needed to be on oxygen around the clock. Our world was turning upside down. Then one bright September morning, our daughter Elizabeth was born, healthy and happy and filling our lives with hope once again. Dee was too weak to come to the hospital, but heroically visited our home just a few days later. She oohed and aahed, cooed and sang, and welcomed our daughter to the world.

A few days later, she convinced my father-in-law to take her shopping. Prior to becoming sick, Dee loved outlet malls and bargain hunting almost as much as stitching. I picture my father-in-law wheeling her through every aisle of the baby superstore, oxygen tank in tow. She selected any baby outfit she liked, knowing she'd probably never see Elizabeth wear them all, and returned home exhausted but happy. Somehow she found the perfect costume for Halloween—a baby bumblebee outfit—and laughed with delight on Halloween afternoon when her granddaughter came to trick or treat.

Soon afterward, she entered the hospital for the final time. Dee, the one who everyone had set their compass by, left us. Though she had only held her grandchild a handful of times, she enjoyed every moment that she could.

Christmas came quickly on the heels of her funeral. My husband and I were still lost in the fog that new babies and nighttime feedings bring, and adrift in a sea of grief. We planned to host everyone on Christmas day as we always had, but this year felt so drastically different. In one year's time we had lost a mother and become parents ourselves.

When my father-in-law arrived Christmas morning, he warned us that we might need a few tissue boxes. While taking out Christmas decorations, he discovered gifts Dee had purchased and hidden months earlier. She'd even labeled the boxes with our names. The presents were sweet and funny, just like she was, and we laughed and cried as we pictured her selecting them. Something that in the past might have been "just a gift" now held deeper meaning; these would be our last gifts from her.

The final package under the tree that morning was for Elizabeth. My father-in-law shifted a little in his seat. His normally strong, baritone voice cracked when he threw the tissue box our way and said, "You're going to need this." We unwrapped the package and gasped. It was the quilt. The baby quilt Dee had started and I had long forgotten.

"Your mom couldn't finish it," he said. "So we asked the lady who was teaching Mom quilting if she wouldn't mind finishing it for us. I got it in the mail last week."

It seemed impossible, but there it was. The quilt that had been born out of expectation and excitement, created for the new life entering our family, was there. All of those pieces that had been left loose were now stitched together: blues and yellows, plaids and flowers, hopes and dreams, beginnings and endings — creating a new work of art.

So much more than a gift, it was a farewell hug. We could wrap the quilt around us and still feel her love.

— Katie O'Connell —

88

My Basement

Create a space in your life to relax, re-energize,
and reconnect with your sacred inner being.
~Melanie Moushigian Koulouris

My basement makes me happy because it is my own personal space — a place for me to be creative. As a mom with a preteen daughter and a husband who works from home, I really appreciate it. However, my basement didn't always make me happy. In fact, when we first moved into this house, this basement made me feel downright depressed.

You see, I had always envisioned having a beautiful finished basement. I wanted a fun space down the stairs (away from real life!) that would be the perfect spot for us to entertain friends and family.

This finished basement of my dreams would be Pinterest-perfect. It would contain many wonderful attributes such as a high-end bar with rich, dark wood and cool pendant lights — maybe even a Tuscan-style wine cellar, complete with a panoramic view of a vineyard painted on one side.

It would also include a fun game area with foosball and air hockey and perhaps a ping pong table. And, of course, the icing on the cake would be the home theater replete with its own popcorn machine, snack bar, and posters of beloved movies tastefully adorning the walls. Plus, there would be a nice, comfortable carpet that warmed up the whole room while providing a cozy place for sleepovers.

Like I said, the house I'm living in now does have a basement.

Alas, it is not the basement with the wine cellar, home theater, popcorn machine, and cozy rug. Instead, this basement sports a gray tile floor, messy boxes of holiday decor and old books, a few pieces of ugly secondhand furniture, and a litter box.

Our basement remains half-finished and, in some areas, not finished at all. It looks as though someone attempted to finish the main room before we moved in. However, they did not do a very good job. The ceiling panels are crooked, and the can lights that were installed are always burning out. Plus, the two other rooms off the main room were not even part of the project, so they remain completely unfinished.

Unfortunately, we have not been able to afford the construction upgrades needed to turn this basement into the basement of anyone's dreams. "One day, we will," my husband promises. "Just be patient!" In the meantime, there it sits... ugly, a little too cold in the winter, and basically unused. That is, until I stopped waiting for my perfect basement to magically arrive and decided to turn this unattractive space into my own personal art cave.

Once I realized that my attitude toward our basement was simply a matter of changing my negative mindset, the rest was easy. First, you have to understand that nobody else comes down to the basement, since I am the one in charge of the laundry and the litter box. My daughter doesn't want to hang out in the basement, preferring her warm and comfy bedroom with its plethora of anime posters and stuffed cats.

So, one day when I was in the basement folding laundry, I suddenly realized that the peace and quiet was sort of... pleasant. There were no cartoons blasting in my ear and no news programs droning on with my husband talking back to them.

Not feeling particularly anxious to head back upstairs, I sat down at the old secondhand desk and pulled out a piece of printer paper. Then I started doodling. Before I knew it (with some guidance from an old picture book of cats), the doodle turned into a picture of a Siamese cat languishing in a garden. I liked the doodle. And I also liked the relaxing time I spent creating it.

The doodle inspired me to take a trip to the local Walmart for some acrylic paints, watercolors, paintbrushes, and glitter. Next thing

I knew, after spending more time down in the basement bundled in a nice thick sweater, I had transformed my doodle into an actual painting. Granted, the printer paper was a little flimsy, but that just inspired me to order some real art pads from Amazon.

I'm not a real artist by any account. The last time I spent so much time creating art was when my daughter was little, and that was only because I didn't need to worry that she would judge my drawings and find them lacking. She loved everything I drew, not caring that my shading wasn't right or the proportions were off. But I haven't really done anything artistic since that time, even though I always enjoyed drawing and painting when I was younger. I guess I never felt confident enough in my abilities.

When my daughter got a little older, she would still paint or make things out of clay with her friends, but I had stopped participating. Getting messy was for kids! Besides, I figured by that point my daughter would catch on that I wasn't very good. So instead, when I am upstairs, you will usually find me cleaning, doing dishes, watching Netflix, or sitting at the computer. However, it is important to note that there is no TV, kitchen sink, or computer down in the basement. There is only me and my art.

The basement has not grown better looking since those early days when it made me feel so depressed. There's no magic spell that's been cast, except for the magic of creativity, I suppose. For instance, the floor is still comprised of the same ugly gray tile that feels like a slab of ice in the winter.

We will replace this tile eventually with that nice, cozy carpet I talked about. However, I'm in no rush. After all, it's much easier to clean paint off a tile floor than it would be to scrub acrylics out of a rug. Besides, a rug might invite the rest of my family down, so I really don't mind the tile… for now.

Also, the furniture situation down here remains less than ideal. One might even call it "sparse." There is a total of one big, clunky desk with a scratched surface and one measly chair, both bought used. There is also a lounge chair purchased at a yard sale a few years back. However, the chair is so incredibly narrow and uncomfortable that nobody uses it… not even the cat!

Nonetheless, this less-than-perfect "lair" is all mine. My finished artwork sits on a shelf that snakes its way around the room. It is a colorful and always changing display of my burgeoning talent. I don't think any of my work is quite good enough to hang upstairs… yet. But for the basement, it's just fine. I can gaze at Purple Cat, Red Elephant, Surreal Deer, Magenta Tulips in Jar, Three Faceless Ballerinas, White Fox, and Love Birds Under Textured Sky any time I want.

Down here, I am the artist I always dreamed of being. Down here, I can make a mess on the scratched table and the tile floor. I spill glitter, and it doesn't matter. I can be creative without listening to the TV or my daughter and husband arguing about messy rooms or politics. Sometimes, our cat, Princess, slinks down to do her "business," but that's okay. I'm the one who cleans out the litter box, so it's just convenient that I'm already here anyway.

As women, we spend so much time worrying about making others happy that it's easy to forget what makes us happy. That's why it's nice, or should I say, essential, to have (as Virginia Woolf called it) "a room of one's own"—somewhere to explore our inner talents, meditate, exercise without feeling foolish, write our hearts out, or paint a picture of a girl in a green hat wearing a pink polka-dot dress, if we so desire.

In my case, that room is my basement. It may not look like paradise to anyone else. But really, paradise is what we make it. For me, it is a room with a cold, gray tile floor, burned-out lights, a few pieces of ugly furniture, a litter box, messy art supplies, and a never-ending display of creativity. I'll take it!

— Nancy Merczel —

89

Traditions

Perhaps all the dragons in our life are princesses who
are only waiting to see us act, just once,
with beauty and courage.
~Rainer Maria Rilke

I parked the car and stared at the Walmart entrance for a minute, not wanting to go in. I avoided Walmart as much as I could these days. It was the second week of November, and we were in full-fledged holiday territory. But I couldn't even consider Thanksgiving or Christmas, because this year I didn't know how to celebrate either of them.

My two-year-old son had been diagnosed with autism only a month earlier, although we'd known for a long time what the diagnosis would be. And, as many in the autism community are painfully aware, sometimes autism comes with peripheral issues — digestive sickness, seizures, allergies, and the like. Our diagnosis came with celiac disease and a host of food sensitivities. Any exposure to gluten, dairy, soy, or corn (even a single bite) would cause copious amounts of vomiting and an otherwise miserable little boy for the next week.

Once I finally made my way inside, I grabbed the dish detergent we needed and made my way across the store to the shampoo aisle. I paused by the newsstand. I saw cover after magazine cover, each heralding holiday tradition and cheer. How to make the perfect Thanksgiving stuffing. How to make the best Christmas cookies. That reminded me of the neighborhood Christmas cookie exchange party.

Half-eaten cookies lying around everywhere, cups of cider waiting to be spilled, plus crowds, tons of noisy children, a grabby gluten-allergic two-year-old, and the probability of epic autistic tantrums. What a logistical nightmare! Probably better not to go. Another thing to avoid.

But it wasn't the lack of cookies, parties, or stuffing themselves that bothered me — it was the lack of tradition. As a kid, I had things I looked forward to every year. Things that were the same every holiday season, even when I came home from college. If it couldn't be extra church services (the crowds are a problem around high holidays), or cookies, or parties, or travel, then what could I give my children? What were Thanksgiving and Christmas going to look like for our family?

By the time I got back to my car, it had started snowing. First snow of the season. I can't say I cared. These magical holiday bits and pieces felt like they would just float by us this year, maybe forever. I cried my way home.

My three-and-a-half-year-old daughter was shouting when I walked in the door.

"Mama, look at the snow. It's snowing outside. There's snow falling out of the sky. The snow is on the ground and on the car and on the stones and on the driveway and on my rock collection and in my room!"

"It's in your room?"

"No. It's outside on the grass and on the roof and on the cat and doggy!"

"Really, you see a dog outside?"

"No. I see the snow. It's snowing outside and everywhere."

Her excitement spilled over until we had her and her brother bundled up and ready to play in the inch of snow on the ground. My husband took them out while I made dinner.

I watched them tumble around and scrounge up enough snow to make a snowman, which they showed me through the kitchen window. They were all rosy-cheeked and runny-nosed, and even my little guy ran back and forth in the snow, tentatively bending over to touch it every five or six paces.

And that's when a sudden inspiration came to me.

My mom had recently made mashed potatoes with almond milk,

and I remembered thinking they tasted normal. Maybe that would work for hot chocolate. Did we have any almond milk?

Check.

Did we still have those allergen-free chocolate chips Grandma got for us?

A third of a bag. Check.

Voila! I poured almond milk in a pan and slowly melted chocolate chips into it. I'd expected them to lump up in a goofy way like most every food substitute seemed to do, but they dissolved like butter. "Ha!" I yelled. My first victory.

My family came tumbling in through the kitchen door, snow flying off scarves and boots, chattering and shouting about how it should snow forever. I triumphantly raised my chocolate spoon and cried out, "Hot chocolate! Who wants hot chocolate?"

The kids paid no attention, but my husband looked at me, shocked.

"You made hot chocolate? Can he have any?"

"Yes, dear. It's safe."

He laughed and started pouring while I began pulling off coats and hats. That's when I realized my daughter was shouting about getting the Christmas tree out.

I looked at my husband. He smiled, and set to work with the kids.

Our boy was running in circles in the light of the Christmas tree, stopping to glance at it every so often and take a swig of hot chocolate from his Sippy cup. He picked up an ornament with bells on it and resumed his running, jingling. My husband and our little girl were clinking their mugs together in a toast to the first snow, Christmas lights glowing off their faces.

There it was. I thought it was completely impossible, but here, I was witnessing our first holiday tradition, everyone participating in his or her own way. And it was beautiful.

— Maura Klopfenstein-Oprisko —

Wise Words

90

Thank You for the Reminder

A gentle answer turns away wrath,
but a harsh word stirs up anger.
~Proverbs 15:1

The bus was full and we'd have to wait more than an hour to get to Mount Vernon, George Washington's home. It had already been quite a journey: a long walk from our hotel and a Metro ride with transfers outside of town to this bus station. We didn't want to waste an hour of valuable touring time, nor stand outside on that hot August Sunday.

There were other people at the bus stop in the same predicament. As my husband and I discussed what to do, we noticed a few taxicabs circling. We started chatting with a woman and her teenage daughter who stood nearby. They were also headed to Mount Vernon, so we suggested we share a taxi.

In the cab we exchanged stories: they had traveled to Washington, D.C. from Washington State and we had come from Arizona. We had all attended a patriotic event at the Lincoln Memorial the day before.

As we talked, Deb shared that she was a recent cancer survivor. I could tell that she had been through a lot: she was thin and her hair was short and fine, possibly having just grown back after chemotherapy. She had a kind spirit and she radiated gratitude for life and appreciation for her family. After their D.C. trip, she and her daughter would fly to Europe for a vacation with some girlfriends.

We ended up getting along so well with Deb and her daughter that we spent most of the day with them at Mount Vernon. Deb began calling us their "cousins."

We told Deb that we had a young daughter ourselves, almost two years old at the time, who was at home with her grandparents. As we stood in line to enter George Washington's home, she told us her most important advice for raising a family, which was liberal use of the phrase, "Thank you for the reminder."

She said it's a rule in her house that whenever a reminder is given or a subsequent request for something is made, she and her family must respond with, "Thank you for the reminder." Deb had gotten tired of hearing "I know!" or "You told me already!" from her husband and kids, so she came up with this response instead. It helped everyone speak more calmly and kindly to one another.

Her daughter chimed in and said that it wasn't always easy to say those words, but they all tried.

After a great day together, we parted ways with our new "cousins" when the estate closed. I am forever grateful to have met them. Deb's advice, those five little words, "Thank you for the reminder," has stuck with me during the six years since we met.

I just love that phrase. It's hard to grumble or speak harshly when you're thanking someone, isn't it? Even if they *are* reminding you of something you already know. Gratitude changes our attitude.

Our family has chosen to adopt this rule—it was a rule from our "cousin," after all. Our daughter is now seven and we also have a four-year-old son whom we are teaching to know and understand the phrase, "Thank you for the reminder." It takes effort of course, lots of modeling and practice! It's often when I fail to use those words that I'm reminded of the difference it makes. I always regret responding sarcastically or pompously because a relational rift often follows.

I don't know what happened to Deb and her family after our meeting in 2010. But if I ever see her again, I'll tell her how grateful

I am for having met her. Her powerful phrase, "Thank you for the reminder," has had a big impact on our family and friends.

Deb, wherever you are… thank you for the reminder!

—Andrea Fortenberry—

91

Snakes in a Bucket

All problems become smaller when you confront
them instead of dodging them.
~William F. Halsey

D ue to my mother's mental illness, I was raised mostly by
my grandmother, who was as intimidating as anyone
you could hope to meet. Imagine, if you will, a real-
life version of Annie Oakley, a woman who had been
born in the late 1800s, grew up in the Wild West and moved onto a
Navajo reservation when she was young as part of a missionary family. Imagine a woman who spent the first five years of her adult life
teaching Apache children in a reservation school. My grandmother
could ride a horse, build furniture, shoot any type of gun and carry
on with the best of them. Almost everything she said seemed so wise
and practical, except for one saying she often directed at me: "Don't
put too many snakes in your bucket." I was at a loss to figure out
what she meant.

One day, I asked her about her experiences with those darn snakes,
thinking that the saying had some literal meaning. And it did. She
was the only teacher to a group of Apache children. And since it was
so far from civilization, the teacher not only taught, but repaired the
schoolhouse, slept in its loft, and basically served every function that
was necessary to keep the school up and running. It was quite common to find various critters and rattlesnakes that had moved in to
escape the bitter cold of a desert night. It was her duty to either kill

or capture them before letting the children in for class. She developed the habit of selling some of what she caught to the local natives for food and leather. She sold others to the zoo or reptile botanical center in Phoenix so they could develop anti-venom for the rattlers' bites. After all, a young teacher made so little pay in those days that every extra dime helped. Hearing that, I figured that explained her strange phrase and let the matter drop.

But several years later, when I was a miserable teenager, my grandmother said it again: "Kamia, you're trying to stuff too many snakes in your bucket." What on earth? There were no snakes around and no bucket to be found.

It only took me a few more weeks to realize that she knew exactly what she was talking about. One day, she decided to illustrate her message while both of us were working at the truck farm my grandparents owned. This was a place carved out of the desert with grit and determination — a place that got its fair share of a wide variety of creatures. Since the farm was organic and committed to being environmentally sustainable, everything that was considered a "critter" had to be relocated. That meant carrying around various buckets and lids, catching whatever turned up, and putting whatever we caught into the buckets to be driven away or donated.

This particular day was immediately after one of the rare rains the desert got, and we found snakes everywhere we went. Most of them were harmless, but seeing one wiggle when we were getting ready to pick something was an inconvenience at best and heart-stopping at worst.

So my grandmother, being the old Western woman she was, began grabbing them and sticking them in the bucket, then plopping the lid back down. At first, it wasn't an issue. The snakes stayed dutifully in the bottom of the bucket. But as the day wore on, and more snakes got plopped in on top of each other, they began trying to get out in earnest. We could hear them striking against the lid time and again. And by the end of the day, there simply was no way to put another snake in the bucket. As soon as we tried to open the lid, heads peeked out all over. When we did finally take them someplace to relocate them and pried off the top of the bucket, it was like a snake explosion, with every one of them slithering off while we stood on a rock high above, making sure we got nowhere near the exodus.

"That's what I meant about you," she said as I watched this drama unfold. "There are all kinds of snakes that will come at you in your life — mean people who want to put you down; bullies who attack; misfortunes you didn't plan on facing; disappointments in life and love; illness, accidents and much more. Right now, you try to deal with how you're feeling about these events by stuffing them into a bucket and pretending they no longer exist. You're trying to present a face to the world that you're tough — too tough to let anything get to you. But that's just like putting these snakes in this bucket. You can push them down all you want, but only for so long. Eventually, if you fail to take them out and deal with them, they will all start pushing to get back out. Usually, your personal lid will blow when you least want it to — often in an inconvenient, embarrassing or even dangerous way.

"Instead of pushing those emotions, conflicts or confrontations away, it's much, much easier to deal with them completely as they come, one by one. Imagine how much easier it would have been to just take a single snake out into the desert and let it go. So, too, will be your life. Remember to stop putting too many snakes in your bucket. Deal with what bothers you as soon as it pushes up its ugly head. You'll be so much happier if you do."

You know what? She was right. I never forgot that graphic illustration, and I never again let my bucket get so full that the lid was pushed off.

— Kamia Taylor —

92

Being Happy Is Enough

*The happiest people don't necessarily have the best of
everything. They just make the best of everything.*
~Author Unknown

Someone on Facebook had shared pictures of her vacation in Europe. The delivery truck had dropped off a gargantuan entertainment system at my neighbor's house. And the kids came home from school raving about the new video game their friends had just gotten.

Meanwhile, we were living in a house furnished mostly with freebies and dressing our kids in secondhand clothes. And even when we and the kids had to go in three different directions at night, we didn't eat out. Ever.

I like to cook, and I'm good at it. But sometimes, you just want to be spared the hassle and the cleanup!

My poor mother-in-law, in town for a visit, got to hear the whole tirade that night. "I feel so resentful sometimes," I told her, as we cleared the table after dinner. "I know we're doing the right thing, living frugally, saving money, but it feels so hard. There are so many things I'd like to have, so many things I'd like to do, and we just can't."

She hummed once or twice, nodding as she folded a cloth napkin in silence. Then she turned to me. "You know," she said, "when you compare yourself to others, it's easy to focus on what you don't have.

Wise Words | 281

But there's one thing you two do that we don't see too much of in other married couples. You two make a priority of going out together and taking time to focus on your marriage. And that's a very important thing. You two have such a great marriage."

I stopped wiping the table and pondered that for a minute. I thought of the movie my husband and I had seen a week earlier, and the English country-dance we'd attended a few weeks before that. I remembered the bike rides and the concerts, the hikes and the picnics. Most of all, I thought of how happy we were together, even after twenty years. How many people can say that?

I looked around my home with new eyes. Our refrigerator is almost too small for a family of six, but it's always filled with food that is both nourishing and delicious. Our kitchen décor is cobbled together, but it comes to us from our grandmothers' homes after they passed away. And our deck overlooks a sycamore grove where our family cooks s'mores in the fire pit every few weeks.

Even without the big TV and the European vacations and the new wardrobe every season, we are... well... happy.

And you know what? That's enough.

—Kathleen M. Basi—

Celebrating the Woman Who Did All the Work

*We often take for granted the very things
that most deserve our gratitude.*
~Cynthia Ozick

When I hung up the phone my heart sank as I thought about my mother, thousands of miles away. Her health had been steadily declining since we'd seen her during our last vacation. I reminded myself that we'd enjoyed her twenty-two years longer than the doctors had predicted. But I still found it hard to imagine my world without her.

With my birthday a week away, Mom had taken over the conversation that day, reliving every detail of my birth. I completely understood what those birthing memories meant to my mother because, when my children's birthdays rolled around each year, I always revisited every detail of their births. That's what mothers do.

Mom's birthday is twenty-two days after mine. If she made it that year, she'd turn eighty-nine. While I tried to remain positive, I needed to do something special for her "just in case," and I already knew what that was. I'd gotten the idea one night while folding laundry and listening to one of Amy Newmark's Chicken Soup for the Soul podcasts.

On this podcast, Amy told a great story by Peggy Purser Freeman called "Deconstructing My Birthday," from *Chicken Soup for the Soul: Think Possible*. In her story, Peggy finds a way to make her birthday more meaningful by giving to others. Amy then talked about how we should celebrate our mothers on our birthdays instead of ourselves. Why not? After all, they carried us for nine months and did all the work to get us here.

Amy's words really hit home. I've never cared much for celebrating my birthday, and I felt the same way Amy did. Not only had my mother gone through nine months of agony to carry me, but when it finally came time to deliver me, the doctor told her he'd have to knock her out cold. I was close to a ten-pounder, and Mom was tiny. I was trouble right away.

After a scary arrival, I mysteriously screamed day and night for several months, causing the doctors and my mother much concern. As a toddler and preschooler, I earned the nickname "Jill the Pill." As I grew, I earned my place as the black sheep of the family. Even though I thought I was a pretty decent kid, I'm probably responsible for almost every gray strand of hair on Mom's head. In fact, I'm sure I still cause her much worry.

If I wanted to pull off this idea by my birthday, I needed to get it out in the next day's mail. I grabbed a generic birthday card from my file box and wrote: "Dear Mom, Happy Birthday to Me!" In the card, I explained that my letter was a birthday present I was giving myself by celebrating the woman who had given birth to me.

My mother got her letter the day before my birthday. And while I knew she'd enjoy it, I was not prepared for her overwhelming response or the emotion in her voice. "You have no idea what a beautiful present you've given me," she said. "I've never received such a priceless gift in my life!"

Out of all the many thoughtful presents I'd given my mother over the years, none touched her so deeply. While I'd always expressed my love and appreciation to my mom, this time I'd gone into great detail, reminiscing about every single thing she had ever done for me as well as stellar moments in my life and even the horrendous times. Mom could see that my childhood wasn't all about me. I'd taken note of all the little as well as the big things that she had a hand in. She mattered a lot! I hadn't forgotten.

Months after my birthday, she was still thanking me. I even received a little note included with money she wasn't supposed to send that said, "Dear Jill, What a beautiful gift you sent me. I will cherish it always."

Not only did that little gift mean more than the world to my mother, it made a huge difference for me. When the day comes that my mother is no longer with me, at least I'll know that I celebrated her in the way that she deserved, and she received memories that meant more to her than any present on earth.

— Jill Burns —

The Tide-Turning Whisper

Forgiveness is the fragrance that the violet sheds
on the heel that has crushed it.
~Mark Twain

From day one, I made my ill feelings toward my mother-in-law crystal clear to my new husband. "Joe, why does the photographer keep inviting your mother into every photo?"

"What? He's not."

"Sure he is. All I keep hearing is, Mrs. Beck, we need you for a photo."

"Annie, he's talking to you. YOU are the Mrs. Beck he wants in the photos."

"Oh," I said, a bit chagrined. I was so certain that the photographer had her in mind as the star of the day instead of me, the bride. And thus it started. My silent declaration of war against my mother-in-law.

Oh Mary Beck was pleasant enough, but she had ulterior motives. I'd been observing her and Joe's relationship for three years. Her slightest whim, once stated, became Joe's main mission. Whatever we had planned always took a back seat to Mary's wants and needs. Or so it seemed to me.

She also incessantly dropped little innuendoes about "her Joe" and always within earshot of me. She knew it got on my nerves. Well, we were married now. Clearly Joe belonged to me and I had the paperwork to prove it.

After our wedding in January of 1984, Joe flew back to Centerville Beach Naval Facility in California. I was not expected to join him until June, after which we would be mother-in-law-free for two whole years. Yay!

About mid-February, Mary invited me to lunch. She wanted to share some wedding photos. Ha! Did she expect me to sit there and act interested in photos she took of "her Joe"? Forget it.

I could have called her to say "no thank you" with a suitable excuse. Instead, I had the audacity to write a letter and explain that I simply wasn't a social person, which shouldn't upset her. In other words, "don't expect to see too much of me, lady."

In June, Joe came home to Philadelphia to collect me and say goodbye to his family. Then we would be off to California. When the day came to say goodbye to his mom, I declined the opportunity. After all, she wasn't my mother. Joe could just go over and say goodbye himself. And so he did, without ever being cross or asking why.

Paradise waited on the other side of the map, where Joe would be mine — all mine. Once settled, Joe called his mom once a week and every time I discretely made my way to the front door and slipped out for a nice long walk.

Two years went by, and before long, we were packing to go home. My sulking started right at the Pennsylvania border. I'd just spent two years avoiding all contact with Mary Beck and now I'd have to face her again.

Joe's mom lived in the city, and as soon as we arrived home, I insisted we get an apartment in the suburbs. When holidays came along, I dutifully purchased a gift and handed it over with a forced smile. Of course I never missed an opportunity to grumble a snarky remark or two, especially if she invited us to come for dinner or worse, suggest that we all go to the movies or a show.

As the months passed and I made no attempt to improve my attitude toward Mary Beck, my relationship with Joe spiraled downward. I repeatedly made mountains out of molehills where she was concerned. Though Joe said nothing about that issue, we grumbled at each other about everything else. As time went on, Joe and I stopped communicating all together and he began sleeping on the couch. That went on for months.

One Saturday I decided I'd had it with him too. I wanted him and everything he owned out the door and out of my life. I was tired of him lying on the couch and ignoring me, and saw no way out other than to split. I told him to pack his things and leave. He changed position on the couch and ignored me some more.

I'll fix him, I thought. So I called his mother and told her flat out that I was through with her son and she'd better get his brothers over to our apartment to collect him and his belongings. She didn't agree to it. She just asked me to give the phone to Joe. When he hung up he said his mother wanted to see us right away.

"Good," I snapped back. "Let's go over and get this move organized. The sooner you're gone the happier I'll be."

Mary opened the door and let us in. Joe headed toward the couch, but before he had a chance to flop down, Mary barked at him in a tone I'd never heard before.

"Oh no, mister, you get right back over here. I want to talk to you."

Joe sheepishly turned and stood beside me.

"Joe, I don't care one bit what this is about. I'm telling you right now, Annie is right and you are wrong. She is the woman who is going to take care of you for the rest of your life. You'll never find anyone who loves you more. Now, listen to me — stop being an idiot and make up."

Then she hugged me and whispered in my ear, "Annie, I learned a long time ago a man will never treat his wife any better than he treats his mother. That's a good thing to remember. Joe will behave himself now he knows I mean business."

And there you have it — the tide-turning, life-changing moment.

Snippets of my past outrageous behavior flashed in my mind as I looked at Joe and saw him smile, and I started to cry.

After years of pushing nothing but snide remarks and selfish behavior in Mary's face, she instantly forgave every transgression and stood up for me. Never was a person less deserving of forgiveness or more grateful for it than I.

Unfortunately we only had about fifteen years to share before Mary passed away, but she and I made the most of it. She loved me as strong and true as any mother could love a daughter, and I returned that love with the same sincerity.

At the very end as Joe and I were at her bedside, I held her hand as she tried to sing something in a whisper, but I couldn't make it out.

Later that evening I asked Joe if he knew what she was trying to sing.

"She was singing, 'So Long, It's Been Good to Know You.'"

What an understatement.

—Annmarie B. Tait—

Messages in a Bottle

The flame never dies because
the commitment never ends.
~Author Unknown

I t was 1940 in the small town of Cleburne, Texas. It didn't take long to spot new people there, and it was my mother who spotted the new milkman making a delivery to the house across the street.

When she told me the story, she explained that the milk bottles rattling in their metal cages sounded like music when he carried them, causing her heart to pound like that of a schoolgirl.

She knew this young man in the crisp, white uniform was the man for her. So she waved the sturdy young man to the porch, introduced herself, and made the proper arrangements.

On the occasion of his first delivery, Dad left an empty bottle along with Mom's two-quart order. A piece of paper curled out of its opening. Mother recalls how her heart beat wildly as she read the note: "Would you consider going out with your milkman?"

Would she!

Exactly six months from the day my father delivered the milk along with its bold message, it was my mother who was dressed in white. The man of her dreams waited at the altar as she made her grand entrance into the town's oldest Christian church to marry him.

As a result of my father's first request, my parents had gotten their wish — each other. The tradition of writing down what you wanted for Christmas and dropping it into that same empty milk bottle began during their first year of marriage. My mother decorated the bottle with a wreath and hand-painted sprigs of holly and mistletoe on its outer surface. The bottle was then displayed at the Thanksgiving table, allowing them both a full month to ponder over whatever the other had asked for.

During my parents' second year of marriage, Mom's note had an unusual Christmas request. She asked my father for a child. She asked him the same thing for three years running, the result being the birth of a girl, a boy, and then in the fourth year, another boy — me.

My siblings and I looked forward to Thanksgiving almost as much as Christmas, for that's when the milk bottle would be brought out and the sugarplums would begin to dance in our heads. We were encouraged to ask for something that would be useful to all of us. That didn't seem like much fun to us kids, but we knew our Christmas goodies weren't restricted to our milk jar requests.

Our house was the center of activity for the whole extended family at Thanksgiving. A wave of hungry relatives always materialized to share in our feast, and then to write their Christmas desires on a small note and drop it into the bottle's glass tummy.

As I grew older, I realized that the reason our relatives loved to come to our house for Thanksgiving was as much about putting their notes in the milk jar as it was about the food and giving thanks. An aunt once told me that my parents' unusual custom represented the milk of human kindness rather than the actual giving of gifts. Judging by the family closeness that has continued all these years, and how my own children took to the custom like little tadpoles in a warm pond, I guess my aunt was right.

Some of my older relatives had suffered greatly during the Depression and the war that followed. My mom and dad became a kind of rallying cry for family unity and my mom's tradition seemed to represent the idea that hopes and dreams were still possible and good will and the spirit of giving were never out of style.

After my dad passed away, my elderly mother seemed to treasure the oft-repeated ceremony all the more. It bridged any generation gap we might have experienced over the years and the tradition has now entered into its fourth generation.

Then one day, Mother chose me to be the guardian of the Christmas bottle and its messages. I assured her I would not let the custom die, no matter how silly it might seem to some.

"Our tradition has brought all of us many wonderful gifts," she reminded me. "The best of them has been those from the heart. The ones in which people ask for no more than love and goodwill."

I vowed that her descendants would not let her down and so we haven't.

Much of the original enamel green and red color my mother painted on the milk jar that first Christmas has now peeled away, but every Thanksgiving through Christmas it still occupies a place of honor in my house. The simple quart jar, representative of my parents' love for family and each other, now sits on a bright Christmas doily with a small wreath around its stubby neck.

The little hands of my grandchildren still drop their thoughtful notes into its mouth in hopes that this magical container will make their Christmas dreams come true. And, on behalf of my parents, I see to it that they do.

—Jay Seate—

96

What You Is

Trust that in living true to yourself, you will attract
people that support and love you, just as you are.
~Jaeda deWalt

When I was in the fourth grade, many years ago, I had an autograph book. It was pink and white, with pinstripes. On the cover was a drawing of two old-fashioned, raggedy little girls. My best friend, Lisa, had given it to me. And, more than anything, I wanted Mamo, my grandmother, to sign it.

"Will you sign my book, Mamo?" I asked one Sunday afternoon. We were visiting in the living room, and the midday sun was falling across the carpet in long, gold bars.

"Why, I'd love to, baby," she said. I handed her the book, and she pawed through her handbag for a pen.

"Now let me think," she said, and she began to write. I remember watching her gentle, soft hands curl around the pen. Mamo always had manicured nails—and a heart of gold. She finished writing, closed the book, and handed it back to me. I could hardly wait to see what she'd written.

But I waited until evening when I was tucked tight into my bed. Then I reached over and snapped on the light. I opened the book to Mamo's page.

The words were captured in my grandmother's scrawl:
Be what you is, and not what you isn't. Because if you is what you

isn't, you isn't what you is.

It was signed, *I love you, Mamo.*

"How odd," I whispered into the night. Somehow, I'd expected more. I didn't even understand the crazy, incorrect grammar. Mamo didn't talk like that. I was disappointed. I'd wanted something to touch my heart. I'd wanted something more.

Decades later, I found pleasure in the pursuit of words. I was finding success as a freelance writer, but I struggled with accepting my own voice. My own style. I'd find a favorite blogger, and I'd want to sound like her. I'd study how an author turned a phrase, and I'd want her voice. I fell in love with writer after writer and voice after voice, and I'd try to imitate those writers I loved.

Then one day, right after we'd moved into our old Victorian and cardboard boxes were stacked through the house like a tall, brown maze, I found the pink striped autograph book. Mamo had long passed away, but the book was nestled between old high-school yearbooks and my bedraggled childhood teddy bear.

I sat on the hardwood floor and opened it with careful hands.

And Mamo's page was right there. *Be what you is...*

Those words washed over me. Dear Mamo. When she'd written them with those kind, soft hands, on that long-lost afternoon, I'd been disappointed. I'd wanted more.

But as I read those words, washed in wisdom and time, they soaked into my soul. I could see Mamo, with her twinkling green eyes, her coiffed auburn hair, and a loving expression on her face. I could almost hear her. "Darling, use your own voice. Sound like yourself. Be who God made you to be. If you're trying to be someone else, you're losing out. You're losing you."

I've taken those words to heart, and I've found my own style. I still want to learn. I still want to grow. And I'll always admire others, too. But I'm happy to be who God made me to be.

There's joy and freedom in just being what I is.

— Shawnelle Eliasen —

97

Truly America

*What is shared in common is infinitely more significant
than what apparently divides.*
~Dave Mearns

It was the first time my mother dragged me to her work — but only because it was the first time I ran out of excuses. As a sixth grader, I was already upset that I had to spend my Saturday afternoon in the basement of a church instead of hanging out with my friends. I never really understood the nature of my mother's work beyond the fact that she was called an "interfaith activist." To me, it was just a label. But little did I know that it would change my outlook on life.

As I lugged posters from our car down the old church stairs, I saw my mother already eagerly placing chairs in a circle. She set up the posters containing information about various religions around the circle of chairs. Like a machine, she did all this work within seconds, while keeping a huge smile on her face. Her excitement got me curious. I wondered, *Who are these chairs for? Why are there so many posters about different religions I have vaguely heard of?* A few minutes later, I heard the sound of the basement stairs creak and got the answers to my questions.

The chairs were meant for teenagers and young adults of various faiths and backgrounds. I sat in awe as I observed the room full of teenage boys wearing turbans and yarmulkes, and women and men wearing traditional clothing. I was surprised to see everyone confidently take a seat within the circle, and I was even more shocked to see my mother getting ready to start a conversation among this diverse group of people.

My mother began by asking everyone to introduce themselves. It was a bit awkward, as everyone, one by one, recited their name, school, and age in a monotone pattern. I was worried that the rest of the time would be just as dull. However, my mother then proceeded to ask us to stand by the poster we identified with most closely. Everyone got up immediately, running in different directions. I stood by the poster that read "Islam" and was greeted with warm smiles from others standing there, too. I saw others standing by posters with the words "Sikh," "Judaism," "Hinduism," "Catholicism," etc. Then we were instructed to break into smaller groups, with each group having individuals from various faiths. My mother instructed us all to share the knowledge we had about our religion with the members of our groups. The room went from silent to loud, as everyone started asking questions and actively engaging. I was intrigued by the discussions of each religion, which made me eager to discuss Islam when it was my turn.

As we regrouped into the big circle of chairs, my mother asked us all to relay information that we gained about a new religion. I was proud to present what I learned about the Sikh faith and smiled when my fellow group member shared what she learned from me about Islam. My mother then asked us to share what we liked about our religion and some struggles we might face. We all realized as everyone went around the room that we shared even more commonalities than differences in our everyday struggles and experiences. In that moment, as I scanned the room and its diverse group of people, I saw what it meant to be an American.

This room not only represented people of different colors, but people of various backgrounds and religions who were able to look beyond their differences to discuss their everyday lives while sharing smiles and laughs. That Saturday afternoon, in the basement of a church, I was proud to be an American.

— Zehra Hussain —

98

The Mom Gene

Accept good advice gracefully as long as it doesn't
interfere with what you intended
to do in the first place.
~Gene Brown

My mother-in-law called to tell me something I already knew. "Now, remember, tomorrow is Labor Day, and that means we won't be getting any mail."

"Thank you for the reminder," I said. But what I wanted to say was, "Yes, Mom, I've lived through forty-three Labor Days now, so I knew that already."

"Now, you need to turn here," she told me when I was driving her to the doctor's office — the same doctor's office I drove her to last month and the month before. "Thanks, Mom," I said, instead of, "Yeah, I know how to get there because I've been to your doctor's office a few dozen times already."

"Do you have a cold?" she said when she heard me sniffle. "Because there's medicine you can take for that. They sell it at Walgreens."

"I'm fine, Mom," I said, instead of, "Yep, I've taken cold medicine before, and they sell it at CVS, Target, and Walmart, too."

My mother-in-law really likes to give me advice, whether I need it or not. And my own mom is not much better.

"Make sure you put jackets on the kids tomorrow," she told me. "It's supposed to be cold."

"Thank you, Mom," I said, instead of, "It's November, and I live in the Midwest. I could've figured out all on my own that my kids would need jackets."

Nearly every day, one of my moms calls me to tell me something that I already know. But I was handling it with aplomb. Until we went on vacation. With both of them. At the same time.

"Can the kids swim? If not, you'll need to put life jackets on them," one mom said.

"And if we're going to be outside, they'll need sunscreen. You know, so they don't get sunburned," my other mom said.

I looked at my husband. "Thank you, Captain Obvious," I whispered.

"Hang in there, love," he said. "They mean well."

My husband was right. They did mean well, and I reminded myself of that fact repeatedly during that vacation — until I'd had enough, and I snapped.

We were eating dinner on the last night of the trip. I'd ordered my meal, as well as a kid's meal for my youngest son. He'd requested fruit as his side dish.

"Does that fruit include grapes?" my mom asked the waitress. "If it does, my daughter will need to cut them in half."

"Oh, yes," my mother-in-law continued. "Grapes are a choking hazard, you know."

"Yes, I do know that," I snapped. I pointed at my oldest son. "He has survived under my care all these years. He is a teenager now, and I never let him choke on a grape or drown in a pool or get stung by a jellyfish or anything. Why can't you guys just trust me to be a good mom?"

My moms' mouths dropped open. "Do you think we don't know you're a good mom?" my mother-in-law said with tears in her eyes.

"You're a great mom," my mom said. "We both know that."

"Then why do you constantly tell me what to do? You both act like I don't know anything."

My moms looked at one another. "We're just trying to help you," one said. "We remember that being a mom is hard, and everyone needs help."

"I'm happy to have your help," I said. "But the unsolicited advice gets to be a little much."

"Oh, we're just reminding you of things you may have forgotten," my mom said. "We're not telling you what to do or anything."

"It makes me feel like you think I can't handle things on my own," I said.

"We're sorry," they said. "You're a wonderful mom. We didn't mean to upset you."

I nodded, feeling sheepish that I'd lost my temper. "It's okay. I appreciate your help."

We hugged it out, and I thanked them both for caring about my family so much.

The next morning, we were getting ready to leave the hotel and make the long drive from the Sunshine State back to the Midwest.

"Did you use the potty?" I asked my younger son. When he nodded, I looked at my older son. "Did you?"

He shook his head. "I don't need to go."

"Are you sure? It's a long drive. We won't be stopping for a few hours, and you'll have to hold it. Maybe you should try. You know, just in case."

My son burst out laughing. He looked at my husband. "It's like a genetic thing. They can't help themselves. I don't think they even know they're doing it."

My husband nodded. "It's the Mom Gene. It's the genetic predisposition to over-parent their children, no matter how old they get." He smiled at me. "And, apparently, it's hereditary."

I started laughing, too. I couldn't help it. Just twelve hours before, I'd gotten mad at our moms for giving unsolicited advice, and now I'd done it to my teenage son.

"I'm sorry, bud," I said. "I shouldn't have said anything. You are old enough to make your own bathroom decisions."

"That's okay, Mom." He looked down and shrugged. "Last night, when you got mad at the grandmas, I understood how you felt."

I nodded. "It's hard to let your kids grow up." And then I realized that my moms probably felt the same way. Just as I loved my kids and wanted to protect them, my moms loved me and wanted only the best for me.

I'd love to tell you that my moms have gotten out of the unsolicited-advice business, but they haven't. They both still call me daily with warnings about the weather, pollen counts, and other concerns, both real and imagined. Mostly imagined.

But oddly, it doesn't bother me as much as it used to. When I start to get irked, I remember the time that I encouraged a teenager who was old enough to drive to use the potty before we traveled. Turns out, I was more like my moms than I want to admit.

We moms love our kids and want the best for them. And sometimes that means we offer unwanted advice.

We can't help it. It's the Mom Gene.

It might be annoying to our children—even our adult children—but we always, always mean well.

— Sarah Williams —

The Secret to Being a Good Hostess

The ornaments of your home are the people who smile
upon entering time and time again.
~Maralee McKee, Manners That Matter for Mom

I remember the day my mother made the comment, "She's learned the secret to being a good hostess." I wanted in on the secret. I was, after all, a grown-up; I had been married for two years.

As a new bride, I had pictured us throwing fantastic parties and delicious sit-down dinners. Tom and I had new dishes, new silverware, new everything. I wanted to entertain. I wanted to have friends over for fancy meals.

I imagined perfect table settings, fresh bouquets of flowers, and tapered candles. I dreamed of memorable dinner parties with gourmet meals like Beef Wellington or Chicken Cordon Bleu. I had never tried those foods, but they sounded classy to me.

One of the hurdles to such entertaining was the fact I was not a great cook. I had not learned the art of having all the components of a meal come out at the same time. Often, our choice was to eat the potatoes hot and the meat later, because cold mashed potatoes are not tasty. Adding to my inadequate cooking ability was the fact we were still in college and couldn't afford fresh flowers to adorn our table. And the only candles we had were those left over from our wedding.

As time wore on, my cooking improved. We managed to have a few people into our home, but each time was stressful for me. I spent hours cleaning the house. I worried over every detail before our guests arrived, fussed about every detail while they were there, and fell into bed exhausted after our guests left.

Then, a few months after moving into a new house, a young couple in our neighborhood invited us over for dinner. They had two small children. Although the house was clean, we had to step over a few toys in the living room. Dinner wasn't quite ready, so Mary Jane asked if I could set the table while the men watched the children. She had made a meatloaf and macaroni and cheese. I watched as she heated green beans from a can in a saucepan and poured a can of peaches into a bowl. After dinner, I covered the leftovers while the men cleared the table and Mary Jane put the children to bed. We all enjoyed the evening talking, laughing, and playing a board game.

"It's funny," I told my mom the next day, "she didn't make anything special, but we had such a good time."

"She's learned the secret of being a good hostess," my mother told me. "Treat your family like company and your company like family."

I took my mother's words to heart. In the forty-plus years my husband and I have been married, I have enjoyed setting our antique dining room table with beautiful linens and interesting centerpieces for our family gatherings. Our daughters, sons-in-law, and grandchildren seem to truly appreciate the time and effort I put into making those occasions special.

But the feet under our kitchen table have belonged to good friends from all walks of life and all over the world. We have entertained everybody from business leaders to local farmers, from square dancers to ministers. We have welcomed friends from China, Korea, Finland, Italy, New Zealand, and India. I've served everything from pot roast to potpies.

Recently, when we needed to meet with a man to discuss publicity for an upcoming convention we were planning, I invited him and his wife to our home for dinner. They had never been to our house before. We made the final arrangements via e-mail.

"How about coming at 6:00?" I typed. "We are taking care of our granddaughter for a few days, and she will need to get to bed early. Just be prepared to step over toys and be treated like family." Again, we had a fun, productive, and memorable evening.

Mary Jane and Mom, did I ever say, "Thank you"?

— Rebecca Waters —

The One Thing We Didn't Have to Unpack

*A memory is what is left when something happens
and does not completely unhappen.*
~Edward de Bono

It was two days before we had to leave our large four-bedroom house and move out of state. I loved this house and all the memories we had made in it. I thought back to raising our son and daughter there. We had brought them home from the hospital to this house. This was where they learned to walk and talk. This was where we watched them play on the lawn as we rocked on the welcoming porch on beautiful spring and autumn days. I had picked apples from the trees in the back yard and learned to make apple pie from scratch in this house. And now we were saying goodbye.

My husband announced that our things would not all fit in our POD. I stood in our driveway while the cicadas screeched like a car alarm. "What's not going to fit?" I asked.

"The sage couches, the kitchen table, the coffee tables, the treadmill, the rocking chairs..."

"We have to take the porch rockers!" Thunder was starting to rumble in the distance, and the wind was picking up, only adding to my sense of urgency. "I nursed our babies in those! We sat in those and counted the fireflies every summer."

"Honey," my husband continued patiently, "they're not going to fit. And even if they did, we're not going to have a porch in California."

We lived east of the Mississippi and all our family was out West, so we were moving out there to be with the people we so desperately missed. We needed our children to be surrounded by people who loved them unconditionally the way only grandparents can. We needed to know that someone had our back and would move heaven and earth to be there if we called. We had flown solo for five years, and although we had made dear friends, there was just no substitute for our parents, Grandma and Grandpa for our kids.

When an opportunity came for my husband to transfer west (to a town that was just a few hours from my parents and a day's drive from his), we knew it was time. We were excited. We would be living in a house half the size of this one, but we didn't care. We would never have to spend Thanksgiving or Christmas alone again. Our children would be able to grow up with grandparents, aunts, uncles, and cousins in the picture.

"Could we get a bigger POD?" I asked, still trying to bring everything along with us.

Jason sighed. "Amy, this is as big as they come."

"But I love the kitchen table," I said.

"Do you want to bring that one instead of the dining room table?"

I thought a moment. "No."

"Honey, we can't take both!" My husband took off his work gloves. He wiped the sweat from his forehead and locked the doors to the POD. The wind was blowing the branches of our pear trees sideways. The thunder boomed. "We have to wait until the storm passes before we can load anything else in the POD. Okay? You think about what you want to take with us." He slipped quietly back into the house.

I stood in the garage and watched the rain run off our driveway. I felt like the sand was running out of our hourglass. We had to say goodbye to the home I loved and the furniture I loved, too.

I sat down on the bumper of my car and called my mom. "Hello?"

"Hi, Mom. It's Amy."

"Hi, honey. What's new? How's the packing going?"

"It's not all going to fit," I said, trying to keep my voice steady and not burst into tears.

"What's not going to fit?"

"The treadmill, the kitchen table, the couches, the porch rocking chairs." I felt hot tears spill down my cheeks. "And I know it's just stuff, and I know stuff doesn't matter, but it's hard! I sat in that rocking chair and read stories to Azure when I was pregnant with Seamus. And I lost the last thirty pounds of my baby weight walking on that treadmill at night after the kids went to bed. And I've sat at that kitchen table every night with my family since we moved into this house…"

"Amy, honey. The stuff isn't the memories. You don't need the rocking chairs to remember reading books to Azure on the front porch when she was small. You don't need your kitchen table to remember family dinners. You will always have those memories, whether the stuff comes with you to your new house or not. And you don't have to worry about losing the memories when you leave your stuff behind. Those you take with you, and you don't even have to worry about boxing them up. Okay?"

"Okay," I said.

"How's your weather?" my mom asked.

"We're having an afternoon thunderstorm." I looked up at the skies. The clouds had thinned and bright blue sky bent around them. "But it looks like the rain has stopped."

"Yeah. You are going to be just fine. Moving is tough, but we are so excited that you are going to be closer."

"We're excited too."

My mom was right. We've been very happy in our new home, half the size of our old one. We have half as much stuff as we did before. We don't miss it, and we have not lost the happy memories of our old home. Those came with us, and they were the only things we never had to box up or unpack.

— Amelia Hollingsworth —

A Puppy of Our Own

My goal in life is to be as good a person
as my dog already thinks I am.
~Author Unknown

We lived on a quiet street with very little traffic so my mom let my brothers and me play out in the front yard a lot. One day we were outside playing when I saw something move under a bush at our neighbor's house. It looked weird so we went over to check it out.

It was a puppy! I sat down in the grass and clapped my hands and it came running over to me and jumped in my lap. I was so happy. I had been begging my parents for a puppy for a long time and here it was. My brothers were going crazy.

I carefully carried the puppy to my house and went inside to look for my mom. "Mom, Mom, guess what I found under the bush next door?" My mom came into the room, looked at me, looked at the puppy and then back at me. "Mom, I think it's lost; it doesn't have a collar or any tags. And Mom, it sure looks hungry."

Mom got a bowl and filled it with water. Then she got some food from the refrigerator and put it in another bowl and put both bowls on the floor. I put the puppy down. She ran right over to the bowls and started eating and drinking. I was right… she was hungry. After she ate she curled up into a ball and went to sleep. My brothers and

I just sat on the floor and watched her sleep.

My mom said that we needed to try and find the owner of the puppy. I didn't want to do that. I wanted to keep the puppy for my own. But Mom said that the owner was probably worried about the puppy and sad that she was gone. She asked me how I would feel if I had lost my puppy. Would I want the person who found it to try and find me? Or just keep the puppy? She was right. We needed to try and find the owner.

We made "Found Puppy" signs and put our phone number on them. We hung the signs up around the neighborhood. My mom put an ad in the newspaper about finding a lost puppy. Every time the phone would ring I would get scared. Almost a week went by and no one had called about the puppy. I was so happy.

Then one day that dreaded phone call came. I could hear my mom asking lots of questions: What does your puppy look like? What does your puppy like to eat? And then I heard her giving our address to the person on the phone and saying we would wait outside for him. I felt sick. I loved this puppy so much and now I might lose her.

The man drove up in his car. There were two kids in the car with him. They all got out of the car and started walking up the front walk to our house. The puppy went wild! It ran to the man and his kids and was jumping all over them. The kids were screaming and laughing and jumping too. The man got down on his knees and the puppy jumped into his arms. There was no doubt that this was their puppy. And the puppy was really happy to see them even though we had been so nice to her.

My mom and brothers and I were sitting on the front porch and the man walked up to us. He was so happy. He thanked us for finding the puppy and for taking such good care of her. He told us that she had gotten out of the yard about a week ago and had run away. Puppies do that. He and his kids had looked all over for her. They had never given up hope of finding her but, since a week had gone by, they weren't sure they would ever see her again. The man wanted to give my mom some money as a reward but my mom said no. She was just glad that we were able to do the right thing and return the puppy to her family. They drove away.

I watched them go and I cried. So did my brothers. We were so sad. We only had the puppy for one week but we loved her so much. My mom was very sad too but she told us to think of how happy the other kids were now that they had their puppy back. And then she told us something that my brothers and I had wanted to hear for a very long time. She and my dad were going to get us a puppy! Our very own puppy! She told us that she was proud of us for taking care of the puppy for the week we had her. And she was proud of us for understanding that giving the puppy back was the right thing to do. My brothers and I started yelling and screaming.

We got our own puppy the very next week. We named her Princess and she ruled our house. My brothers and I took good care of her and we didn't ever have to worry about having to give her up. She was OUR puppy. Keeping that other family's puppy would have never felt right to us. Princess was like our reward. We got her because we did something that was hard to do but it was the right thing to do.

—John Berres—

Meet Our Contributors

We are pleased to introduce you to the writers whose stories were compiled from our past books to create this new collection. These bios were the ones that ran when the stories were originally published. They were current as of the publication dates of those books.

Kristi Adams is a travel writer who has written about llamas in Europe, the trials of using German GPS, adventure caves, and more. She lives in Germany with her husband and a curmudgeonly rescue cat and is a proud seven-time contributor to the *Chicken Soup for the Soul* series. Read more of her work at www.kristiadamsmedia.com.

Monica A. Andermann lives and writes on Long Island where she shares a home with her husband and their little tabby Samson. Her writing has been included in such publications as *Woman's World*, *Sasee* and *Guideposts* as well as many *Chicken Soup for the Soul* books.

Allison Andrews is an Emmy award-winning producer who left a career in television news to help other people tell their stories and find more time to tell her own. She has a teenage daughter and is preparing to visit fifty places she's never been the year she turns fifty!

Peggy Archer is the author of picture books for children, including *Turkey Surprise*, a New York Times bestseller. Besides writing, she enjoys walking, line dancing, and time with her grandchildren. She and her husband have six children and eleven grandchildren. They live in O'Fallon, MO. Visit her at peggyarcher.com.

Suzanne Baginskie lives on the west coast of Florida with her husband, Al. Recently retired, she enjoys writing and has been published in various *Chicken Soup for the Soul* books. Her other interests include traveling, reading, and watching movies. She is currently working on an inspirational romantic suspense novel.

Nancy King Barnes is a registered practicing nurse who lives with her husband in Rowlett, TX. Chicken Soup for the Soul has served as a wonderful venue to express her life's experiences that God has provided.

Writing is a hobby and she is thankful to this publication for allowing her to share her heart.

Kathleen M. Basi is the quintessential jack-of-all trades writer: composer-songwriter, columnist, feature writer, essayist, novelist, and author of three short nonfiction books for families. In her "spare" time, Kate juggles disability advocacy, directing a church choir, and turning her four kids into foodies.

Jan Bono's new cozy mystery series set on the southwest Washington coast is now available! She's also published five humorous personal experience collections, two poetry chapbooks, nine one-act plays, a dinner theater play, and has written for magazines ranging from *Guideposts* to *Woman's World*. Learn more at www.JanBonoBooks.com.

Jackie Boor began her freelance writing career in 1968. She went on to raise three children and build a distinguished career as a large group facilitator, mediator, civic engagement specialist, speaker and award-winning author. Besides gardening and golf, Jackie enjoys educational adventures with colleagues and family.

Jane Brzozowski comes from a family of writers, including her husband Steve and her daughters Kat and Sally. Her sister, Lava Mueller, got her hooked on the *Chicken Soup for the Soul* series.

John P. Buentello is the author of many published essays, short stories, nonfiction and poetry. He is currently at work on a mystery novel and can be contacted via e-mail at jakkhakk@yahoo.com.

Jill Burns lives in the mountains of West Virginia with her wonderful family. She's a retired piano teacher and performer. She enjoys writing, music, gardening, nature, and spending time with her grandchildren.

Connie Sturm Cameron is a freelance writer and speaker who lives in her country empty nest with her husband Chuck. She has been published in dozens of periodicals and is the author of the book *God's Gentle Nudges*. Contact her at P.O. Box 30, Glenford, OH 43739; www.conniecameron.com; or conniec@netpluscom.com.

Matt Caprioli lives in New York City. His essays have appeared in *Mr. Beller's Neighborhood*, *Cirque*, and *Opossum Magazine*. Matt was a journalist in Alaska for three years and has contributed to the *Huffington Post*, *Worn in New York*, and *The Paris Review Daily*. He holds an MFA in creative writing from Hunter College.

Eva Carter is a freelance writer and amateur photographer. Her background is in telecommunications where she spent twenty-three years in finance. She and her husband live in Dallas, TX. E-mail her at evacarter@ sbcglobal.net.

Emily Parke Chase speaks at conferences and retreats and has authored six books, including *Help! My Family's Messed Up* (Kregel 2008) and *Standing Tall After Falling Short* (WingSpread, 2011). She enjoys reading, cooking and spoiling her grandchildren. Visit her at emilychase.com.

Kim Childs is a Boston-area life and career coach specializing in Positive Psychology (aka The Science of Happiness), creativity and sacred living. She also publishes a blog, "A Pilgrim on the Path," and teaches workshops on The Artist's Way: A Spiritual Path to Higher Creativity. Please visit her at www.KimChilds.com.

Erika Chody lives in Austin, TX with her husband and a house full of pets. Erika teaches 7th and 8th grade English as a Second Language and is working on completing her Master's degree in Reading Education at Texas State University.

Cindy Armeland Clemens graduated from the University of Windsor. Her story "Shoe Shoe Train" appeared in *Chicken Soup for the Soul: O Canada The Wonders of Winter*. She's had a diverse career, but her most important title is Jacob and Jonathan's mom. She and her husband Mark live on a hobby farm. E-mail her at cindyclemens@hotmail.com.

Cj Cole lives between the Chesapeake Bay and the Atlantic on the eastern shore of Virginia. She has been a radio personality on the shore for fourteen years and was a weekly advice/opinion columnist for twelve years.

Courtney Conover is a freelance writer and yoga practitioner who resides in Michigan with her husband, Scott. The couple eagerly awaits the birth of their first child this fall. This is Courtney's fourth contribution to the *Chicken Soup for the Soul* series. Learn more at www.courtneyconover.com.

D'ette Corona is the Associate Publisher for Chicken Soup for the Soul. She received her Bachelor of Science in business management.

Barbara D'Amario is a retired executive secretary who honed her skills writing accommodation letters and personnel evaluations. She belongs to two writing groups, attends workshops and enjoys cooking, reading and painting.

Gwen Daye is a wife, homemaker, dog rescuer, parent of two teenagers, and is thrilled to have her second piece accepted into the *Chicken Soup for the Soul* series.

John Dorroh taught high school science for thirty years. Currently he works part-time as an educational consultant, writes poetry, short fiction, and business and restaurant reviews. He travels and makes photo notecards for friends... and still writes old-fashioned letters.

Cheryl Edwards-Cannon has been a giver of care for more than ten years and is currently writing a book about her experience. She is also a Care Consultant to those who are struggling with the challenges of elderly care. E-mail Cheryl at clearpathpartners14@gmail.com.

Shawnelle Eliasen and her husband Lonny live in an old Victorian in a small Illinois town on the Mississippi River. They have five sons, and Shawnelle home teaches the youngest two. She blogs, writes inspirational stories for publication, and hopes to begin a book soon.

RoseAnn Faulkner is a retired teacher from Yuma, AZ. She enjoys documenting family history through her stories. Her mother Dorothy Faulkner, the inspiration for this story, passed away in 2005. RoseAnn and her husband, Stan Smith, have been married for thirty-two years. E-mail her at roseannfaulkner@gmail.com.

David Fingerman is a retired court clerk who now devotes his time to writing. He lives in Minneapolis and finds Zen in shoveling snow. He's sure one day a relative will write a story in a book about crazy families and it will be about him.

Inspired by her grandmother, **Kris Flaa** obtained an M.A. in Gerontology before she left corporate management to write, see the National Parks, and spend more time with her family and friends. She recently completed her first novel and lives near Minneapolis with her partner and their charming Westie. E-mail her at kmflaa@comcast.net.

James Foltz graduated from Penn State, and like many English degree graduates, he is writing the "Great American Novel." He enjoys "date nights" with his wonderful wife and playing "wrestle-house" with his two young boys while trying to avoid serious injury. His book *All the Past We Leave Behind* will be available in 2015.

Andrea Fortenberry lives near Phoenix, AZ with her husband and two children. She writes and speaks on relationships, family and faith. She was also a contributor to *Chicken Soup for the Soul: Devotional Stories for Wives*. Connect with Andrea at andreafortenberry.com.

University of Pennsylvania graduate **Sally Schwartz Friedman** has been an essayist for over three decades, sharing the sounds of her life. Her husband, three daughters and seven grandchildren provide those sounds. Her work has appeared in *The New York Times*, *The Philadelphia Inquirer*, *AARP Magazine*, and numerous national and regional publications. E-mail her at pinegander@aol.com.

Cynthia M. Gary is a Physician Assistant in rural North Carolina, where she is blessed to help people achieve physical and mental wellness. She balances her challenging profession with dance, writing, scrapbooking, and outdoor activities. She is forever grateful to her parents, Mary and John Gary. E-mail her at CynCynCreates@gmail.com.

Grace Givens has only recently begun writing about the many serendipitous occurrences in her life. A veteran performer, she is a cancer survivor who sings through her exams, tests and treatments. She and her husband Robert reside in Houston, TX. E-mail her at gracegivens@gmail. com or view her at youtube/gracegivens/survive.

Donna Goering is a Registered Dental Hygienist. She volunteers in the Awana program at her church. She enjoys spending time with husband Marvin, daughter Rachel and Charlotte the puppy. She enjoys reading, watching sci-fi, drinking hot tea and eating chocolate.

Freelance writer **Wendy Hobday Haugh** has had hundreds of articles, stories, and poems for adults and children published in more than three dozen national and regional publications. Mother to three grown sons and grandmother to two spunky kids, Wendy lives with her husband Chuck and their two eccentric, elderly cats.

Amelia Hollingsworth wishes everyone could have a friend like Lois Thompson Bartholomew. When Amelia told Lois that she was interested in writing, Lois encouraged her. She mentored Amelia, and even sent her the submission guidelines that led to Amelia's first publication in *Chicken Soup for the Soul: Just for Preteens*.

Mark A. Howe is a native of Topeka, KS and has been living in northern Indiana since 1999, when he met his wife on a dating website. Neither of them thinks that's especially weird. They have two sons, Matthew and Michael, and he is a writer with the *Times-Union* in Warsaw, IN.

Carol Huff is a frequent contributor to the *Chicken Soup for the Soul* series. She has also had her work published in other national magazines and currently has a novel available as an ebook. Her spare time is spent taking care of her thirty-plus animals on her farm in Georgia. Contact her via e-mail her at herbiemakow@gmail.com.

Zehra Hussain is currently a senior at the University of North Texas in Denton, TX. She is pursuing a Bachelor of Arts in Political Science with a minor in Medical Anthropology. Zehra is an aspiring physician and hopes to combine both her passion for medicine and politics in order to shape global health.

Kim Kelly Johnson is a Southern girl at heart, a loving wife and a mother to three kids. Writing became her prime outlet while studying at Valdosta State University. Her beloved mother, Linda, passed away from pancreatic cancer in 2015 but continues to be Kim's inspiration each and every day — both in writing and in life.

Lori D. Johnson has an M.A. in Urban Anthropology from The University of Memphis. Her work has appeared in a variety of publications, including *Chapter 16*, *Mississippi Folklife*, *The Root*, *Memphis* magazine, and *Obsidian II: Black Literature In Review*.

Sandy Kelly is a communications specialist from Alberta, where she has enjoyed a successful career as a reporter and nonfiction writer for over twenty years. Her lifelong love affair with the written word has made her an avid reader and dabbler in fiction writing, and she is currently working on her second novel.

Published author **Roger Dean Kiser's** stories take you into the heart of a child abandoned by his family and abused by the system. Through his stories, he relives the sadness and cruelty of growing up an orphan in the early 1950s.

Maura Klopfenstein-Oprisko and her husband are proud parents to a four-year-old autistic son and a six-year-old gifted daughter. She has a B.A. degree in professional writing and writes a restricted diets column for *Crawfordsville's Journal Review*. Unsolicited hugs from her kids bring her indescribable joy.

Kimber Krochmal lives in rural North Carolina. She has a large family consisting of not only her own children but other children she "adopted" over the years. They keep her young and are a constant source of inspiration.

Cathi LaMarche has contributed to over twenty anthologies. As a composition teacher, novelist, and writing coach, she spends most days immersed in the written word. In her spare time, she enjoys gardening, cooking, and hiking. She resides in Missouri with her husband, two children, and three dogs.

With the passing of her mother, **Cindy Legorreta** has fulfilled one task — that of caregiver. Now she intends to keep a promise made. She will begin her "second life," post retirement, and relocate with hubby, Ric, to his home city of New Orleans. There Cindy plans to focus her energies — guiding and mentoring NOLA youth at risk.

Lisa Leshaw recently retired from the mental health profession. She's spending her days building new bridges, freelance writing, and conducting empowerment workshops for women of every age.

Janeen Lewis is a writer living in Kentucky with her husband, Jesse, and two children, Andrew and Gracie. She has been published in several *Chicken Soup for the Soul* anthologies. When she isn't refereeing her kids, she loves reading and knitting. E-mail her at jlewis0402@netzero.net.

Nikki Loftin writes in the Texas Hill Country, surrounded by dogs, chickens, and small, loud boys. She studied fiction writing at The University of Texas at Austin (M.A. '98). Her first novel, *The Sinister Sweetness of Splendid Academy*, will be published by Razorbill/Penguin in Summer 2012. Learn more at www.nikkiloftin.com.

Barbara LoMonaco has worked for Chicken Soup for the Soul as an editor since 1998. She has co-authored two *Chicken Soup for the Soul* book titles and has had stories published in numerous other titles. Barbara is a graduate of the University of Southern California and has a teaching credential.

Betty Maloney is a multi-award-winning painter and artist. A widow, she is surrounded by wonderful grandchildren and Boston Terriers.

Tiffany Mannino is a sixth grade teacher and breast cancer survivor living in Bucks County, PA. Tiffany loves to feed her artistic spirit by traveling abroad, writing, decorating, dancing, and laughing. She also has a story published in *Chicken Soup for the Soul: New Moms*. E-mail her at tlorindesigns@gmail.com.

Alicia McCauley is a first grade teacher and a teacher consultant for the Writing Project. She's happily married to her high school sweetheart. Alicia is President of Vigilante Kindness, a non-profit organization dedicated to bringing sustainable education opportunities to students in developing countries.

Caroline McKinney is semi-retired from the School of Education at the University of Colorado where she has been an adjunct for over twenty years. She spends time with her seven grandchildren and hiking Colorado's trails with her big dog. She enjoys writing poetry for religious publications.

Kate Tanis McKinnie grew up in Roanoke, VA and attended college at Appalachian State University. She now lives in Nashville, TN and has built a career in the non-profit sector doing fundraising and event planning. She is married to Ryan, has two stepchildren, Savannah and Ryland, and a dog named Archie.

Nancy Merczel lives in Illinois with her husband and (senior) cat. She is currently writing a book for tween girls.

Since being diagnosed with age-related macular degeneration over nine years ago, **Priscilla Miller** continues to pursue her passion for writing and has just published her first children's book, *McGillicutty: A Very Special Bear*.

Greg Moore has spent his life in broadcast radio; he is frequently heard on morning radio shows across the country as a creator of comedic vignettes and parody songs. He lives in Oklahoma City.

Elizabeth Moursund received a Bachelor of Arts in Theatre from Providence College in 1998. She lives with her husband and three boys in Southern Oregon. She spends her time volunteering with the PTA as well as chauffeuring her kids to sports and music practices. She finds time to write while waiting in the school pick-up line.

Kimberly Noe studied journalism at Oklahoma State University and currently works as advertising director at a suburban weekly newspaper in central Oklahoma. She and her nine-year-old daughter love to travel and play with friends and family. Kim often writes personal columns and is working on her first novel. E-mail her at kimnoe@gmail.com.

Katie O'Connell is a writer, teacher, mother of two, and lover of all things creative and inspiring. She is passionate about observing life's little moments and the lessons they reveal if we give them our attention. Katie is currently completing a children's book about her grandfather.

Tiffany O'Connor, Ph.D., holds a Doctorate in Philosophy and a Master of Business Administration degree. She is an accomplished freelance writer. Tiffany is married to her high school sweetheart and is the mother of two amazing boys. She chronicles her experiences raising boys at hashtaglifewithboys.com.

Sharon Pastore is a forty-one-year-old entrepreneur and avid dreamer whose purpose is to help people "wake up," follow their dreams and believe in the magic. She now runs a dream circle called Dreamgirls, which uses night dreams to help daydreams come true. She lives in Havertown, PA with her super cool husband and two precious girls.

Lori Phillips has a B.A. in communications/journalism and an M.A. in education. She enjoys writing both nonfiction and children's nonfiction, gardening, learning languages, trying new recipes for her family, and visiting all types of museums. She lives in Southern California with her family.

Cheryl Pierson is a freelance editor who lives in the Oklahoma City area. She teaches classes on novel and short story writing for adults and teens. Cheryl is currently working on her sixth novel, including a screenplay adaptation. E-mail her at cheryl@westwindsmedia.com.

Rachel Elizabeth Printy is blessed to have grandparents such as Magee and Pagee who have shaped her in countless ways. Both they and her parents, Tom and Debbie Printy, are a huge encouragement to her during the ups and downs of her writing journey. She would also like to wish Shannon and Nick Schell a lifetime of adventures together.

Founding director of a non-profit agency serving residents in care facilities, **Carol McAdoo Rehme** is a twenty-five-year volunteer and advocate for the frail elderly. During her lifetime, she has found herself as both caregiver and care recipient. A veteran editor and author, she publishes prolifically in the inspirational arena.

Sauni Rinehart is a writer, speaker, and teacher. She teaches literature and composition online for Liberty University. She has self-published four books, and her work has appeared in several anthologies. She and her husband live in East Tennessee and enjoy hiking, kayaking, and traveling.

Nan Rockey lives in Bloomington, IN with her writer husband and her non-writer dog, Padfoot. She loves playing the ukulele and spending time with her wonderful in-laws.

Alicia Rosen's stories have appeared in journals, magazines and anthologies throughout America. She lives in a tiny apartment in Brooklyn with her pup and more than 1,000 books.

Tammy Ruggles is a legally blind freelance writer, finger painter, and photographer based in Kentucky. Faith, family, and friends are important to her. She also writes screenplays and poetry, and welcomes e-mail at tammyruggles@yahoo.com.

Jay Seate writes everything from humor to the macabre, and is especially keen on transcending genre pigeonholing. He lives in Golden, CO with the dream of enjoying the rest of his life traveling and writing.

Jodi L. Severson earned a Bachelor's degree in Psychology from the University of Pittsburgh. She resides in Wisconsin with her husband and three children. Check out her other stories in these *Chicken Soup for the Soul* books: *Sister's Soul*, *Working Woman's Soul*, *Girlfriend's Soul*, and *Shopper's Soul*. Reach her at jodis@charter.net.

Mickey Sherman is a criminal defense lawyer in Greenwich, CT.

He has been a legal commentator on most every TV network except *The Food Channel*. His first book, *How Can You Defend Those People?*, has been universally praised by the legal and literary community. Learn more at mickeysherman.com or e-mail him at ms23@aol.com.

Shanna Silva is an author, freelance writer and Tony-nominated producer. Her work is found in the *Multiples Illuminated* anthology, on Kveller, and her first children's book, *The Passover Scavenger Hunt*, will be published in early 2017. E-mail her at shanna@2ndchapter.net.

Harvey Silverman is a retired physician living in Manchester, NH, who writes mostly for his own amusement. E-mail him at HMSilverm@ yahoo.com.

Linda St.Cyr is a writer, blogger, activist, and short story author. When she isn't writing or raising her kids with her life partner, she is busy being vocal about feeding the hungry, sheltering the homeless, and bringing attention to human rights violations all over the world.

Amy L. Stout is a wife, mommy, and autism advocate who loves travel, coffee houses, books and especially Jesus! As a child of the King, her tiara is often missing, dusty, bent out of shape, or crooked, but she will always be his treasured princess. Contact her at histreasuredprincess. blogspot.com or Brightencorner@hotmail.com.

Annmarie B. Tait lives in Conshohocken, PA with her husband Joe Beck. Annmarie has been published in more than twenty *Chicken Soup for the Soul* books as well as various other magazines and anthologies. Annmarie and her husband enjoy singing and recording Irish and American folk music. E-mail her at irishbloom@aol.com.

Kamia Taylor has been writing since she was a very young child, and spent over twenty years drafting legal documents. She now lives on an organic farm and wildlife sanctuary with eight rescued dogs, enjoying nature, continuing to write and trying to make sense of her earlier life.

Lisa Timpf is a graduate of McMaster University in Hamilton, Ontario. Lisa enjoys writing, nature walks, and organic gardening, and has published a collection of creative nonfiction and poetry entitled *A Trail That Twines*.

Julia M. Toto shares stories of hope, forgiveness, and second chances. She is a published author of inspirational fiction and a previous contributor to the *Chicken Soup for the Soul* series. Learn more at www.juliamtoto.com.

Shawna Troke-Leukert is a published writer and an Infinite Possibilities trainer. She grew up in Sydney, Nova Scotia and today lives in beautiful Codroy Valley, Newfoundland with her husband Eric and two dogs. She enjoys gardening, working on writing projects, and visiting her mother Viola every summer in Nova Scotia.

Jennifer Waggener works for the Alzheimer's Association West Virginia Chapter. She and her husband enjoy adventures in travel and are quite infatuated with learning the fine art of excellent grandparenting under the careful guidance of their first grandchild, Henley.

Sarah Wagner lives in West Virginia with her husband and two young sons. Her work has appeared in *The Front Porch*, *Celebrations: Love Notes to Mothers*, and *A Cup of Comfort for Cat Lovers*. You can find her online at www.sarahwagner.domynoes.net.

Roz Warren is the author of *Our Bodies, Our Shelves: A Collection of Library Humor*. She writes for everyone from *The New York Times* to *Funny Times*, and has been featured on both *Today* and *Morning Edition*. This is the sixth time her work has appeared in a *Chicken Soup for the Soul* book.

Rebecca Waters has been a writer most of her life. Her first published work was a story in the school newspaper she wrote in second grade. Her first novel, *Breathing on Her Own*, was released in 2014. Her second novel, *Libby's Cuppa Joe* is due out in March of 2019.

David M. Williamson is a grateful husband, father of four, and Air Force aircrew veteran living on Okinawa, Japan. He writes songs, plays piano, and drinks unhealthy amounts of coffee. When not at work or playing online games, he writes fantasy novels, short stories, and the occasional haiku.

Jennifer Zink received her Bachelor of Arts degree from Rowan University, Glassboro, NJ, in 2012. She is married with three children: Mike, age twenty; Kimmy, age eighteen; and Daniel, age sixteen. Jen loves to read and write, spend time with her family, and travel.

Meet Amy Newmark

Amy Newmark is the bestselling author, editor-in-chief, and publisher of the *Chicken Soup for the Soul* book series. Since 2008, she has published 165 new books, most of them national bestsellers in the U.S. and Canada, more than doubling the number of Chicken Soup for the Soul titles in print today. She is also the author of *Simply Happy*, a crash course in Chicken Soup for the Soul advice and wisdom that is filled with easy-to-implement, practical tips for enjoying a better life.

Amy is credited with revitalizing the Chicken Soup for the Soul brand, which has been a publishing industry phenomenon since the first book came out in 1993. By compiling inspirational and aspirational true stories curated from ordinary people who have had extraordinary experiences, Amy has kept the twenty-seven-year-old Chicken Soup for the Soul brand fresh and relevant.

Amy graduated *magna cum laude* from Harvard University where she majored in Portuguese and minored in French. She then embarked on a three-decade career as a Wall Street analyst, a hedge fund manager, and a corporate executive in the technology field. She is a Chartered Financial Analyst.

Her return to literary pursuits was inevitable, as her honors thesis in college involved traveling throughout Brazil's impoverished northeast region, collecting stories from regular people. She is delighted to have come full circle in her writing career — from collecting stories "from the people" in Brazil as a twenty-year-old to, three decades later, collecting stories "from the people" for Chicken Soup for the Soul.

When Amy and her husband Bill, the CEO of Chicken Soup for

the Soul, are not working, they are visiting their four grown children and their grandchildren.

Follow Amy on Twitter @amynewmark. Listen to her free podcast — "Chicken Soup for the Soul with Amy Newmark" — on Apple Podcasts, Google Play, the Podcasts app on iPhone, or by using your favorite podcast app on other devices.

Sharing Happiness, Inspiration, and Hope

Real people sharing real stories, every day, all over the world. In 2007, *USA Today* named *Chicken Soup for the Soul* one of the five most memorable books in the last quarter-century. With over 100 million books sold to date in the U.S. and Canada alone, more than 250 titles in print, and translations into nearly fifty languages, "chicken soup for the soul®" is one of the world's best-known phrases.

Today, twenty-seven years after we first began sharing happiness, inspiration and hope through our books, we continue to delight our readers with new titles, but have also evolved beyond the bookshelves with super premium pet food, television shows, a podcast, video journalism from aplus.com, licensed products, and free movies and TV shows on our Popcornflix and Crackle apps. We are busy "changing the world one story at a time®." Thanks for reading!

Share with Us

We all have had Chicken Soup for the Soul moments in our lives. If you would like to share your story or poem with millions of people around the world, go to chickensoup.com and click on Submit Your Story. You may be able to help another reader and become a published author at the same time. Some of our past contributors have launched writing and speaking careers from the publication of their stories in our books!

We only accept story submissions via our website. They are no longer accepted via mail or fax. Visit our website, www.chickensoup.com, and click on Submit Your Story for our writing guidelines and a list of topics we are working on.

To contact us regarding other matters, please send us an e-mail through webmaster@chickensoupforthesoul.com, or fax or write us at:

Chicken Soup for the Soul
P.O. Box 700
Cos Cob, CT 06807-0700
Fax: 203-861-7194

One more note from your friends at Chicken Soup for the Soul: Occasionally, we receive an unsolicited book manuscript from one of our readers, and we would like to respectfully inform you that we do not accept unsolicited manuscripts, and we must discard the ones that appear.

Changing the world one story at a time®
www.chickensoup.com